T0155874

Communications in Computer and Information Science 1460

More information about this series at http://www.springer.com/series/7899

Rafael Valencia-García ·
Martha Bucaram-Leverone ·
Javier Del Cioppo-Morstadt · Néstor Vera-Lucio ·
Emma Jácome-Murillo (Eds.)

Technologies and Innovation

7th International Conference, CITI 2021
Guayaquil, Ecuador, November 22–25, 2021
Proceedings

 Springer

Editors
Rafael Valencia-García 🆔
Universidad de Murcia
Espinardo, Spain

Martha Bucaram-Leverone 🆔
Universidad Agraria del Ecuador
Guayaquil, Ecuador

Javier Del Cioppo-Morstadt 🆔
Universidad Agraria del Ecuador
Guayaquil, Ecuador

Néstor Vera-Lucio 🆔
Universidad Agraria del Ecuador
Guayaquil, Ecuador

Emma Jácome-Murillo 🆔
Universidad Agraria del Ecuador
Guayaquil, Ecuador

ISSN 1865-0929   ISSN 1865-0937 (electronic)
Communications in Computer and Information Science
ISBN 978-3-030-88261-7   ISBN 978-3-030-88262-4 (eBook)
https://doi.org/10.1007/978-3-030-88262-4

This Springer imprint is published by the registered company Springer Nature Switzerland AG
The registered company address is: Gewerbestrasse 11, 6330 Cham, Switzerland

Preface

The 7th International Conference on Technologies and Innovation (CITI 2021) was held during November 22–25, 2021, in Guayaquil, Ecuador. The CITI series of conferences aim to be an international framework and meeting point for professionals who are mainly devoted to research, development, innovation, and university teaching within the field of computer science and technology applied to any important area of innovation. CITI 2021 was organized as a knowledge-exchange conference consisting of several contributions about current innovative technology. These proposals deal with the most important aspects and future prospects from an academic, innovative, and scientific perspective. The goal of the conference was to examine the feasibility of investigating advanced and innovative methods and techniques, and their application in different domains, in the field of computer science and information systems, which represents innovation in current society.

We would like to express our gratitude to all the authors who submitted papers to CITI 2021, and our congratulations to those whose papers were accepted. There were 36 submissions this year. Each submission was reviewed by at least three Program Committee (PC) members. Only the papers with an average score of ≥ 1.0 were considered for final inclusion, and almost all accepted papers had positive reviews. Finally, the PC decided to accept 14 full papers.

We would also like to thank the Program Committee members, who agreed to review the manuscripts in a timely manner and provided valuable feedback to the authors.

November 2021

Rafael Valencia-García
Martha Bucaram-Leverone
Javier Del Cioppo-Morstadt
Néstor Vera-Lucio
Emma Jácome-Murillo

Organization

Honor Committee

Martha Bucaram-Leverone	Universidad Agraria del Ecuador, Ecuador
Javier Del Cioppo-Morstadt	Universidad Agraria del Ecuador, Ecuador
Emma Jácome-Murillo	Universidad Agraria del Ecuador, Ecuador
Teresa Samaniego Cobo	Universidad Agraria del Ecuador, Ecuador

Organizing Committee

Rafael Valencia-García	Universidad de Murcia, Spain
Martha Bucaram-Leverone	Universidad Agraria del Ecuador, Ecuador
Javier Del Cioppo-Morstadt	Universidad Agraria del Ecuador, Ecuador
Néstor Vera-Lucio	Universidad Agraria del Ecuador, Ecuador
Emma Jácome-Murillo	Universidad Agraria del Ecuador, Ecuador

Program Committee

Jacobo Bucaram Ortiz	Universidad Agraria del Ecuador, Ecuador
Martha Bucaram-Leverone	Universidad Agraria del Ecuador, Ecuador
Rina Bucaram-Leverone	Universidad Agraria del Ecuador, Ecuador
Rafael Valencia-García	Universidad de Murcia, Spain
Ricardo Colomo-Palacios	Ostfold University College, Norway
Ghassan Beydoun	University of Technology Sydney, Australia
Antonio A. López-Lorca	University of Melbourne, Australia
Chunguo Wu	Jillin University, China
Siti Hajar Othman	Universiti Teknologi Malaysia, Malaysia
Anatoly Gladun	V.M. Glushkov of National Academy Science, Ukraine
Aarón Ayllón-Benítez	Université de Bordeaux, France
Giner Alor-Hernández	Instituto Tecnológico de Orizaba, Mexico
José Luis Ochoa	Universidad de Sonora, México
Ana Muñoz	Universidad de Los Andes, Venezuela
Miguel Ángel Rodríguez-García	Universidad Rey Juan Carlos, Spain
Lucía Serrano-Luján	Universidad Rey Juan Carlos, Spain
Eugenio Martínez-Cámara	Universidad de Granada, Spain
José Antonio García-Díaz	Universidad de Murcia, Spain
José Antonio Miñarro-Giménez	Universidad de Murcia, Spain

Miguel Vargas-Lombardo	Universidad Tecnologica de Panama, Panama
Denis Cedeño Moreno	Universidad Tecnologica de Panama, Panama
Viviana Yarel Rosales Morales	Instituto Tecnologico de Orizaba, Mexico
Claudia Victoria Isaza Narvaez	Universidad de Antioquia, Colombia
Raquel Vasquez Ramirez	Instituto Tecnologico de Orizaba, Mexico
Janio Jadán Guerrero	Universidad Indoamérica, Ecuador
Yordani Cruz Segura	Universidad de las Ciencias Informáticas. Cuba
Freddy Tapia León	Universidad de las Fuerzas Armadas ESPE, Ecuador
Nemury Silega Martínez	Universidad de las Ciencias Informáticas, Cuba
Astrid Duque Ramos	Universidad de Antioquia, Colombia
Nelson Becerra Correa	Universidad Distrital Francisco José de Caldas, Colombia
Alireza Khackpour	Ostfold University College, Norway

Local Organizing Committee

Katty Lagos Ortiz (General Coordinator)	Universidad Agraria del Ecuador
Teresa Samaniego Cobo	Universidad Agraria del Ecuador, Ecuador
Andrea Sinche Guzmán	Universidad Agraria del Ecuador, Ecuador
Verónica Freire Avilés	Universidad Agraria del Ecuador, Ecuador

Sponsoring Institution

Contents

Semantic Technologies and Machine Learning

Approach Based on Text Processing and Ontology Applied to the Health Domain of Palliative Care in Panama

Denis Cedeno-Moreno[1]([✉])(iD), Miguel Vargas-Lombardo[1](iD),
and Daniela Moctezuma[2](iD)

[1] Grupo de Investigación en Salud Electrónica y Supercomputación (GISES),
Universidad Tecnológica Panamá, Panama City, Panama
{denis.cedeno,miguel.vargas}@utp.ac.pa
[2] Centro de Investigación en Ciencias de Información Geoespacial,
Mexico City, Ags, Mexico
dmoctezuma@centrogeo.edu.mx

Abstract. Natural language processing (NLP) is a discipline of artificial intelligence (AI) and computational linguistics. NLP facilitates the user's work and communicating with the computer, as well as to analyze unstructured data such as textual documents. In Panama, doctors in palliative care units write their diagnoses, observations and medications in textual documents, which represents a problem to properly handle the information. The development of an expert system to support clinicians in decision-making for palliative care patients is presented. It uses NLP techniques to extract information from plain textual documents. The information extracted from the textual documents was organized in an ontological domain that can be accessed to feed an efficient information system that manages the information of palliative care patients. The evaluation of the platform was carried out through a case study in a hospital in Panama. The results are favorable, since the data extracted from the created ontology produces responses similar to those of the experts. Therefore, this platform can help clinicians make better decisions regarding the treatment of patients in palliative care.

Keywords: Natural language processing · Ontology · Palliative care · Expert health system · Knowledge

1 Introduction

An increasing number of patients present multiple morbidities and conditions in the final moments of their life, current medicine through palliative care manages a set of programs for these patients that aims to maximize the quality of life (QoL) to the last stage of life [1].

Nowadays, in Panama health organizations need to manage reliable patient data. However, even in many organizations the doctor writes patient information

© Springer Nature Switzerland AG 2021
R. Valencia-García et al. (Eds.): CITI 2021, CCIS 1460, pp. 3–17, 2021.
https://doi.org/10.1007/978-3-030-88262-4_1

or medical history on a sheet and stores it in a folder on the computer. These patient data are found in an unstructured or incompatible format, which makes it difficult to extract and systematize knowledge, which is a problem. The processing of large volumes of data to extract knowledge requires the application of a series of techniques that include information retrieval (IR) and information extraction (IE), that is, specific tasks of NLP.

Recently, health information systems include, for example, from a basic medical device to those involving hospital networks and interoperability [2]. Common elements such as user interfaces, databases, use of computer networks [3] can be highlighted. Despite these advances in Panama we do not have the development of expert systems in medicine, this action leads us to conclude that it is necessary to build information systems that make contributions beyond the usual, that use artificial intelligence tools, such as NLP and make it an extraordinary advance [4]. NLP has two foundations: natural language understanding and the generation of knowledge that emanates from the text [5].

Knowledge management is a concept applied in organizations. The representation of knowledge has the fundamental objective of managing knowledge in a way that facilitates inference, that is, drawing correct conclusions from said knowledge. In the early 1990s, ontologies began to be an area of common interest for some research groups, especially those related to knowledge [6]. Ontologies [7] can be used to structure information. An ontology is defined as "a formal and explicit specification of a shared conceptualization" [8]. There are few technological proposals in the country that promote NLP tools and knowledge based on ontologies, to deepen and improve knowledge in this case of expert systems in medicine, especially in the area of palliative care patients [9]. Furthermore, ontologies have become an important tool for developing semantically rich applications. We can carefully construct ontologies from texts to express knowledge clearly and precisely [10,11]. This is a critical process, which can be done manually, but is tedious, expensive, and time-consuming.

This article describes the development of an expert health system that makes use state-of-the-art technologies such as: NLP and IR to extract and organize information. A domain ontology is created and populated as a suitable and reliable knowledge base. The ontology is then accessed as a software agent to generate different useful user interfaces so that palliative care health professionals can use patient information in a more appropriate and friendly way. The palliative care ontology generated serves to share knowledge and use as a resource between physicians and researchers. A case study was carried out with a data set of Panamanian patients which served as the basis for the evaluation of the system, obtaining good results.

The rest of the manuscript is structured as follows, Sect. 2 describes literature review on NLP and ontologies. Section 3 describes the proposed platform showing the resources and tools used, Sect. 4 shows case of study, Sect. 5 shows the results and discussion, and Sect. 6 the conclusions are presented.

2   Related Work

There is significant progress in recent years in the application of NLP techniques, to cope with the large volume of information in the rapidly growing area of medical literature. However, it is not common to find applications of NLP in the area of clinical information systems [12,13].

Some other related proposals has been published in the NLP area. For instance, in [14] authors present a framework to populate instances of relationships in ontologies from natural language that contains a structured model of machine learning (ML). The proposed framework applies to the novel problem of mapping natural language in spatial ontologies. In their work [15] present a semi-automatic framework to populate ontologies for the E-commerce domain, especially attribute values related to product information from semi-structured texts or web stores. The method then contains a lexicon along with patterns for classifying products, mapping properties, and creating instance values.

In [16] authors introduced a system for learning and population of ontologies, which combines statistical and semantic methodologies to generate terminological ontologies for a given semantic domain. As a contribution, the reported experimental results demonstrated the effectiveness of the proposed system in terms of quality of the ontologies in comparison with those generated manually by experts. Another proposal is presented in [17], called Apponto-Pro. The framework consists of an incremental process that manages to build and populate an application ontology in the domain of family law, has the ability to generate a file OWL with elements of the ontology such as classes, taxonomy, non-taxonomic relations, instances, properties, and axioms. Researchers [18] propose a methodology that allows populating ontologies with event instances. Two ontologies are used in the methodology, the extraction ontology and the domain ontology. The main contribution is related to the exploration of the flexibility of linguistic rules and the representation of the knowledge domain through its manipulation and integration with a reasoning system. The documents to be processed must be treated with a deep linguistic analysis program and then represented in OWL with the POWLA data model.

A new method is presented in [19] that guides the population process of ontology by identifying instances of properties mentioned in texts. By guiding the population of ontologies through the identification of property instances, it contributes to solving problems of ambiguity of the terms and inferring information implicit in the ontology. Finally, the authors demonstrate that with this information they can extract instances of classes implicitly or explicitly. The work presented in [20] developed an approach for the generation of ontologies, which include class axioms and instances automatically extracted from texts in English. Techniques such as NLP, clustering algorithms and IE are used. The approach combines WordNet synsets and contextual information to create a set of queries that are sent to a web search engine. Finally, the built ontology is manually compared with the reference or gold standard ontology. A generic domain-independent method for automatic ontological population from textual sources is proposed in [21]. As input is needed a corpus and an empty ontology.

The tasks performed by the method are using NLP techniques and statistical models. Finally, the classification of instances is performed which requires the classifier and the annotated corpus as inputs and then uses NLP and ML to assign the instances to classes, properties and relationships.

In their work [22] present a methodology to resolve the problem of how to keep biomedical ontologies update and how to enrich them. The system is fed with a biological domain ontology enriched with text instances in natural language. The process has three layers: the first layer shows the top-level ontologies which define the basic semantic relationships to be mapped within resources that allow labeling semantic roles; the second layer presents the ontology of the domain to be populated which is related to the ontological model; and the third layer the ontology of the populated domain through ontological models and linguistic resources.

Carla Faria et al. [23] presented a process for the automatic population of ontology from text extracted with techniques of NLP and IE taking advantage of the advances in both fields to acquire and classify instances of ontologies. The most important contribution of this work is that it is part of HERMES, a research project that seeks techniques and tools to automate the learning process and population of ontologies.

Another proposal for the extraction of instances of relationships is presented in [24]. In addition, it works in a sports domain in soccer specifically. The process populates the instances and relationships of the domain ontology with a corpus extracted from the web. Hee-Geun Yoon et al. [25] proposed an automatic method for population of ontologies with data in structured format. Instances are pulled from web pages using wrappers or sentences using NLP techniques. The method requires an ontology and seed instances extracted from documents semi-structured. A system was also developed that discovers automatically pair a predicate and property to resolve instance and concept.

In [26] authors presented a method for automatically extracting information from the web that uses hand-made patterns for the classes and relationships. The patterns are queried on Google where the results are used to search for other instances. They contribute to create of an algorithm that given a domain of interest, extracts, structures and combines the information from the Internet. The work presented in [27] authors created an ontological support system for medical decision-making, called OntoDiabetic that assesses risk factors for the health of patients with diabetes and hypertension and suggests appropriate treatments. In the ontology, a semantic profile of the patient is applied that collects information on signs, nutritional history and values of laboratory tests. In [28] authors proposed a platform to support the diagnosis and detection of Alzheimer's disease where ontologies and semantic reasoning play a fundamental role. The work contributes to helping physicians in the early detection of the disease through the use of multidisciplinary knowledge. Ontologies are used as supporting knowledge structures and a semantic reasoning system for the decision-making process.

The work presented in [29] proposes a methodology that use ontology created and focused on the palliative care domain, the ontology is built with the purpose of managing information and then it is also used to complement a relational database with which interacts as a tool for the design of palliative care systems. The ontology was designed using an adaptation of the Uschold and King methodology. In [30] where the ontology uses a controlled vocabulary to facilitate the exchange of information. It works in four domains of palliative care. Process of care delivery, patient and family care, governance, and program administration and support. The system makes it possible to automatically extract coded information from the clinical health record, makes use of speech point labeling information during tokenization and uses ontological knowledge during concept extraction.

As can be seen, many of the studies analyzed in the literature focus on several areas, presenting decision support systems that are based on ontologies, some focused on commerce, tourism, law, and others, only a few were found that tackle the palliative care domain. As a summary, in Table 1 is presented a comparison of the most relevant aspects from each work described in this section.

Table 1. Comparison of the aspects of the works described tables.

Work	Author	Type of Text	Techniques	Ontology generation
[14]	Kordjamshidi	Unstructured	ML	YES
[15]	Nederstig	Semi-structured	Patterns	NO
[16]	Colace	Unstructured	Statistics and semantics	YES
[17]	Santos	Unstructured	Incremental Cycle by Objectives	YES
[18]	DeAraujo	Unstructured	NLP and IE	YES
[19]	Sadoun	Unstructured	ML	YES
[20]	Ríos	Unstructured	NLP-IE	YES
[21]	Faria	Unstructured	NLP-IE	YES
[22]	Ruiz-Martínez	Unstructured	NLP	YES
[23]	Faria	Unstructured	NLP	YES
[24]	De Boer	Semi-structured	Co-occurrence on the web	YES
[25]	Yoon	Unstructured	NLP	YES
[26]	Geleijnse	Semi-structured	Patterns	YES
[27]	Sherimon	Semi-structured	EI	YES
[28]	Sanchez	Semi-structured	EI	YES
[29]	Kusiemsky	Semi-structured	EI	YES
[30]	Barrett	Semi-structured	NLP	NO

The works above propose a variety of solutions to the ontologies population problem, in general, it can be stated the ontologies have been used to build decision support systems in different domains. However, very few have developed expert health system in the area of palliative care. Most of the analyzed works use ontologies as the main mechanism to represent the knowledge of experts and they differ in the techniques used for construction.

Thus we see that the works reported in [14] and [19] use ML techniques for the development of their work. Others like [15] and [26] manage to identify patterns in the text, which makes the work develop in a semi-structured way. Other, like [18,20–23], and [25] use some technique related to NLP, which leads to a certain similarity with our proposed work, only focused on other domains. In the works [27] and [28] deal with the medical area, one for Diabetes the other for Alzheimer's disease, they also generate ontologies. And only in the work presented in [29] and [30] is tackled the area in palliative care.

3 Proposed System

Health organizations in Panama, specifically physicians in palliative care units, have used an archaic way of managing patient data without a defined format or structure. It is an important amount of data that is wasted, because its handling is not dynamically managed. It cannot be used to: obtain real statistics, carry out health strategies, make future projections, contribute to decision making, help as a basis for research.

For these reasons, the main objective of our proposal is to support the decision-making of doctors by managing and disposing of knowledge efficiently through an expert system that is also available to the researcher where they can later access to obtain valuable information. The proposed system has user interfaces that allow the physician a visualization of the information of a patient and functionalities that help to monitor this information. For this, an ontology was used as the knowledge base [31]. In a nutshell, the system is made up of a series of elements that are described in the following sections. Figure 1 depicts the architecture of the proposed system.

3.1 Dataset

The data set used to evaluate the proposed system is a text file, composed of 70 documents of palliative care patients in natural language. It has a varied length and written in Spanish. These documents contain general information about the patient, his companions, clinical diagnoses, medications, history, referring service, and other problems collected by the treating physician and stored on the disk of his computer. This dataset provided valuable data to build a health information system that allow medicals to manage patient information quickly and efficiently. This because is real-life data and it was acquired in a practical environment as a hospital.

3.2 Natural Language Processing

This module receives as input the dataset with the patient's information written in natural language, explained before. Its objective is to analyze the text in a linguistic way. For this first the text is divided into sentences, words, it also applies to eliminate unnecessary words (for example 'a', 'an', 'the', 'of'). Second, the standard task of word segmentation is performed with the application programming interface provided in the development framework for the NLP called GATE (General Architecture for Text Engineering). The GATE development framework provides the necessary components to perform text segmentation into

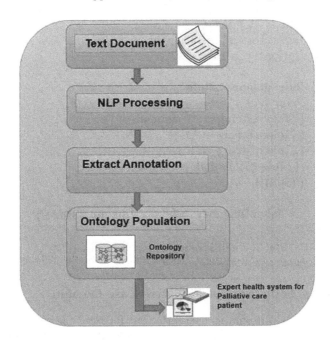

Fig. 1. System architecture of expert health system.

sentences and words. These components are easily assembled to achieve a more complex pipe-based application, where the annotation extraction component is added [32]. In this work tokens can be words, numbers, symbols, and punctuation marks. The tokens separate the content from the text to be able to extract the annotations.

3.3   Extract Annotations

In the extraction of information for the labeling of the annotations two GATE components called JAPE Transducer and Gazetteer were used which were responsible for compiling and executing a set of rules based on JAPE (Java Annotation Pattern Engine) grammar [33]. A set of 41 semantic rules were built and encoded in the JAPE grammar in order to extract the necessary annotations. Figure 2 presents an example of rule generated using JAPE language that extracts the diagnosis of a patient.

The generated rule is used to find the diagnosis of a palliative care patient within the formatted document. The Gazetteer's task is to identify entity names based on a series of predefined lists. Lists are flat files with one input per line that are compiled using finite state machines and are used to give some memory to the system. Besides the above-mentioned process the JAPE Transducer process is performed which is based on IE and annotation techniques. It receives as a parameter a file which contains a list of JAPE language grammars.

```
Phase: Diagnosys
Input: Token Lookup Split
Options: control = brill

Rule: diagnosysRule
Priority: 5
( {Token.string == "Diagnostico" })
( {Token.string == "1"})
( {Token.string == ":"})?
(( {Token})*):label
( {Split})

--> :label.Diagnosys = {rule = "diagnosysRule"}
```

Fig. 2. An illustration of Jape language rule.

3.4 Ontology Population in Palliative Care Domain

The population or automatic instantiation focuses on enriching through instances, classes and relationships of our ontology that was created prior to this process. The importance of the population of ontologies resides fundamentally in the fact that existing ontologies need periodic updates, the ontological fabric is broad enough to cover numerous specialized domains and the instantiation of the ontologies that comprise it supposes a qualitative leap in tasks such as IR [34].

In Fig. 3 it can be observed that in ontology there are different classes and sub-classes. The entire hierarchy of ontology originates from the Thing class then the relationships between each concept or class are established the PalliativePatient class is presented as the central concept of the domain ontology. This concept is the one that has the greatest number of relationships with the other concepts or classes in the ontology. The Address class represents the concept of origin and direction of the patient that is why it has two subclasses, ComingFrom and CurrentAddress.

In this sense, an annotation is inserted into the ontology as individuals of one or more classes. Likewise, the values of its attributes and relationships are identified. If an instance had not been previously inserted, then the system instantiates the ontology with the extracted information thus creating a new individual. For this module it was used a Java API called JENA [35]. JENA is a framework for building applications for the semantic web. The following functions can be implemented using the JENA framework reading and parsing resource description framework (RDF) documents creating and writing RDF documents browsing and searching an RDF chart querying an RDF data set using SPARQL and making inferences using ontologies [36]. With the information extracted the health information system is fed so that the data of palliative care patients can be viewed more efficiently separated by groups including general data,

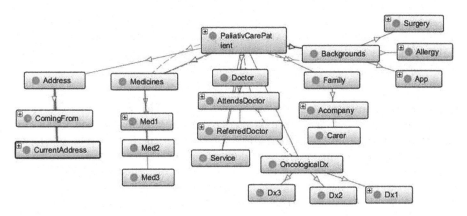

Fig. 3. An illustration of class hierarchy of the created domain ontology.

the doctors who have treated them, their diagnoses the medications. Figure 4 shows the system's interface.

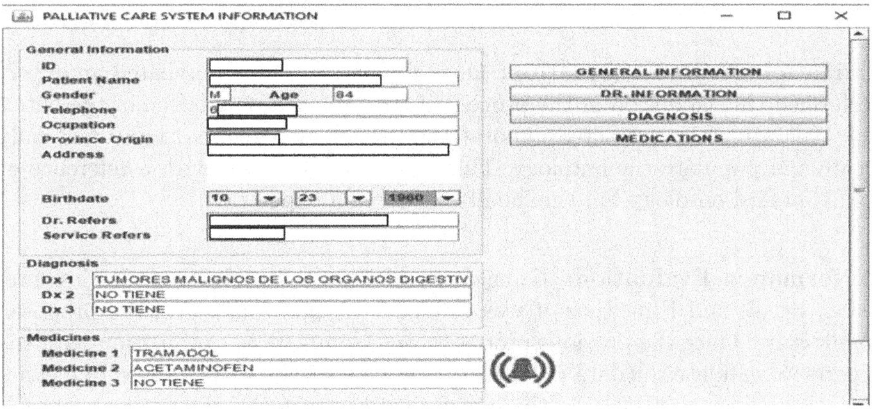

Fig. 4. A illustration one of the system interfaces.

The application that was developed gathers important elements, it manages to automatically process the text, the creation and instantiation of the ontology and visualization of the results so that doctors can make effective decisions.

4   Case of Study

In this section we describe the experimentation we have carried out through a case study conducted to validate the tasks of the system and its contribution to palliative care. The methodology followed was the following:

Data Collection: A group of people was in charge of collecting all the documents of the palliative care patients for processing. The first phase was the cleaning of data in the text documents and then it was organized by completing those data that did not exist.

Data Preparation: A data set in spanish was used for the experiment. This data set is from 55 palliative care patients of which 25 have a second follow-up, 12 a third follow-up and 5 a fourth follow-up. From these data sets attributes are obtained such as: id, name, sex, date of birth, ethnicity, origin, caregiver, doctor, service, type, and intensity of pain, diagnosis, treatment, indications, dose, frequency. We believe that this dataset provided valuable data to build a health information system that would allow doctors to manage patient information quickly and efficiently.

Data Entry to the Application: For the experiment, the application was used on a computer. The data set was entered into the application and the ontology was automatically populated. Annotations are inserted into the ontology as individuals of one or more classes. Likewise, the values of its attributes and relationships are identified.

Validation of the Information: Once the ontology was populated an expert performed the validation of the process of creation and population of the ontology. Validating the extracted annotations the set of concepts to automatically create and populate the ontology. This was then compared with a reference or gold standard ontology built manually by domain experts.

Performance Evaluation: Using a set of standard evaluation metrics: precision, recall, and F-measure it was evaluate the performance of the proposed architecture. Once the previous processes were complete in conjunction with the experts we validate the data in terms of precision, recall, and F-Measure metrics of the experiment reflected in the interface of the system.

5   Results and Discussion

As mentioned before, the precision, recall, and F-measure [37] metrics were used for evaluation. This set of metrics are very common in the evaluation processes of NLP systems in conjunction with the retrieval and extraction of information [38]. The evaluation was done in each of the following phases that make up the architecture: the extraction of annotations in the creation and population of the ontology. The log extraction process is performed after the NLP process has finished. Its objective is to identify within the data of the palliative care patient, those words that will have a meaning or importance for the other tasks, that is, for the construction and population of the ontology. In addition, we have split the information into the different sections into which the patient data is broken down, that is: general data, diagnostic data, and medication data. The metrics were calculated for each section considered, in this way, for the data sets corresponding to the section. The true positives (TP) are the data that were correctly related to the section, that is, those data from sections that were correctly extracted. False positives (FP) are data that were incorrectly related to the corresponding section. In other words it extracted information that was not from that section. Finally, false negatives (FN) are the data related to a different section that is the data that was not related to the correct section [39]. The following formulas describe how these metrics are calculated:

$$Precision = \frac{TP}{TP + FP} \tag{1}$$

$$Recall = \frac{TP}{TP + FN} \tag{2}$$

$$F - measure = \frac{(2 * Precision * Recall)}{(Precision + Recall)} \tag{3}$$

Table 2 shows the experimental results for the extraction of annotations of the documents from the palliative care medical domain. The results obtained for each section of the corpus, a total of 2784 annotations were obtained, in the three sections described: general, medication, and diagnosis. Also, it can be seen the total number of annotations that were executed correctly per section (TP), the number of annotations that were extracted per section, but were not what was expected (FN), and the number of annotations that were not extracted per section (FP).

Table 2. Results of the set of annotations.

Section	Total	TP	FN	FP	Precision	Recall	F-measure
General	2154	1945	109	100	0.9511	0.9469	0.9490
Diagnosis	320	280	22	18	0.9395	0.9215	0.9333
Medications	310	275	20	15	0.9482	0.9322	0.9401
Average					0.9494	0.9430	0.9462

In the evaluation of the creation and population of the ontology we can see that the extracted annotations, the set of concepts or elements have been chosen to automatically create and complete the ontology built by the system. Then we have compared those elements against a reference or gold standard ontology. The gold standard ontology was created by an expert of the domain and with it we have been able to know if what the system has created is correct or not. Table 3 shows the results of the set of concepts or elements automatically built by the system compared with the established by the human experts.

Table 3. Results of the set of concepts.

Concept	Systems extract	Gold standard	Precision
Class	8	8	1
Subclass	14	15	0.9333
Data	20	22	0.9090
Object	7	8	0.8750
Property	51	53	0.9622

Here, it can be seen both the values extracted by the system and the ontology created by the team of experts which resulted with high precision which indicates that the creation and the ontological population is adequate and will help doctors in making decisions for patients in palliative care. Although it is necessary to improve certain details regarding the extraction of concepts in the ontology, for example, the doctor writes something syntactically wrong, this represents an exception to our rules. The precision measure for the extraction of annotations, in the palliative care domain, has been equal to 1, this is because almost all the annotations identified by the system are relevant. Regarding the precision, recall, and scores of F-measure, the annotations from the General data section had the best results, and the annotations from the diagnostic data section had the lowest ones. In general terms we consider that the extractions of the proposed model and its results are promising with an average precision of 0.9494, recall of 0.9430 and, F-measure of 0.9462.

For the results obtained in the process of extraction of annotations defined in our methodology it can be concluded that were outstanding results. The evaluation was performed based on the comparison of the learned ontology against a reference ontology. As it can be seen in the different results obtained in the experiments for the medical domain used, the key to the correct operation of the proposed methodology is found in the first phase of the process, the extraction of annotations, hence if everything is fine the creation and population of the ontology is satisfactory. The objective of the IE in unstructured documents is to extract specific information from the problem and then convert it into a structured form that can be used directly by the computer system for its due process. Due to several disadvantages of unstructured texts such as lack of grammatically being poorly written or disparity in upper or lower case it poses greater challenges for the extraction of information.

6   Conclusions

Populating an ontology can be done manually, but this causes several cost and time-consuming problems. This proposed system represents an attempt to reduce the ontology creation processes. The importance of the ontology population is that the ontologies must be constantly updated, otherwise it would be static information. This article describes the way in which through textual documents it is possible to generate a system for decision-making by physicians in palliative care units through a palliative care ontology and the use of NLP techniques, we have shown that our ontology has clinical relevance by showing that the elements contained in the ontology are capable of representing the guidelines and acting as a tool for the design of palliative care systems. The system proposed obtained encouraging results with a precision range closer to 1, and F-Measure results also near to 1 in the comparison of the learned ontology with a reference ontology. The main contribution of this work is the development of an ontology for palliative care patients with their general characteristics, symptoms, treatments, and medications. Furthermore, this system is intended as a guide for future development or software agents. Currently, there are very few ontological learning systems aimed at mastering palliative care patient information for the construction of ontologies, making research in this field increasingly important.

Acknowledgments. The authors would like to thank the National Secretariat of Science, Technology and Innovation of Panama (SENACYT, SNI) for the support given in the development of this research. Also, GISES-CIDITIC and the Regional Center of West Panama of the Technological University of Panama (CRPO-UTP).

References

1. Ngwenya, N., Mills, S.: The use of weblogs within palliative care: a systematic literature review. Health Inform. J. **20**, 13–21 (2014)
2. Maldonado, J.: Using the ResearchEHR platform to facilitate the practical application of the EHR standards. J. Biomed. Inform. **45**, 70–73 (2012)
3. Normand, L., Paternó, F., Winckler, M.: Public policies and multilingualism in HCI. Interactions **21**, 70–73 (2014)
4. Yang, Q., Zhang, Y.: Transfer learning in natural language processing. Transf. Learn. **45**, 234–256 (2020)
5. Akusok, A., Bjork, K.: High-performance extreme learning machines: a complete toolbox for big data applications. IEEE Access **3**, 1011–1025 (2015)
6. Holzinger, A., Geierhofer, R.: Semantic information in medical information systems: utilization of text mining techniques to analyze medical diagnoses. J. Univers. Comput. Sci. **14**, 3781–3795 (2008)
7. Castellanos-Nieves, D., Fernandez-Breis, J., Valencia-Garcia, R., Martinez-Bejar, R., Iniesta-Moreno, M.: Semantic web technologies for supporting learning assessment. Inf. Sci. **181**, 1517–1537 (2011)
8. Ijntema, W., Sangers, J.: A Lexico-semantic pattern language for learning ontology instances from text. J. Web Semant. **10**, 37–50 (2012)
9. Khan, S., Safyan, M.: Semantic matching in hierarchical ontologies. Comput. Inf. Sci. **26**, 247–257 (2014)
10. Choukri, D.: A new distributed expert system to ontology evaluation. Procedia Comput. Sci. **37**, 48–55 (2014)
11. Bilgin, G., Dikmen, I., Birgonul, M.: Ontology evaluation: an example of delay analysis. Procedia Eng. **85**, 61–68 (2014)
12. Heinze, D., Morsch, M., Holbrook, J.: Mining free-text medical records. Proc. AMIA Symp. **14**, 254–258 (2001)

13. Stavrianou, A., Andritsos, P.: Overview and semantic issues of text mining. ACM SIGMOD **36**, 18–23 (2007)
14. Kordjamshidi, P.: Global machine learning for spatial ontology population. J. Web Semant. **30**, 3–21 (2015)
15. Nederstigt, L., Aanen, S., Frasincar, F.: FLOPPIES: a framework for large-scale ontology population of product information from tabular data in E-commerce stores. Decis. Support Syst. **59**, 296–311 (2014)
16. Colace, F., De Santo, M., Moscato, V.: Terminological ontology learning and population using latent Dirichlet allocation. J. Vis. Lang. Comput. **25**, 818–826 (2014)
17. Santos, S., Picariello, A.: Apponto-pro: an incremental process for ontology learning and population. In: 9th Iberian Conference on Information Systems and Technologies (2014). https://doi.org/10.1109/CISTI.2014.6876966
18. De Araujo, D., Rigo, S., Muller, C.: Automatic information extraction from texts with inference and linguistic knowledge acquisition rules. Intell. Agent Technol **3**, 151–154 (2013)
19. Sadoun, D.: From natural language requirements to formal specification using an ontology. In: 2013 IEEE 25th International Conference on Tools with Artificial Intelligence, pp. 755–760 (2013) https://doi.org/10.1109/ICTAI.2013.116
20. Rios-Alvarado, A., Lopez-Arevalo, I.: Learning concept hierarchies from textual resources for ontologies construction. Expert Syst. Appl. **40**, 5907–5915 (2013)
21. Faria, C., Serra, I., Girardi, R.: A domain-independent process for automatic ontology population from text. Sci. Comput. Program. **95**, 26–43 (2014)
22. Ruiz-Martínez, J., Valencia-García, R., Martínez-Béjar, R., Hoffmann, A.: BioOntoVerb: a top level ontology based framework to populate biomedical ontologies from texts. Knowl. Based Syst. **36**, 68–80 (2012)
23. Faria, C., Girardi, R., Novais, P.: Using domain specific generated rules for automatic ontology population. Int. Conf. Intell. Syst. Des. Appl. ISDA **95**, 297–302 (2012). https://doi.org/10.1109/ISDA.2012.6416554
24. De Boer, V.: A redundancy-based method for the extraction of relation instances from the Web. Int. J. Hum. Comput Stud. **65**, 816–831 (2007)
25. Yoon, H., Han, Y.: Ontology population from unstructured and semi-structured texts. In: Proceedings of the 6th International Conference on Advanced Language Processing and Web Information Technology, ALPIT 2007, vol. 65, pp. 135–139 (2007). https://doi.org/10.1109/ALPIT.2007.30
26. Geleijnse, G., Korst, J.: Automatic ontology population by googling, Belgian-Netherlands. Artif. Intell. **6**, 120–126 (2005)
27. Sherimon, P.C., Krishnan, R.: OntoDiabetic: an ontology-based clinical decision support system for diabetic patients. Arab. J. Sci. Eng. **41**(3), 1145–1160 (2015). https://doi.org/10.1007/s13369-015-1959-4
28. Sanchez, E., et al.: A knowledge-based clinical decision support system for the diagnosis of Alzheimer disease. In: IEEE 13th International Conference on e-Health Networking, Applications and Services, pp. 351–357 (2011). https://doi.org/10.1109/HEALTH.2011.6026778
29. Kuziemsky, C., Lau, F.: Ontology-based information integration in health care: a focus on palliative care. Elev. Annu. Int. Work. Softw. Technol. Eng. Pract. **1**, 164–172 (2004)
30. Barrett, N., Weber-Jahnke, J., Thai, V.: Engineering natural language processing solutions for structured information from clinical text: extracting sentinel events from palliative care consult letters. Stud. Health Technol. Inform. **192**, 594–598 (2013)

31. Cimiano, P., Unger, C., McCrae, J.: Ontology-based interpretation of natural language. Synth. Lect. Hum. Lang. Technol. **7**, 1–178 (2014)
32. Pande, V., Khandelwal, A.: A survey of different text mining techniques. IBMRD's J. Manag. Res. **3**, 125–133 (2014)
33. Wyner, A., Schneider, J., Atkinson, K., Bench-Capo, T.: Semi-automated argumentative analysis of online product reviews. In: COMMA, vol. 245, pp. 43–50 (2012)
34. Ochoa, J., Valencia-García, R., Perez-Soltero, A.: A semantic role labelling-based framework for learning ontologies from Spanish documents. Expert Syst. Appl. **40**, 2058–2068 (2013)
35. Zhou, S., Ling, H., Han, M., Zhang, H.: Ontology generator from relational database based on Jena. Comput. Inf. Sci. **3**, 263–267 (2010)
36. Rui, L., Maode, D.: A research on E - learning resources construction based on semantic web. Phys. Procedia **25**, 1715–1719 (2012)
37. Krallinger, M., Morgan, A., Smith, L.: Evaluation of text-mining systems for biology: overview of the Second BioCreative community challenge. Genome Biol. **9**, 1–9 (2008)
38. Min, H., Park, J.: Identifying helpful reviews based on customer's mentions about experiences. Expert Syst. Appl. **39**, 1830–1838 (2012)
39. Othman, M., Hassan, H., Moawad, R., Idrees, A.: Using NLP approach for opinion types classifier. J. Comput. **9**, 400–410 (2018)

Data Governance, a Knowledge Model Through Ontologies

Ana Muñoz$^{(\boxtimes)}$ (iD), Luis Martí (iD), and Nayat Sanchez-Pi (iD)

Inria Chile Research Center, Av. Apoquindo 2827, Las Condes, Santiago, Chile
{ana.munoz,lmarti,nayat.sanchez-pi}@inria.cl
http://www.inria.cl

Abstract. Ontologies have emerged as a powerful tool for sharing knowledge, due to their ability to integrate them. A key challenge is the interoperability of data sources that do not have a common schema and that were collected, processed and analyzed under different methodologies. Data governance defines policies, organization and standards. Data governance focused on integration processes helps to define what is integrated, who does it and how it is integrated. The representation of this integration process implies that not only the elements involved in the integration of metadata and their data sets need to be represented, but also elements of coordination between people and knowledge domains need to be included. This paper shows the ontology that describes the data governance processes, the elements that make it up and their relationships. For its development, the methodology based on competency questions and definition of terms is used. The data governance ontology creates a context to support the interaction of different data sources. The ontology is instantiated by means of a case study for Data Governance in Mining Inspection for the Geology and Mining Service of the Chilean government.

Keywords: Data governance · Knowledge representation · Ontology · Interoperability

1 Introduction

Digital transformation in an organization involves complete digitization and correct governance of the whole information that the operation generates. Data governance consists of establishing internal processes in an organization which allow to guarantee data safety, quality, integrity consistency and availability of an organization throughout its life cycle. Data governance is "the exercise of shared authority, control and decision making (planning, monitoring and application) on data management as an asset". Due to the enormous growing of data that nowadays organizations create, collect and store, the concept of data governance

This project was supported by the Mining Management of Sernageomin through the 0 Accidents project.

R. Valencia-García et al. (Eds.): CITI 2021, CCIS 1460, pp. 18–32, 2021.
https://doi.org/10.1007/978-3-030-88262-4_2

has increased in its importance and usage in the recent years. Organizations are aware of the need to establish rules to govern their groups of data as an asset, besides they are also concerned about risks regarding security, privacy and legal aspects. Integral data treatment is a way to ensure performance, quality, sustainability and stepping in an organization. Its last goal is to achieve an effective data governance through trustworthy and safe data. The efficient data governance should be promoted and aligned with business objectives. It involves knowing how to deal with processes in the organization, which leads us to think about the representation of this knowledge. The data management process faces many challenges, not the least of which are the diverse formats resulting from the diversification of data models and the proliferation of data management systems and data warehousing. A key challenge is the integration of data sources that do not have a common schema and were collected, processed and analyzed using different methodologies. Data exchange between disparate sources encounters several constraints during integration, data heterogeneity and semantic heterogeneity [7]. Data heterogeneity represents variations in the structure of definitions including attribute formats, precision or types [9]. While semantic heterogeneity represents similarities in data schema or representation of terms with unique meaning. Semantic analysis helps to validate the contextual information of data using knowledge sources. The main goal of data integration is to generate a global schema by integrating the multiple different schemes. During the construction of the global schema, the lack of understanding of semantic heterogeneity leads to inaccurate search results [7]. Data governance defines policies, organization and standards in data management for efficient access to different data sources and their data sets. Data governance focused on integration processes helps to define what is integrated, who integrates and how it is integrated. The representation of this integration process implies that not only the elements involved in the integration of metadata and their data sets must be represented, but also elements of coordination between people and knowledge domains must be included. Ontology-based data integration has emerged as an active research area to overcome the limitations of these mentioned problems [2]. Therefore, utilizing and sharing existing domain knowledge through ontology is crucial for interoperability and data integration. Standardization and formalization based on domain ontologies support high-level interoperability between systems. An ontology is a formal representation of knowledge on a field of interest for the organization, expressed in terms of objects, concepts, relationships among objects and concepts relations. The ontology of an organization data governance can fulfill different functions. It represents specific vocabulary for data governance with its related definitions, which describe concepts, relations among them, and rules combining them. These definitions avoid ambiguity and are specified in the OWL2 language [14]. They are also represented by a hierarchy and formal logic that adds axioms to limit possible meanings and allow reasoning. We focus on the fact that ontology can be a generalized governance model that leads to policy and organization on its data for its different scopes and objectives. This work propose data governance based on ontology as a promising path to approach the challenges involved in data governance interoperability from data semantics. The key idea of ontological model for data governance has been defined by a three-layer structure: organization, data management and tools. The rest of this paper is organized as follows. Section 2 shows the state-of-the-art with some studies related to data governance, interoperability and ontology. The next two sections show the design and implementation of the ontology, using Mine inspection as study case; and finally, Sect. 5 shows the technological architecture that will support the ontological model.

2   State of the Art

Various research related to data governance and ontology is found in literature and the most important associated with our work are described below. Abraham, R. et al. [1] provided an overview of the state-of-the-art data governance and identified a research agenda. Two research questions framed his literature review: What are the building blocks of data governance? Where is the knowledge about data governance lacking? They answered the first question by developing a conceptual framework for data governance that comprises six dimensions: governance mechanisms, organizational scope, data scope, domain scope, antecedents, and data governance consequences. Furthermore, they reply to the second question by analyzing the gaps within the dimensions of a conceptual framework and deriving areas for which more research is required. They identified five promising fields for future research: Governance mechanisms, the scope of data governance, history of data governance, consequences of data governance, and new research that strengthens the generalized and applicability of results. Brennan, R. et al. [5] created an ontology that can be used to markup Slack channel conversations about data governance topics in terms of the data as- sets, processes, roles and policies of an organization. This ontology is based on the Collibra Data Governance Operating Model. It required the creation of eight main OWL classes (GovernanceAsset, BusinessAsset, DataAsset, TechnologyAsset, Role, Issue, and User) and parent classes for assets and data governance execution and monitoring concepts. In addition, a data management task class was created to hold the frequent references to data management activities (e.g., importing, copying, and backing up data) that are showed in the Slack channel. This last class was an extension of the Collibra data governance operating model as these activities are not separately modeled from business processes within that model. Also, three relation types from the Collibra model are included: the generic relation between assets, the use of asset relation and the one that is governed by relation. Then these upper data governance terms were linked to the World Wide Web Consortium (W3C) provenance ontology by defining all odgov:Asset as subclasses of prov:entity, odgov:DataAssets as subclasses of dataid:dataset, dgov:DataManagementTask as a subclass of prov:Activity and odgov:User as a subclass of prov:Activity. A set of machine-readable metadata fields were defined so that the ontology is publishable via the live OWL documentation environment. Lee, S. U. [12] identifies data governance factors for platform ecosystems through literature review. The study then surveys the data governance state of practice of four platform ecosystems: Facebook, YouTube, eBay and Uber. It describes nineteen governance models in industry and academia. Calvanese et al. [6] use the technology developed for Ontology-Based Data Access (OBDA) to govern data-aware processes through ontologies. Alongside that, the Semantically-Governed Data-Aware Processes (SGDAP) are introduced, in which they merge these two approaches by enhancing a relational layer constituted by a Data-Centric Dynamic Systems (In DCDS-based system the processes operate over the data of the system and evolve it by executing actions that may issue calls to external services), with an ontology, constituting a semantic layer. The ontology captures the domain in which the SGDAP is executed, and allows for seeing the data and their manipulation at a conceptual level through an ontology-based data access (OBDA) system. Specifically, an SGDAP is constituted by two main components: (i) an OBDA system which includes (the intentional level of) an ontology, a relational database schema, and a mapping between the ontology and the database; (ii) a process component, which characterizes the evolution of the system in terms of a process specifying preconditions and effects of action execution over the relational layer. The ALIGNED project [16], presents a suite of ontologies to align the divergent processes encapsulating data and software engineering. This ontology suite aims to support the generation of combined software, data engineering processes, and tools for improved productivity, agility and quality. The suite contains linked data ontologies/vocabularies designed to: (1) support semantics-based model driven software engineering, by documenting additional system context and constraints for RDF-based data or knowledge models in the form of design intents, software life-cycle specifications and data life-cycle specifications; (2) support data quality engineering techniques, by documenting data curation tasks, roles, data sets, work owns and data quality reports at each data life-cycle stage in a data intensive system; and (3) support the development of tools for unified views of software and data engineering processes and software/data test case interlinking, by providing the basis for enterprise linked data describing software and data engineering activities (tasks), agents (actors) and entities (artifacts) based on the W3C provenance ontology. The work [8] is focused on the data governance problem that was caused by rich relationships while the systems grew. The rich relationships that need to be captured in order to reflect how data relate differently to different parties, systems, and initiatives; ontology is a suitable approach to model these complex relationships. They proposed an approach using an ontology-based linked data technique that was used to increase data awareness and data quality. Alkhamisi and Saleh [2] proposed a data integration study using the concept of ontology to solve semantic heterogeneity. They describe heterogeneous data types and different categories of ontology-based integration with their advantages. They analyze the opportunities and challenges in issues related to ontologies and data integration. Finally, they conclude that ontology-based data integration has become an important area of research in both academic and industrial applications.

The above research defines elements of data governance from different points of view. The data governance ontology in [5] is used to define data governance entities and relationships. It acts as an upper ontology for data governance concepts and draws heavily on the Collibra data governance operating model. The [6] ontology describes changes to the data in a relational database in real-time, and provides the data context. The De Stefano's work [8], proposed an approach using ontology-based linked data technique that was used to increase data awareness and data-quality. In [2] describe the challenges in data integration from different aspects of ontologies, and provides different perspectives in ontology-based data integration. This work proposes the data governance ontology as a knowledge base that provides a quality model for data governance and interoperability for different data sources. It is based on the fact that ontology could be a generalized data governance model which leads organization and policies about data for different scopes or goals in any organization, it represents a complement to the above proposals. The next section presents a description of the methodology for the development of the ontology.

3   Methodology

Two methodologies are used in this work, the one used for data governance and ontology engineering for the development of ontologies.

3.1   Data Governance Methodology

Describe activities performed for data governance. Eight stages as an iterative cycle are described, it can be executed as a whole or part of this cycle many times. These stages are: Scope and Initiation, Asses, Vision, Align and Business Value, Functional Design, Governing Framework Design, Road map, and Roll out and Sustain. Each step builds upon the previous one. However, the steps can also be conducted as a "stand-alone" process if the required artifacts or information for that step are available [11].

3.2   Ontology Methodology

For the design and evaluation of our data governance ontology, we followed a methodology proposed by [10]. Briefly, this methodology proposes: first, to define the requirements of the ontology through informal questions. Then, ontology terminology, such as classes and relations, is specified using first-order logical language. This, language must provide the necessary terminology to formally restate the informal competition questions. This allows us to formulate the competence questions as entailed queries regarding the ontology's axioms. In this sense, the ontology and claim that it is adequate can be evaluated. Ontology is developed in the OWL 2 [14] ontology language using the Protégé tool [15]. Data governance ontology offers a knowledge frame about concepts and their relations on data governance, creating a shared vocabulary used by data governance users and could inter-operate systems that exchange data from different sources and as a knowledge base for the creation and use of applications.

4 Ontology Design

In this section, elements conforming concepts and relations involved in data governance ontology are described. The outline of Fig. 1 defines a frame with elements that make up the data governance ontology. We provide a data-oriented architecture, and consider that data life cycle to be the central element of the structure. The Ontology describe three layers: Organization, Data Management and Tools.

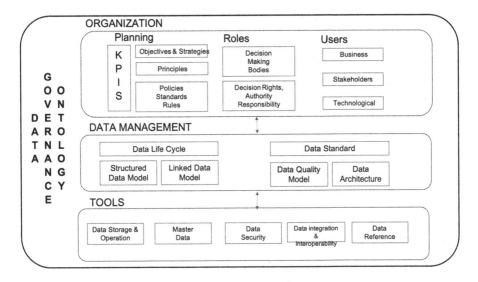

Fig. 1. Ontology data governance framework.

Organization. Organization is planning, oversight, and control over data management, the use of data and data-related resources [13]. Organization must specify who has decision-making rights and responsibilities in the processes related to the data, as well as establishing a consensual model, under which these processes are executed, describing who, what, when and under what circumstances and methods should be used. In addition, it must orchestrate (and therefore affect) users and roles. Organization also must be coherent with the mission, strategy, norms and culture, so that it would be able to manage its data as a strategic asset.

Planning. This is the incorporation of activities aimed at the management of change and culture in the environment, sharing responsibilities and addressing principles and ethical aspects. The elements of planning are:

- Goal: goal to be achieved with data governance.
- Objectives and Strategies: consist of the objectives and strategies of the data governance program, as well as the principles that explain and clarify how data governance supports the structure, culture and goals of the organization.

- Policies, Standards and Rules: Policies must cover all data issues such as data security and risk, metadata management and data quality. The policies must specify how data is governed at the different levels of vertical and horizontal integration along the organization's value chain. Standards define the rules required to ensure that policies are properly implemented, so data fits its purpose. Processes and procedures provide details about how standards must be executed.

Roles. Identifies the business users involved in decision-making on data and its management at different integration levels. Thus, it is necessary to define the roles and assign them rights on decision-making, responsibility and authority in the data governance. Users. Identify the different types of users according to service and data usage. The types of users are:

- Business, are those users who define use, manage and standards of data.
- Stakeholders, are all those general users of the data, such as Commercial organizations, Non-profit organizations, Government and Citizens.
- Technological, are those users related to technological data management.

Transforming corporate data policies into processes and procedures to ensure its compliance. It is about defining how these policies and standards are implemented, translating them into processes and activities. This means describing what the organization should do and how it would do it. Here, it is necessary to choose the adequate technologies, models and standards.

Data Management. The data management layer has two elements, the data life-cycle for structured data models and linked data models. And the data standards defined for data quality models and data architecture.

Data Life-Cycle. Identify each data and be able to trace its evolution, to know when it is displays or generated in the system, the transformations it suffers, where it can be found, in what tasks and processes it is involved in, and its relationship with the strategic business objectives. *Structured Data Model.* This model [3] is used to represent data as XML, CSV, SQL etc. For this Model, the Data Life Cycle has six stages: Creation, Processing, Analysis, Preservation, Access and Reuse. *Linked Data Model.* This model is used to represent data published as Linked Data. The different stages of the Linked Data life-cycle include: Storage, Authoring, Interlinking, Classification, Quality, Evolution/Repair, and Search/Browsing/Exploration.

Data Standard. It is a technical specification that describes how data should be stored or exchanged for the consistent collection and interoperability of that data across different systems, sources, and users. Data standards are typically made up of discrete data standards components. There are conformed by two components Data Quality Model and Data Architecture. *Data Quality Model,* represents and capture the business requirement. Data quality meets six dimensions: accuracy, completeness, consistency, timeliness, validity, and uniqueness. *Data Architecture.* The process of discovering, analyzing, representing, and communicating data requirements in a precise form called the data model [13].

Tools. Describes the technological tools that support data governance, like: Data storage and operation, Master Data, Data Security, Data Integration and Interoperability, and Data Reference.

Competence Question. Competence questions allow us to first overview ontology and help with the validation the ontology. Some of these competence questions are presented in Table 1. Answers to these questions can change during the process of ontology design, but they help us to limit the scope of ontology at any time.

Table 1. Competence question.

Q_n	Competence question
Q_1	What are the elements of data governance ontology?
Q_2	What are the elements that compose the Organization?
Q_3	What are the planning elements?
Q_4	What are the roles of data governance?
Q_5	Who are the users?
Q_6	How is the data life cycle defined?
Q_7	What are the data quality standards?
Q_8	What are the tools that support data governance?

5   Data Governance Ontology Implementation

Data governance ontology is created from structure previously described, using Protégé [11] as ontology editor and OWL2 [10] language representation tool. Figure 2 shows the Data Governance Ontology. The data governance concepts are represented by the rectangles and some of them are: Organization, Data Management and Tools. The relationships between concepts are shown through the Arc Types, and the instance of the Organization is shown through the violet rhombus. Figure 3 below, shows the concepts and relationships to describe how data standards define the organization from the data, through: data quality, data architecture and data models.

5.1   Axioms

The axioms represent the relationships that exist between the elements of the ontology. They are shown below in Table 2 through natural language sentences and first order logical.

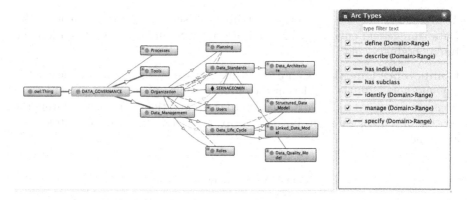

Fig. 2. Data governance ontology model. The data governance concepts are represented by the rectangles and some of them are: Organization, Data Management and Tools.

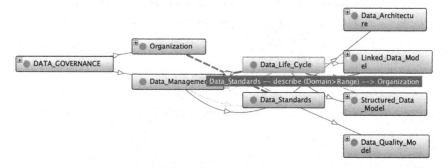

Fig. 3. Relationship between Organization and Data Management. Data standards describe the behavior of the organization.

5.2 Data Governance for National Service of Geology and Mines of Chile

The Ontology is evaluated through of data governance for Mine Inspection of Geology and Mining Service of the Chilean government, Sernageomin (Servicio Nacional de Geología y Minería, by its Spanish acronym). Mine Inspections are critical processes for the control and reduction of accidents in mining. The inspection process carries out activities to inspection mining facilities so that they comply with mining safety regulations, which helps preventing accidents. They also describes the updated status of mining sites through the findings and their causes during the mine inspection. A finding is an element that indicates that a safety standard is not met and that it could lead to an accident. These findings capture valuable information that indicates their nature, the possible causes behind such findings, and the corrective actions to be taken. All this information provides a critical view of mining facilities and supports the decision-making process to avoid accidents. Information systems that support inspection activities store structured data according to a defined data model, but cannot

Table 2. Axioms.

Natural language sentences	First order logical
Data Governance has Organization and has Data Management and has Tools	$\forall x DataGovernance(x) \Rightarrow has(x, Organization) \wedge$ $has(x, DataManagement) \wedge has(x, Tools)$
Data Governance has Organization and has Data Management and has Tools	$\forall x DataGovernance(x) \Rightarrow has(x, Organization) \wedge$ $has(x, DataManagement) \wedge has(x, Tools)$
Organization has Planning and has Roles and has Users	$\forall x Organization(x) \Rightarrow has(x, Planning) \wedge has(x, Roles) \wedge$ $has(x, Users)$
Planning has Goal and has Objectives and has Strategies and has Principles and has Policies and has Standard and has Rules	$\forall x Planning(x) \Rightarrow has(x, Goal) \wedge has(x, Objectives) \wedge$ $has(x, Strategies) \wedge has(x, Principles) \wedge$ $has(x, Policies) \wedge has(x, Standard) \wedge has(x, Rules)$
Roles has Decision Making Bodies and has Decisions Rights and has Authority and has Responsibility	$\forall x Roles(x) \Rightarrow has(x, DecisisonMakingBodies) \wedge$ $has(x, DecisionRights) \wedge has(x, Authority) \wedge$ $has(x, Responsability)$
Data Management has Data Life Cycle and has Data Standards	$\forall x DataManagement(x) \Rightarrow has(x, DataLifeCycle) \wedge$ $has(x, DataStandards)$
Data Life Cycle has Structured Data Model and has Linked Data Model	$\forall x DataLifeCycle(x) \Rightarrow has(x, StructuredDataModel)$ $\wedge has(x, LinkedDataModel)$
Structured Data Model has Data Creation and has Data Processing and has Data Analysis and has Data Preservation and has Data Access and has Data Reuse	$\forall x StructuredDataModel(x) \Rightarrow has(x, DataCreation) \wedge$ $has(x, DataProcessing) \wedge has(x, DataAnalysis) \wedge$ $has(x, DataPreservation) \wedge has(x, DataAccess) \wedge$ $has(x, DataReuse)$
Linked Data Model has Storage and has Authoring and has Interlinking, and has Classification, and has Quality, and has Evolution and has Search-Browsing-Exploration	$\forall x LinkedDataModel(x) \Rightarrow has(x, Storage) \wedge$ $has(x, Authoring) \wedge has(x, Interlinking) \wedge$ $has(x, Classification) \wedge has(x, Quality) \wedge$ $has(x, Evolution) \wedge has(x, SearchBrowsingExploration)$
Data Architecture is expressed by Data Model and is expressed by Data Rules and is expressed by Metadata	$\forall x DataArchitecture(x) \Rightarrow isExpressedBy(x,$ $DataModel) \wedge isExpressedBy(x, DataRules) \wedge$ $isExpressedBy(x, Metadata)$

store the knowledge that is generated during inspection activities in real time. This knowledge is generated by the practice for the inspectors handle ac- cording to their experience. It is frequently stored in text files or reports that are difficult to process to consolidate all the information related to the inspection. Mine inspection is a complex process. In Chile there have been established specifications for conducting inspections through the mining safety regulations for mining projects. The Sernageomin is the country's authority in terms of mining facility inspections. Sernageomin mainly relies on the applicable mining safety specifications to inspect safety in mines, develop inspection knowledge and gain experience over time and practice. Most inspection practices are recorded in information systems and distributed files that are isolated and not integrated, this creates information silos with information named in different ways according to who uses it. One of the key elements that help the integration of these diverse data in different systems is data governance. And for this purpose, the mining inspection data governance program was created. From the point of view of business processes, the following Fig. 4 shows the existing systems and how they are in information silos.

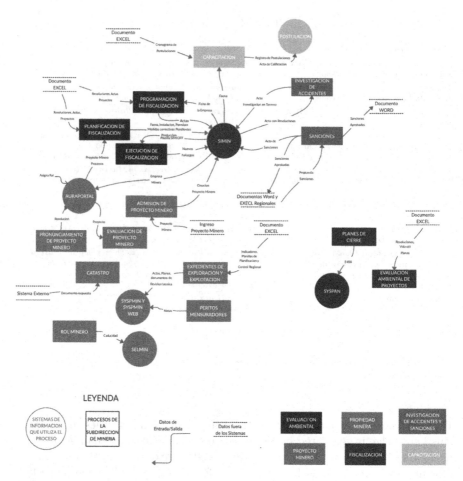

Fig. 4. Information systems containing data for mine inspection management. This approach is from the business processes.

5.3   Instances

Next, the ontology validation elements are shown, such as its overview and then some instances that show how the data governance ontology behaves for the Sernageomin. The following Fig. 5 shows an overview of the Data Governance ontology from Protégé OWL.

Figure 6 shows the business processes that have some relationship with mine inspection. For these processes, data governance is performed, from data management and the elements that integrate the organization.

Figure 7 shows an instance of the Ontology, which describes that SIMIN System belonging to the Data Architecture, contains the Metadata (inferred class) Finding, Risk Condition, Inspection Records, Executed Inspection, Inspection Evidence, Corrective Measures, Scheduled Inspection.

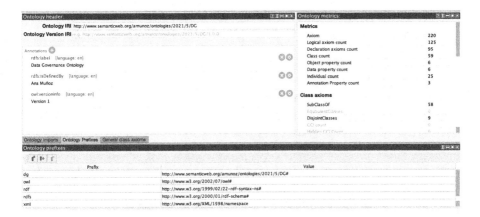

Fig. 5. Ontology overview. Annotations, ontology prefix and metrics in Protégé OWL.

Fig. 6. Business processes of inspection mine

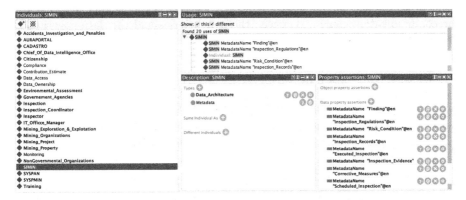

Fig. 7. Description of SIMIN instance. SIMIN have a finding, risk condition, inspection records, executed inspection, inspection evidence, corrective measures and scheduled inspection metadata.

6   Technological Architecture of Data Governance Knowledge Model

In this work, a cloud-based technological architecture is proposed, which offers advantages of simplified software installation and centralized maintenance and version control. As can be seen in Fig. 8, the architecture is composed of three layers: the presentation layer, the knowledge management layer, and the data layer.

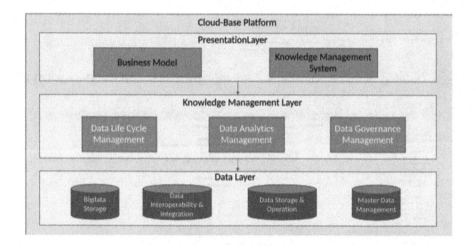

Fig. 8. Technological architecture of data governance knowledge model.

Presentation Layer. This layer is made up of the business model and knowledge management systems. The business model is related to activities the creation of knowledge for data governance. Knowledge management systems are the communication element between the beneficiaries and the data governance processes. The main goal of this layer is to establish communication between users, share processes and resources for data governance.

Knowledge Management Layer. This layer is made up of three main elements, the Data Life-cycle, the Data Governance Management, and Smart Data Management. The data life cycle represents the elements and processes around the data value chain. Smart data represents all the elements and processes related to the intelligent data analysis. Finally, the Data Governance Management represents the knowledge about the activities and resources to manage the quality, interoperability and integrity of data.

Data Layer. The data layer is made up of all those elements that will support the processes of data governance, data life cycle and intelligent data treatment, some of them are: big data storage, data interoperability and integration, data storage and operation and master data management among others.

7   Conclusions and Future Work

Data Governance Ontology describes knowledge elements that should be taken into account during data management. Data Governance support data organization and data quality along its existence, knowing where, who, and how to find data. When describing concepts involved in data processing from the very beginning until removal, culture around data as an active is created. It allows a significant data management for each process of an organization can be achieved. Ontology offers a knowledge base which will support decision making, as well as a base line for the creation of intelligent applications as support system to decisions. This ontology works as a knowledge base for the creation of knowledge graphs that allow solving problems related to interoperability and integration. Ontology can be transformed in a standard to show the steps to follow in a governance program which could link different technologies supporting the activities performed during the data life cycle. The Data Governance Ontology is the basis for creating a knowledge management system through knowledge graphs. Knowledge graphs are recognized as an efficient approach to data governance, metadata management, and data enrichment, and are increasingly being used as a data integration technology [4]. Ontologies are based on the open world hypothesis, which implies that more knowledge can always be added. The conceptual model, and in a semantic knowledge graph it is represented by an ontology. The scope of the domain to be represented by the conceptual model can be calculated by means of competence questions. Subsequently, the domain knowledge can be made available as a machine-processed domain model, in order to largely automate the extraction and linking of data from data sources in any given repository. In [4] three elements that make up a knowledge graph are identified: Ontology: conceptual model; Taxonomy: linguistic model, and Data graph: instances of data sets and metadata, documents and annotations. The development of the knowledge graph is a future work that supports the semantic inter operation of data sources for different organizations. On this basis, advanced knowledge discovery and data analysis applications can be developed using the knowledge graph as the semantic layer.

References

1. Abraham, R., Schneider, J., Vom Brocke, J.: Data governance: a conceptual framework, structured review, and research agenda. Int. J. Inf. Manage. **49**, 424–438 (2019)
2. Alkhamisi, A.O., Saleh, M.: Ontology opportunities and challenges: discussions from semantic data integration perspectives. In: 2020 6th Conference on Data Science and Machine Learning Applications (CDMA), pp. 134–140. IEEE (2020)
3. Ball, A.: Review of data management lifecycle models. Citeseer (2012)
4. Blumauer, A., Nagy, H., Nagy, H.: The Knowledge Graph Cookbook. Edition mono/monochrom (2020)

5. Brennan, R., Quigley, S., De Leenheer, P., Maldonado, A.: Automatic extraction of data governance knowledge from slack chat channels. In: Panetto, H., Debruyne, C., Proper, H.A., Ardagna, C.A., Roman, D., Meersman, R. (eds.) OTM 2018. LNCS, vol. 11230, pp. 555–564. Springer, Cham (2018). https://doi.org/10.1007/978-3-030-02671-4_34

6. Calvanese, D., De Giacomo, G., Lembo, D., Montali, M., Santoso, A.: Ontology-Based governance of data-aware processes. In: Krötzsch, M., Straccia, U. (eds.) RR 2012. LNCS, vol. 7497, pp. 25–41. Springer, Heidelberg (2012). https://doi.org/10.1007/978-3-642-33203-6_4

7. Chromiak, M., Grabowiecki, M.: Heterogeneous data integration architecture-challenging integration issues. Annales Universitatis Mariae Curie-Skłodowska. Sectio AI, Informatica 15(1), 7–11 (2015)

8. DeStefano, R., Tao, L., Gai, K.: Improving data governance in large organizations through ontology and linked data. In: 2016 IEEE 3rd International Conference on Cyber Security and Cloud Computing (CSCloud), pp. 279–284. IEEE (2016)

9. Gandomi, A., Haider, M.: Beyond the hype: big data concepts, methods, and analytics. Int. J. Inf. Manage. 35(2), 137–144 (2015)

10. Grüninger, M., Fox, M.S.: Methodology for the design and evaluation of ontologies (1995)

11. Ladley, J.: Data Governance: How to Design, Deploy, and Sustain an Effective Data Governance Program. Academic Press, Cambridge (2019)

12. Lee, S.U., Zhu, L., Jeffery, R.: Designing data governance in platform ecosystems. In: Proceedings of the 51st Hawaii International Conference on System Sciences (2018)

13. Mosley, M., Brackett, M.H., Earley, S., Henderson, D.: DAMA guide to the data management body of knowledge. Technics Publications (2010)

14. Motik, B., et al.: OWL 2 web ontology language: structural specification and functional-style syntax. W3C Recommendation 27(65), 159 (2009)

15. Parsia, B., Patel-Schneider, P., Motik, B.: OWL 2 web ontology language structural specification and functional-style syntax. W3C, W3C Recommendation (2012)

16. Solanki, M., Božić, B., Freudenberg, M., Kontokostas, D., Dirschl, C., Brennan, R.: Enabling combined software and data engineering at web-scale: the ALIGNED suite of ontologies. In: Groth, P., et al. (eds.) ISWC 2016. LNCS, vol. 9982, pp. 195–203. Springer, Cham (2016). https://doi.org/10.1007/978-3-319-46547-0_21

On Intelligent Fingerprinting of Antique Buildings from Clay Composition

Elena Marrocchino[3], Guido Sciavicco[1], Estrella Lucena-Sánchez[1,2(✉)], and Carmela Vaccaro[3]

[1] Department of Mathematics and Computer Science, University of Ferrara, Ferrara, Italy
{guido.sciavicco,estrella.lucenasanchez}@unife.it
[2] Department of Physics, Informatics, and Mathematics, University of Modena and Reggio Emilia, Modena, Italy
[3] Department of Physics and Earth Science, University of Ferrara, Ferrara, Italy
{elena.marrocchino,carmela.vaccaro}@unife.it

Abstract. Materials research in archaeological ceramic artifacts is a consolidated practice that helps architectural heritage preservation. Ancient buildings located within the historic centres, in particular, mark the image and history of each city at different periods, and when damaged historical masonry needs restoration actions, a good characterization of both new and old material is crucial to forecast the behaviour of the system. In this paper we consider 9 antique buildings and constructions of the Medieval city of Ferrara (NE Italy), and the geochemical characterization of samples from their bricks and *terracottas*. We apply an intelligent fingerprinting technique to major and trace elements, along with some of their ratios, with the purpose of identifying the smallest and more accurate subsets that allow to uniquely identify one building from all others. We obtain very encouraging results, with accuracies over 80% even with very small fingerprints.

Keywords: Feature selection · Fingerprinting · Material research

1 Introduction

Materials research applied to the study of archaeological ceramic artifacts is now a consolidated practice, and during the last decades the interest of scientists, architects, engineers, and archaeologists towards architectural heritage preservation has risen. The ancient buildings within the historic centres mark the image and history of each city at different periods, and when damaged historical masonry needs restoration actions, a good characterization of both new and old material is crucial to forecast the behaviour of the system. Historical understanding is not only useful to analyse and preserve objects but also to investigate the knowledge and skills used to produce and use them. In this light, the main goals of the building materials characterization are preservation and

R. Valencia-García et al. (Eds.): CITI 2021, CCIS 1460, pp. 33–47, 2021.
https://doi.org/10.1007/978-3-030-88262-4_3

restoration, which include [26]: *(i)* origin of historical raw materials, *(ii)* processes and changes in archaeological artifacts, *(iii)* determination of original firing temperature, and *(iv)* reconstruction of firing techniques and manufacturing technologies. Bricks and ceramics can be considered artificial rocks fired in kilns and, under this point of view, mineralogical, petrological and geochemical study approaches can be useful tools for the study of archæological ceramic materials. Bricks in ancient buildings preserve the trace of the claystone geological formation used to create them and geology influences raw material availability and thus building methods.

The Medieval city of Ferrara (NE Italy) is located in the eastern part of the Po alluvial plain and its geographical position, situated on a major waterway at a natural crossroads between the Adriatic Sea and the Po alluvial plain, contributed to the flourishing of the city, which peaked during the Renaissance period. Ferrara reached the top of Renaissance architecture and prestige with the dominion of the Estense family [10,29,30,36]. The Estense family considered the urban layout inside the first defensive walls inappropriate to represent their greatness and their dominance over the territory. This was the reason they decided to radically modify the city's layout, changing its structure and appearance with a further fortification of the wall ring and embellish of the city centre with numerous sumptuous palaces. These buildings utilized bricks (*cotto ferrarese*) and mortars as the dominant building materials. The use of these construction materials is related to the geographical position and the geomorphological framework of the Ferrara area, which is characterized by the widespread presence of silico-clastic sediments [1]. Historical bricks and terracotta decorations from some important Medieval and Renaissance buildings of Ferrara were collected and studied [7,28]. The chemical characterization of their bricks and *terracotta* elements were used to evaluate the nature of the original raw material (i.e. clay-rich sediment of local provenance). As a result of that study it was shown that characterizing the old construction materials used, as well as establishing the causes of the decay (when possible), could be useful for the planning of suitable restoration treatment and to identify and characterize the materials that were used to make these architectural elements [5,38]. This was motivated by the need of giving the restorer adequate information for choosing suitable new materials when replacement is necessary and to avoid incorrect restoration materials. The data obtained defined some technological information regarding the manufacture and some information regarding the different provenance of the raw materials. Such results were compared with the chemical-mineralogical data available for the sediments of the area [6,8] in order to define the nature and provenance of the original raw materials. In this paper, instead, we use them to establish the *geochemical fingerprint* of these building, effectively proving that it is possible to distinguish one building from another by the composition of its clay. Fingerprinting is a well-known problem in geology [18], and geochemical fingerprints for the classification of natural environments are being used more and more often, as (semi-)automatic, artificial intelligence based techniques improve in accuracy and diffusion. Chemical and geological fingerprinting is applied across many fields, but it is particularly prominent in forensic studies, mineral exploration, and in tracking the source of environmental pollutants. Other applications include petroleum science, geology, botany, food and agricultural science. Geochemical fingerprints are used in different ways: to differentiate among different mantle reservoirs, to characterize magmatic rocks from different geotectonic settings, to distinguish different water types, among others. In this particular case, we fingerprinting antique buildings helps in their restoration, conservation, and historical studying and placement.

In this paper, we define the geochemical fingerprinting problem as a *feature selection for classification* problem, and we solve it via an optimization problem, similarly to [12]. In particular, we: *(i)* study the basic statistical characterization of major and trace elements in bricks and *terracottas* of the buildings; *(ii)* define an optimization problem that allows us to establish which of them can be used to uniquely identify one building from another; and *(iii)* solve such an optimization problem via an evolutionary algorithm.

2   Background

Feature Selection. *Feature Selection* is a machine learning technique for data preprocessing, usually employed to eliminate those features, or attributes, that are considered irrelevant or noisy for the problem at hand [17]. On the one side, feature selection is meant to be used in order to improve the interpretability of the data, or sometimes to reduce the space requirement to store them. But feature selection is itself a learning process: the selected features provide a valuable information on the data themselves, as the fact that they have been selected implies their importance in the process being analyzed. This is particularly true in fingerprinting, that is, in essence, a feature selection process in which we want to understand which features do form a fingerprint, and how good such fingerprint performs. In some cases, feature selection models consider the various features *individually* during the selection process; these are called *univariate* methods, and they consist in applying some criterion to each pair feature-response and measuring the individual power of a given feature with respect to the response independently from the other features. In *multivariate* methods, on the other hand, the choice is performed *by subset* of features rather than single features. Among the several different approaches to feature selection, the most versatile ones are those that define the selection problem as an *optimization* problem. A *multi-objective optimization problem* (see, e.g. [9]) can be formally defined as the optimization problem of simultaneously minimizing (or maximizing) a set of k arbitrary functions:

$$\begin{cases} \min/\max \ f_1(\bar{x}) \\ \min/\max \ f_2(\bar{x}) \\ \dots \\ \min/\max \ f_k(\bar{x}), \end{cases} \tag{1}$$

where $\bar{x}$ is a vector of decision variables. A multi-objective optimization problem can be *continuous*, in which we look for real values, or *combinatorial*, in which we look for objects from a countably (in)finite set, typically integers, permutations, or graphs. Maximization and minimization problems can be reduced to each other, so that it is sufficient to consider one type only. A set $\mathcal{F}$ of solutions for a multi-objective problem is *non dominated* (or *Pareto optimal*) if and only if for each $\bar{x} \in \mathcal{F}$, there exists no $\bar{y} \in \mathcal{F}$ such that *(i)* there exists i $(1 \leq i \leq k)$ that $f_i(\bar{y})$ improves $f_i(\bar{x})$, and *(ii)* for every j, $(1 \leq j \leq k, j \neq i)$, $f_j(\bar{x})$ does not improve $f_i(\bar{y})$. In other words, a solution $\bar{x}$ *dominates* a solution $\bar{y}$ if and only if $\bar{x}$ is better than $\bar{y}$ in at least one objective, and it is not worse than $\bar{y}$ in the remaining objectives. We say that $\bar{x}$ is *non-dominated* if and only if there is not other solution that dominates it. The set of non dominated solutions from $\mathcal{F}$ is called *Pareto front*. Optimization problems can be approached in several ways; among them, *multi-objective evolutionary algorithms* are a popular choice (see, e.g. [14,20,32]). Feature selection can be seen as a multi-objective optimization problem, in which the solution encodes the selected features, and the objective(s) are designed to evaluate the performances of some model-extraction algorithm; this may entail, for example, instantiating (1) as:

$$\begin{cases} \max\ Performance(\bar{x}) \\ \min\ Cardinality(\bar{x}), \end{cases} \tag{2}$$

where $\bar{x}$ represents the chosen features; Eq. 2 can be referred to as a *wrapper*.

Fingerprinting. Physical and chemical *fingerprinting* is a well-known problem in geology and other affine disciplines. The most accepted definition refers to a geo-chemical fingerprint as a *signal that provides information about the origin, the formation and/or the environment of a geological sample* [18]. Geochemical fingerprints for the classification of natural environments are also characterized by the fact that their original composition is usually preserved, or in case of small changes during later geological history, must preserve its main geochemical characteristics to an extent that the original chemical signature is still recognizable. The use of geochemical fingerprints has a long tradition in Earth sciences, and a necessary prerequisite for applying geochemical fingerprints is that suitable analytical methods exist which allow the detection of fingerprints. The typical *by hand* process for fingerprinting is very expensive and entails an elevated risk of mistake due to potential loss of information, manual loading of data, and prolonged analysis time. In recent times, several statistical methods have been applied to aid the traditional geochemical investigation to understand, for example, pollution sources via fingerprinting, possible correlation among elements, and, in some cases, the nature of the contamination [4,21,40]. Examples of fingerprinting include recent works focused on protection of groundwater against pollution, deterioration, and for input pollution identification include applying geographical information systems and decision analysis [33,34], logistic regression model learning [27], univariate and multivariate analysis [31], and multiple regression models [15]. More in general, machine learning is emerging as an effective, less complicated and less expensive [19], empirical approach for both regression and/or classification of nonlinear systems, ranging from few to thousands of variables, and they are ideal for addressing those problems where our theoretical knowledge is still incomplete but for which we do have a significant number of observations, such as in fingerprinting analysis. In the past decades, it has proven useful for a very large number of applications, and among the techniques most commonly used we may mention artificial neural networks [2,24,39,42], support vector machines [3], but also self-organizing map, decision trees, ensemble methods such as random forests, case-based reasoning, neuro-fuzzy networks, and evolutionary algorithms [23].

3   Intelligent Fingerprinting

Classification. In this paper, we approach the fingerprinting problem of antique buildings by using an intelligent, machine learning-based novel methodology, based on defining the fingerprinting problem as a *feature selection for classification* problem. In data mining *classification* is an essential task for assigning the class values of new instances. Fingerprinting can be seen as a classification problem because we can interpret the existence of a model for classification as a proof that the identification is possible. As we shall see, each building will be represented by a set of samples, each of which, in turn, is described by a set of values of chemical elements and compounds. We interpret every sample as an instance, classified with the (unique) identification of the building from which it was taken. A classification model of such a dataset is an implicit fingerprinting method that, as we have explained, proves that those values contain enough information to distinguish one building from the others.

Feature Selection and Evaluation. Three problems must be addressed as this point. The first one concerns the evaluation method. Classification can be evaluated using different classical *metrics* (such as, for example, *accuracy, accuracy by class, area under the ROC curve*, and so on) combined with different *evaluation methods*, whose statistical value depends on the numerosity of dataset and the type of pre-processing. In our case, as we have explained, obtaining clay samples from antique buildings is an expensive and time-consuming process, resulting in having relatively small datasets. Small datasets are difficult to evaluate, being the most suitable method the so-called *leave-one-out cross validation* (*LOOCV*), which is a variant of the more general *cross validation* (*CV*). In cross validation, we randomly divide a dataset into k disjoint folds with approximately equal size, and each fold is in turn used to test the model induced from the other $k-1$ folds by a classification algorithm. The performance of the classification algorithm is evaluated by averaging the performances of the k models, and hence the level of averaging is assumed to be at fold. The leave-one-out version is used to estimate the performance of a classification algorithm by setting k to be the number of examples in the dataset, making it the best choice in the case of small datasets, and is able to produce robust enough estimates of model performance as each instance is given an opportunity to represent the entirety of the test dataset. The second problem concerns the dimension of the fingerprints.

Classification per se extracts models that use all attributes, that is, the entire chemical spectrum of samples. On the one side, good performances of a classification model in our problem proves that fingerprinting is possible, which is not obvious. On the other hand, useful fingerprints should also be small, so that they can be graphically visualized, discussed, and evaluated within the current theory. For this reason, intelligent fingerprinting of building requires minimizing the number of attributes. Finally, it so happens that the chemical interactions that describe a particular clay may not be all linear. In other words, good fingerprint may depend on *ratios* of elements instead of elements themselves; this should be taken into account in data preparation.

A Model for Building Fingerprinting. Summing up, our strategy for building fingerprinting is to use an evolutionary algorithm to solve the following optimization problem:

$$\begin{cases} \max \ Performance - LOOCV(\bar{x}) \\ \min \ Cardinality(\bar{x}), \end{cases} \tag{3}$$

where $\bar{x}$ represents the set of possible chemical values or ratios between chemical values that describe the instances.

4   Data

Origin. The data used for this study consist of 113 samples of clays and bricks from 9 different antique palaces located in the province of Ferrara. These included the Monastery of Sant'Antonio in Polesine (built in several phases during the 12th–16th centuries), the Church of Santa Maria in Vado (founded in the 10th century and extensively modified in the 15th–16th centuries), the Church of Santo Stefano (founded in the 10th century, but rebuilt in the 15th–16th centuries), the Cathedral of Ferrara (apse, 15th–16th centuries), the Schifanoia Palace ('Hall of Stuccoes', 15th–16th centuries), the surrounding city walls (15th century), the Palazzo Roverella (built in the 16th century), the Monastery of Santa Maria delle Grazie (built in several phases starting from the 14th century) and the church of San Andrea (built around the year 1000, in the east part of the Byzantine Castrum, but nowadays of the ancient splendor only the aisle with small semicircular apses and a small portion of the apse remain). Geochemical characterisation of their *terracottas* was carried out through X-ray fluorescence (XRF). The preparation of all the samples and the following analyses were carried out in the laboratories of the Department of Physics and Earth Sciences of the University of Ferrara. All the samples were pulverized using an agate pestle until a powder with a particle size less than 2 μm was obtained; part of the powder of each sample was used for loss on ignition (LOI) calculation where the powders were first dried in an oven at 110 °C, and then placed in the ceramic crucibles and subjected to a temperature of 1000 °C for one day. After that, 0.5 g of each powder was prepared by pressing a tablet on boric acid support for obtaining the chemical composition, determined by XRF with a wavelength dispersion spectrometer ARL Advant-XP (Thermo Fisher Scientific, Waltham, MA, USA) and consisted of an X-ray tube with a Mo target and an SSD Peltier-cooled detector (10 mm^2 active area and resolution of <155 eV at 10 $kcps$) according to [16,35]. The maximum voltage and current of 50 kV and 1500 μA, respectively, were used to excite the secondary fluorescence X-rays. A collimator with a diameter of 1 mm was used to collect the emitted secondary X-rays from a surface area of about 0.79 mm^2 in air. This allowed the major elements to be determined, expressed as a percentage by oxide weight: SiO_2, TiO_2, Al_2O_3, Fe_2O_3, MnO, MgO, CaO, Na_2O, K_2O, P_2O_5. Moreover, it allowed to extract trace elements, reported in ppm: V, Cr, Ni, Cu, Zn, Ga, Rb, Sr, Zr, Ba, La, Ce, Pb, Sc, Co, Th, Y, Nd, S. The accuracy of the instrument, estimated on the basis of the results obtained on international standards of geological samples, and the precision, expressed as standard deviation of replicated analyses, were between 2% and 5% for the major elements, and between 5% and 10% for the trace elements. The detection limit (0.01% for major oxides) was estimated to be close to 10 ppm for most trace elements, except for S for which 50 ppm was considered. The processing of the acquired intensities and the correction of the matrix effect were performed according to the model proposed in [22,25,37].

Basic Statistical Analysis. In the context of fingerprinting via feature selection for classification, the relevant elements and the relevant ratios among elements can be considered as variables. Some relevant statistical measures of our variables are shown in Table 1. They can be classified by their behaviour in three major groups according to a Shapiro normality test: *(i)* *normal* ones (that follow a normal distribution), that is, SiO_2, P_2O_5, LOI, MgO, Zn, Ni, La, MgO/Cr, SiO_2/TiO_2, SiO_2/Al_2O_3, SiO_2/CaO, SiO_2/Na_2O, SiO_2/K_2O and Cr/Ni; *(ii)* *quasi normal* ones (that do not follow a normal distribution, but with low values of skewness and kurtosis), that is: Cr, Y and V; *(iii)* *non-normal* ones: K_2O, TiO_2, Al_2O_3, Fe_2O_3, MnO, CaO, Na_2O, K_2O, Pb, Co, Th, Zr, Rb, Sr, Ba, and Nb. As always, such an analysis highlights that more often than not real data are difficult to treat with standard statistical tools, such as PCA, justifying the application of frequency-based approaches such as the one used here.

5   Experiments and Results

Parametrization. To instantiate (2), we used three different classifiers, in order to compare which type of classification shows the best performances for this particular problem. In particular we used a *single decision tree* (J48), a *random forest* (RF), and a *logistic regression algorithm* (LR), all from the implementation of the Weka package [41], and all with their standard parametrization. Because our purpose is fingerprinting, the choice of the particular learning algorithm used in the wrapper is not very important. Decision trees are one example of interpretable learning method; random forest can be considered quasi-interpretable (as they are set of trees, but the decision are taken functionally); logistic regression is an example of functional, non-interpretable method. Our purpose is to prove that in this case fingerprinting can be solved regardless the characteristics

Table 1. Descriptive statistical analysis of the data.

Feature	Mean	P-value	Kurtosis	Skewness
SiO_2	52.27	0.023	$4.08 * 10^{+14}$	-0.32
TiO_2	0.68	0.576	$2.68 * 10^{+14}$	-0.11
Al_2O_3	14.34	0.749	$2.62 * 10^{+13}$	-0.09
Fe_2O_3	5.93	0.636	$2.71 * 10^{+14}$	0.17
MnO	0.12	0.105	$2.71 * 10^{+14}$	0.04
MgO	4.45	$0.921 * 10^{-3}$	$3.81 * 10^{+14}$	-0.73
CaO	10.80	0.555	$3.70 * 10^{+13}$	-0.02
Na_2O	1.47	1.349	16.46	$3.14 * 10^{+14}$
K_2O	2.51	9.433	24.34	$3.51 * 10^{+14}$
P_2O_5	0.24	0.003	3.33	0.71
LOI	6.96	0.013	2.25	0.29
Pb	43.47	0.729	17.60	$3.36 * 10^{+12}$
Zn	114.45	$1.273 * 10^{-7}$	75.39	$8.02 * 10^{+14}$
Ni	146.47	$0.564 * 10^{-3}$	4.21	-0.70
Co	19.49	0.212	3.00	-0.25
Cr	205.36	0.0428	3.34	-0.55
V	102.53	0.001	5.89	0.88
Th	9.84	0.322	3.15	-0.23
Nb	8.49	1.237	-	-
Zr	134.68	0.023	2.79	-0.46
Rb	118.15	0.576	52.23	$5.62 * 10^{+14}$
Sr	297.80	0.749	3.87	-0.18
Ba	417.82	0.636	25.51	$3.10 * 10^{+14}$
Y	25.34	0.105	-	-
La	31.22	$0.921 * 10^{-3}$	3.18	0.63
Ce	52.26	0.555	4.33	0.58

of the underlying learning algorithm; using their standard parameters, as provided in the package, allows the experiments to be reproduced. The performances of each classification model have been measured in LOOCV mode (as explained above), and models are all multi-classes (one class per building). In terms of optimization problem, we used *accuracy* to instantiate $Performance(\bar{x})$. To solve the optimization problem we used the evolutionary algorithm NSGA-II (Nondominated Sorted Genetic Algorithm) [11], which is available as open-source from the suite *jMetal* [13]. NGSA-II is an elitist Pareto-based multi-objective evolutionary algorithm that employs a strategy with a binary tournament selection and a rank-crowding better function, where the rank of an individual in a population is the non-domination level of the individual in the whole population.

Table 2. Results of the shortest fingerprinting.

Classifier	Name	Fingerprint	Acc	ROC
J48	F1	Fe_2O_3, P_2O_5	0.75	0.75
	F2	$MgO, Na_2O, P_2O_5, Nb, Zr$	0.80	0.79
	F3	$TiO_2, Na_2O, P_2O_5, Zr, La$	0.78	0.81
	F4	Na_2O, K_2O, Nb, Ce	0.78	0.82
	F5	Na_2O, Nb, Rb	0.78	0.85
RF	F6	P_2O_5, Cr, Nb	0.81	0.91
	F7	Pb, Nb	0.67	0.80
	F8	Na_2O, Nb	0.72	0.84
	F9	Na_2O, P_2O_5	0.71	0.85
	F10	P_2O_5, Nb	0.74	0.90
LR	F11	Al_2O_3, Nb, Ba	0.78	0.89
	F12	P_2O_5, Zr	0.74	0.85
	F13	Ni, Nb, La, Ce	0.81	0.91
	F14	Al_2O_3, Co, Nb	0.73	0.86
	F15	P_2O_5, Ce	0.65	0.80

We used the standard parameters in each experiment, and used a simple binary representation (zero means that the feature is discarded and one that the feature is selected) of each solution with standard mutation and crossover. We used an initial population of 10 individuals, each evolving 1000 times; each experiment has been run 10 times and the best absolute solution has been considered, in terms of accuracy of the classification model.

Results. In Table 2 we show the results of the experiments. In particular, we show five selected elements from the Pareto fronts of each group of experiments; we selected them as the most accurate fingerprints per each group with less than six features each. This additional constraint allows us to deal with fingerprints that can be interpreted, yet being still accurate enough. From Table 2 we can initially conclude that the fingerprinting problem *per se* can be solved, as the average accuracies in leave one out cross-validation mode range from 65% to 81%. More specifically, though, we can also observe that interpretable and quasi-interpretable models seem to work slightly better than non-interpretable ones, in this case, considering that, across all selected fingerprints, their average accuracy is slightly higher. Moreover, we can analyze the behaviour of fingerprints for specific buildings in Table 3. We find that some buildings are more recognizable than others. This is the case for example of Palazzo Roverella and Santa Maria delle Grazie, which can be identified with accuracies over 90%. In the same way, some buildings such as Santa Maria in Vado present a more complex situation, and only the classifier based random forest is able to reach (an unimpressive) 66%. This proves that while our technique is able to solve the problem, there

Table 3. Results of the shortest fingerprinting with metrics by class.

Name	F1				F2				F3				F4				F5				Class
Classifier	acc	sens	spec	roc	acc	sens	spec	roc	acc	sens	spec	roc	acc	sens	spec	roc	acc	sens	spec	roc	
J48	0.70	0.45	0.95	0.65	0.69	0.45	0.92	0.63	0.64	0.36	0.91	0.63	0.80	0.63	0.96	0.67	0.59	0.27	0.91	0.80	Polesine
	0.48	0.00	0.96	0.49	0.65	0.33	0.97	0.58	0.76	0.55	0.97	0.70	0.74	0.55	0.93	0.70	0.59	0.22	0.96	0.79	MariaInVado
	0.64	0.28	1.00	0.75	0.85	0.71	0.98	0.89	0.63	0.28	0.97	0.60	0.63	0.28	0.97	0.60	0.93	0.85	1.00	0.91	Stefano
	0.76	0.54	0.98	0.77	0.64	0.36	0.91	0.67	0.70	0.45	0.94	0.75	0.71	0.45	0.97	0.75	0.76	0.54	0.97	0.83	Schifanoia
	0.87	0.85	0.88	0.82	0.86	0.81	0.91	0.79	0.84	0.76	0.91	0.83	0.70	0.43	0.96	0.83	0.77	0.57	0.97	0.81	Duomo
	0.77	0.71	0.82	0.75	0.91	0.85	0.96	0.89	0.86	0.78	0.92	0.83	0.86	0.86	0.86	0.83	0.88	0.86	0.89	0.85	Pietro
	0.99	0.75	0.99	0.85	0.97	0.62	0.95	0.77	1.00	1.00	0.99	1.00	0.98	0.87	0.97	1.00	0.97	0.75	0.94	0.96	Roverella
	0.92	0.87	0.97	0.90	0.94	0.87	1.00	0.94	0.93	0.87	0.99	0.94	1.00	1.00	0.99	0.94	0.79	0.62	0.96	0.98	Grazie
	0.49	0.00	0.98	0.98	0.50	0.00	1.00	0.71	0.50	0.00	1.00	1.00	0.50	0.00	1.00	1.00	0.50	0.00	0.99	0.86	Andrea

Name	F6				F7				F8				F9				F10				Class
Classifier	acc	sens	spec	roc	acc	sens	spec	roc	acc	sens	spec	roc	acc	sens	spec	roc	acc	sens	spec	roc	
RF	0.69	0.45	0.93	0.86	0.67	0.36	0.97	0.82	0.56	0.18	0.94	0.69	0.60	0.27	0.92	0.80	0.79	0.63	0.95	0.90	Polesine
	0.66	0.33	0.98	0.75	0.60	0.22	0.98	0.74	0.63	0.33	0.93	0.85	0.63	0.33	0.93	0.67	0.61	0.22	0.99	0.70	MariaInVado
	0.79	0.57	1.00	0.98	0.77	0.42	0.99	0.97	0.77	0.57	0.97	0.87	0.63	0.28	0.97	0.88	0.85	0.71	0.98	0.99	Stefano
	0.71	0.45	0.97	0.85	0.76	0.54	0.97	0.90	0.58	0.18	0.97	0.74	0.71	0.45	0.96	0.81	0.66	0.36	0.96	0.88	Schifanoia
	0.85	0.86	0.85	0.89	0.68	0.71	0.65	0.61	0.71	0.67	0.75	0.72	0.67	0.47	0.87	0.84	0.84	0.86	0.82	0.86	Duomo
	0.92	0.89	0.95	0.98	0.78	0.64	0.92	0.91	0.82	0.68	0.95	0.95	0.74	0.60	0.87	0.97	0.83	0.71	0.94	0.95	Pietro
	0.99	0.62	0.98	0.96	0.97	0.25	0.96	0.78	0.98	0.25	0.97	0.75	0.98	0.87	0.97	0.91	0.93	0.12	0.92	0.92	Roverella
	0.87	0.75	0.98	0.89	0.55	0.12	0.97	0.84	0.80	0.62	0.97	0.96	0.80	0.62	0.97	0.93	0.61	0.25	0.96	0.88	Grazie
	0.50	0.00	0.99	0.91	0.50	0.00	0.99	0.70	0.50	0.00	0.99	0.98	1.00	1.00	1.00	0.42	0.75	0.50	0.99	0.99	Andrea

Name	F11				F12				F13				F14				F15				Class
Classifier	acc	sens	spec	roc	acc	sens	spec	roc	acc	sens	spec	roc	acc	sens	spec	roc	acc	sens	spec	roc	
LR	0.65	0.36	0.94	0.86	0.78	0.63	0.93	0.91	0.73	0.54	0.91	0.91	0.56	0.18	0.94	0.86	0.67	0.45	0.88	0.86	Polesine
	0.58	0.22	0.93	0.73	0.50	0.00	0.99	0.62	0.48	0.00	0.95	0.75	0.52	0.11	0.92	0.75	0.50	0.00	1.00	0.44	MariaInVado
	0.91	0.86	0.97	0.84	0.78	0.43	0.99	0.84	0.78	0.57	0.98	0.73	0.71	0.43	0.99	0.73	0.70	0.43	0.97	0.89	Stefano
	0.73	0.54	0.91	0.93	0.72	0.54	0.89	0.94	0.66	0.36	0.96	0.87	0.77	0.64	0.90	0.87	0.48	0.00	0.96	0.77	Schifanoia
	0.80	0.71	0.89	0.85	0.87	0.81	0.93	0.94	0.90	0.86	0.93	0.87	0.72	0.62	0.81	0.87	0.68	0.52	0.84	0.79	Duomo
	0.98	1.00	0.96	0.93	0.86	0.86	0.87	0.88	0.93	0.89	0.96	0.91	0.96	0.96	0.96	0.91	0.73	0.68	0.79	0.83	Pietro
	0.98	0.00	0.98	0.82	0.95	0.25	0.94	0.85	0.99	0.75	0.98	0.97	1.00	0.00	1.00	0.97	0.96	0.50	0.94	0.93	Roverella
	0.80	0.62	0.98	0.96	0.73	0.50	0.96	0.88	0.93	0.87	0.98	0.98	0.54	0.12	0.95	0.98	0.73	0.50	0.95	0.91	Grazie
	0.50	0.00	1.00	0.41	0.50	0.00	1.00	0.44	0.74	0.50	0.98	0.98	0.75	0.50	0.99	0.98	0.49	0.00	0.98	0.71	Andrea

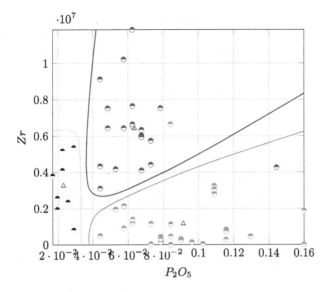

Fig. 1. Fingerprint representation of solution 12 (Duomo building in red, Pietro building in green and Roverella building in yellow; centroids are represented with a triangle) (Color figure online)

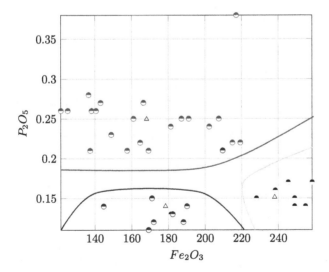

Fig. 2. Fingerprint representation of solution 1 (Grazie building in blue, Duomo building in red and Roverella building in yellow; centroids are represented with a triangle). (Color figure online)

are situations that deserve more attention; possible strategies include the use of ratios of elements, instead of simple elements. Finally, our approach can be completed with a graphical account of selected solutions. We show two examples in Fig. 1 and 2, in which we have displayed only the buildings that separate best from each other. As it can be observed, separating lines are highly non-linear: this can be taken as an empirical proof that non-automatized approaches to this problem are unfeasible, as fingerprints cannot be easily noticed by visual examination of the data.

6   Conclusions

Materials research applied to the study of archaeological ceramic artifacts is a consolidated practice that raised the interests of scientists, architects, engineers, and archaeologists towards architectural heritage preservation during the last decades. The main goals of the building materials characterization are their preservation and restoration. In some cases, material research is conducted with the help of accurate statistical analysis of the geochemical compositions of samples. Such an analysis can be carried on by visual exploration of the data, or by semi-automated techniques. The classical statistical tools to this end, however, often require a certain numerosity of samples, as well as that the statistical variables described by such samples behave in some specific way, in order to be applied. Artificial intelligence methods, on the other hand, are frequency-based, and do not require any specific hypothesis to be applied, resulting in a more realistic range of applicable cases. In this paper, we proved that geochemical characterization of antique building by means of clay composition analysis can be seen as a feature selection for classification problem. Using only few available samples of clay composition of bricks and *terracottas* of 9 different building in the city of Ferrara (NE Italy) we were able to devise unique geochemical fingerprints of the building themselves, within a reasonable statistical reliability of the results. Not only our results are important in the context from which they are obtained, but they are also an empirical evidence that in most cases, with real-world, expensive data (in this case, samples were collected in a period that spans 10 years) intelligent techniques must, and can, adapt to the situation in a better way compared to classical approaches.

As future work, we want to extend this research to include a second fingerprinting step which would allow us to establish which type of clay has been used for each building. This can be done starting from *typical clay samples* of the area surrounding Ferrara, and using an adaptation of our technique to establish which samples is the closest one to actual composition of the clay taken from the buildings. Such a fingerprinting process, if successful, can help the historians in their job, and could be replicated in other, less historically clear situations around Italy and the world.

Acknowledgments. E. Lucena-Sánchez and G. Sciavicco acknowledge the support of the project *New Mathematical and Computer Science Methods for Water and Food Resources Exploitation Optimization*, founded by the Italian region Emilia-Romagna.

References

1. Amorosi, A., Centineo, M., Dinelli, E., Lucchini, F., Tateo, F.: Geochemical and mineralogical variations as indicators of provenance changes in late quaternary deposits of SE Po plain. Sediment. Geol. **151**(3–4), 273–292 (2002)
2. Atkinson, P., Tatnall, A.: Introduction: neural networks in remote sensing. Int. J. Remote Sens. **4**(18), 699–709 (1997)
3. Azamathulla, H., Wu, F.: Support vector machine approach for longitudinal dispersion coefficients in natural streams. Appl. Soft Comput. **2**(11), 2902–2905 (2011)
4. Belkhiri, L., Mouni, L., Narany, T.S., Tiri, A.: Evaluation of potential health risk of heavy metals in groundwater using the integration of indicator kriging and multivariate statistical methods. Groundwater Sustain. Dev. **4**, 12–22 (2017)
5. Benedetto, C.D., Graziano, S., Guarino, V., Rispoli, C., Munzi, P., Morra, V., Cappelletti, P.: Romans' established skills: mortars from d46b mausoleum, porta Mediana necropolis, CUMA (Naples). Mediterr. Archaeol. Archaeom. **18**, 131–146 (2018)
6. Bianchini, G., Laviano, R., Lovo, S., Vaccaro, C.: Chemical-mineralogical characterisation of clay sediments around Ferrara (Italy): a tool for an environmental analysis. Appl. Clay Sci. **21**(3–4), 165–176 (2002)
7. Bianchini, G., Marrocchino, E., Moretti, A., Vaccaro, C.: Chemical-mineralogical characterization of historical bricks from Ferrara: an integrated bulk and micro-analytical approach. Geol. Soc. Lond. Special Publicat. **257**(1), 127–140 (2006)
8. Blo, G., Conato, C., Contado, C., Fagioli, F., Vaccaro, C., Dondi, F.: Metal content in river suspended particulate matter: data on PP river. Ann. Chim J. Anal. Environ. Cult. Herit. Chem. **94**(5–6), 353–364 (2004)
9. Collette, Y., Siarry, P.: Multiobjective Optimization: Principles and Case Studies. Springer, Berlin (2004). https://doi.org/10.1007/978-3-662-08883-8
10. Dean, T.: Land and Power in Late Medieval Ferrara: The Rule of the Este, pp. 1350–1450. No. 7, Cambridge University Press, Cambridge (1987)
11. Deb, K.: Multi-objective optimization using evolutionary algorithms. Wiley, London (2001)
12. Di Roma, A., Lucena-Sánchez, E., Sciavicco, G., Vaccaro, C.: Towards automatic fingerprinting of groundwater aquifers. In: Valencia-García, R., Alcaraz-Marmol, G., Del Cioppo-Morstadt, J., Vera-Lucio, N., Bucaram-Leverone, M. (eds.) CITI 2020. CCIS, vol. 1309, pp. 73–84. Springer, Cham (2020). https://doi.org/10.1007/978-3-030-62015-8_6
13. Durillo, J., Nebro, A.: Jmetal: a Java framework for multi-objective optimization. Adv. Eng. Softw. **42**, 760–771 (2011)
14. Emmanouilidis, C., Hunter, A., Macintyre, J., Cox, C.: A multi-objective genetic algorithm approach to feature selection in neural and fuzzy modeling. Evol. Optim. **3**(1), 1–26 (2001)
15. Farhadian, H., Katibeh, H.: New empirical model to evaluate groundwater flow into circular tunnel using multiple regression analysis. Int. J. Mining Sci. Technol. **27**(3), 415–421 (2017)
16. Franzini, M., et al.: Revisione di una metodologia analitica per fluorescenza-x, basata sulla correzione completa degli effetti di matrice (1975)
17. Guyon, I., Elisseeff, A.: An introduction to variable and feature selection. J. Mach. Learn. Res. **3**, 1157–1182 (2003)
18. Hoefs, J.: Geochemical fingerprints: a critical appraisal. Eur. J. Mineral. **22**, 3–15 (2009)

19. Jang, W.S., Engel, B., Yeum, C.M.: Integrated environmental modeling for efficient aquifer vulnerability assessment using machine learning. Environ. Model. Softw. **124**, 104602 (2020)
20. Jiménez, F., Sánchez, G., García, J., Sciavicco, G., Miralles, L.: Multi-objective evolutionary feature selection for online sales forecasting. Neurocomputing **234**, 75–92 (2017)
21. Kozyatnyk, I., Lövgren, L., Tysklind, M., Haglund, P.: Multivariate assessment of barriers materials for treatment of complex groundwater rich in dissolved organic matter and organic and inorganic contaminants. J. Environ. Chem. Eng. **5**(4), 3075–3082 (2017)
22. Lachance, G.: Practical solution to the matrix problem in X-ray analysis. Can. Spectrosc. **11**, 43–48 (1966)
23. Lary, D., Alavi, A., Gandomi, A., Walker, A.: Machine learning in geosciences and remote sensing. Geosci. Front. **7**(1), 3–10 (2016)
24. Lary, D., Muller, M., Mussa, H.: Using neural networks to describe tracer correlations. Atmos. Chem. Phys. **4**, 143–146 (2004)
25. Liu, H., Zhou, X., Zhang, X., Wu, K., Lu, C.: Experimental study and matrix effect correction of pseudobinary samples in XRF analysis. In: IOP Conference Series: Materials Science and Engineering. vol. 389. IOP Publishing (2018)
26. López-Arce, P., Garcia-Guinea, J., Gracia, M., Obis, J.: Bricks in historical buildings of Toledo city: characterisation and restoration. Mater. Character. **50**(1), 59–68 (2003)
27. Mair, A., El-Kadi, A.: Logistic regression modeling to assess groundwater vulnerability to contamination in Hawaii, USA. J. Contamin. Hydrol. **153**, 1–23 (2013)
28. Marrocchino, E., Telloli, C., Vaccaro, C.: Geochemical and mineralogical characterization of construction materials from historical buildings of Ferrara (Italy). Geosciences **11**(1), 31 (2021)
29. McIver, K.A.: The ESTE monuments and urban development in renaissance Ferrara **13**, 230–233 (1999)
30. McIver, K.A., Rosenberg, C.M.: The ESTE monuments and urban development in renaissance Ferrara **29**, 121 (1998)
31. Menció, A., et al.: Nitrate pollution of groundwater; all right.., but nothing else? Sci. Total Environ. **539**, 241–251 (2016)
32. Mukhopadhyay, A., Maulik, U., Bandyopadhyay, S., Coello, C.C.: A survey of multiobjective evolutionary algorithms for data mining: Part I. IEEE Trans. Evol. Comput. **18**(1), 4–19 (2014)
33. Ozdemir, A.: Gis-based groundwater spring potential mapping in the Sultan Mountains (Konya, Turkey) using frequency ratio, weights of evidence and logistic regression methods and their comparison. J. Hydrol. **411**(3), 290–308 (2011)
34. Pizzol, L., Zabeo, A., Critto, A., Giubilato, E., Marcomini, A.: Risk-based prioritization methodology for the classification of groundwater pollution sources. Sci. Total Environ. **506**, 505–517 (2015)
35. Potts, P.: X-ray fluorescence analysis: principles and practice of wavelength dispersive spectrometry. In: A Handbook of Silicate Rock Analysis. pp. 226–285. Springer, Dordrecht (1987). https://doi.org/10.1007/978-94-015-3988-3_8
36. Rosenberg, C.M.: The ESTE monuments and urban development in renaissance Ferrara (1997)
37. Rousseau, R.M.: Corrections for matrix effects in X-ray fluorescence analysis-a tutorial. Spectrochim. Acta Part B Atom. Spectrosc. **61**(7), 759–777 (2006)

38. Sanfilippo, G., Aquilia, E.: Multidisciplinary process aimed at the diagnosis and treatment of damages in stony cultural heritage: the balustrade of villa cerami (catania). Mediterr. Archaeol. Archaeom. **18**(5) (2018)

39. Shahin, M., Jaksa, M., Maier, H.: Artificial neural network applications in geotechnical engineering. Aust. Geomech. **1**(36), 49–62 (2001)

40. Singh, C.K., Kumar, A., Shashtri, S., Kumar, A., Kumar, P., Mallick, J.: Multivariate statistical analysis and geochemical modeling for geochemical assessment of groundwater of Delhi. India J. Geochem. Expl. **175**, 59–71 (2017)

41. Witten, I., Frank, E., Hall, M.: Data Mining: Practical Machine Learning Tools and Techniques, 3rd edn. Morgan Kaufmann, Elsevier (2011)

42. Yi, J., Prybutok, V.: A neural network model forecasting for prediction of daily maximum ozone concentration in an industrialized urban area. Environ. Pollut. **3**(92), 349–357 (1996)

Natural Language Processing

Emotional Corpus, Feature Extraction and Emotion Classification Using the Parameterized Voice Signal

Miriam Martínez-Arroyo[1] , Vicente Bello-Ambario[1] ,
José Antonio Montero-Valverde[1] , Eduardo de la Cruz-Gámez[1] ,
Mario Hernández-Hernández[2] , and José Luis Hernández-Hernández[3]([envelope])

[1] Division of Research and Graduate Studies, TecNM/Technological Institute of Acapulco, Acapulco, Mexico
{miriam.ma,ponente.msc,jose.mv,eduardo.dg}@acapulco.tecnm.mx
[2] Faculty of Engineering, Autonomous University of Guerrero, Chilpancingo, Mexico
mhernandezh@uagro.mx
[3] Division of Research and Graduate Studies, TecNM/Technological Institute of Chilpancingo, Chilpancingo, Mexico
joseluis.hernandez@itchilpancingo.edu.mx

Abstract. The recognition and classification of human emotions through voice analysis, it is a very interesting research area, due to the wide variety of applications: telecommunications, learning, human-computer interface, entertainment, etc. In this investigation a methodology is proposed for the recognition of emotions analyzing voice segments. The methodology is mainly based on the fast Fourier transform (FFT) and Pearson's correlation coefficients. The tone (pitch), the fundamental frequency (Fo), the strength of the voice signal (energy) and the speech rate have been identified as important indicators of the emotion in the voice. The system consist of a graphical interface that allows user interaction by means of a microphone integrated into the computer, which automatically processes the data acquired. In our environment, human beings are programmed to let our voice flow, in multiple ways to communicate and to capture through it emotional states. There are various investigations where the Berlin database is used, which is free and many researchers have used it in their research. However, the creation of an emotional corpus with Spanish phrases, was needed for testing that provide clearer results. The corpus contains 16 phrases per emotion created by 11 users (9 women and 2 men) with a total of 880 audio samples. The following basic emotions were considered: disgust, anger, happiness, fear and neutral. Results obtained indicate that the emotion recognition algorithm offers an 80% of effectiveness.

Keywords: Emotional state · Parameterization · Statistical models · Pattern recognition

1 Introduction

The most relevant research would be directed to the study of emotions through facial expressions, although in 1872 Charles Darwin himself pointed out the importance of

R. Valencia-García et al. (Eds.): CITI 2021, CCIS 1460, pp. 51–64, 2021.
https://doi.org/10.1007/978-3-030-88262-4_4

non-verbal aspects, vocal behavior and situations where the individual uses speech as a means of expression [2]. Technical difficulties leading to evaluation of vocal behavior and the merger with respect to its status as non-verbal behavior; are two of the reasons that have led to this mismatch with respect to facial expression [3, 4].

Studies on vocal expression of emotion can be classified into two large groups:

- **Expression Studies**. They have as basic objective determine how an emotional state is expressed or is externalized through the voice of the subject [5], its evaluation can be carried out at two levels: acoustic analysis and perceptual judgments of acoustic parameters.
- **Recognition Studies**. They try to know to what extent the receiver is able to identify, through the non-verbal aspects of the speaker's voice and the emotional state expressed by him.

One of the main problems what research on voice emotion recognition has faced [6], has been the separation of the verbal channel from the vowel, so that the linguistic content of the message does not determine making judgments on the affective state of the transmitter. It has been established that speech is an acoustic event, containing important information on the functioning of the central nervous system, and therefore carries information about the emotional state of a person.

Emotions are physically "reactions that represent modes of adaptation to certain stimuli in the individual and that affect the responses of different biological systems, including the voice" [7]. Emotions a very powerful force in human behavior, in addition to having a great influence on people's health, both physical and mental. A clear example of this fact is that a person who is excited, is able to do some action that never would do during a stable emotional state that is paralyzed by fear or sadness. However, one of the problems encountered by researchers when working with emotions, is that they present a high degree of subjectivity. This is due to the way they express themselves and it depends largely: of the speaker, culture of origin and of the environment.

Each emotion generates a set of reactions, they are automatic affective states and complexes that are unleashed in our body, which also fulfil a beneficial function of adaptation of the organism, by favoring our reaction to a stimulus. The emotions considered in this research are known as primary emotions established in Ekman's model (surprise, disgust, sadness, anger, fear and happiness) that cause a set of reactions in the human being [8–10]. A brief description of the primary emotions is provided below:

- **Surprise**. This is an emotional reaction to an unexpected situation and its main function is to make the nervous system adjust to an unforeseen change in the environment, eliminating the possible interferences that could appear.
- **Disgust**. It is characterized by a low medium tone, a wide range, the slowest speech rate y with big pauses. This gesture blocks the nostrils in case of perceiving an unpleasant substance and to facilitate the need to expel it.
- **Sadness**. Sad speech exhibits a medium tone lower than normal, a narrow range and a slow speed of speech. Energy decreases, motivation is reduced, metabolism is reduced and social isolation is increased. Sadness arises after the occurrence of an emotionally

damaging situation. Responds to survival instinct, as it alerts us to a harmful situation. In addition, promotes the search for social support.

- **Anger**. It is defined as "the unpleasant and annoying impression that occurs in the mood". This is a negative emotion that prioritizes sending blood to the hands and legs. Adrenaline levels are elevated, is associated with hostility, the fury and in the most extreme cases; with a pathological and permanent hatred.
- **Afraid**. This primary emotion is a way of warning us that a danger is approaching for which we are not prepared. Fear is awakened after a stimulus that makes us anticipate such danger. Helps the person perform some behavior to distance themselves from potential danger, therefore promotes escape behaviors, avoidance and prevents dealing with dangerous situations.
- **Happiness**. Manifests itself in an increase in the mean tone and in your range; as well as an increase in the speed of locution and in intensity. It is associated with positive feelings such as pleasure, the euphoria and the suppression of negative feelings. It is produced therefore, a sense of calm and well-being.

For an emotion to be considered primary, it must meet the following requirements:

- Have a specific neural substrate and that differentiates it from the rest. That is to say, that the neurons involved are specific ones.
- That the facial expression representing that emotion is unique and distinctive.
- That the feelings underlying the emotion, namely; the thoughts and the way we feel, they are characteristics of that emotion.
- It has an evolutionary and survival purpose.
- It has adaptive functions in a certain situation.

There are several research papers, where they indicates that some emotions are better recognized than others. Fechner [11] argues that the better recognition of negative emotions can be explained in terms of their greater survival value. In another case, in studies with adults, Scherer [3] handle the hypothesis which points out that anger is often the most widely recognized emotion, followed by sadness, indifference and happiness.

A corpus was built that contains 16 sentences per emotion created by 11 users (9 women and 2 men) with a total of 880 audio samples. Are considered the following basic emotions: disgust, anger, happiness, fear, and neutral. The algorithm of Emotion recognition gives 80% effectiveness in the results obtained.

2 Related Work

Several works have been carried out related to the identification of basic emotional states by analyzing audio segments in different languages.

In [22] Meftah et al. designed an emotional corpus in Arabic language in order to identify the following emotional states: neutral, sadness, happy, surprised, and questioning, for this the authors building and selected 16 sentences that were read by 20 male and female native speakers. In this sense, a similar work was developed by Constantini et al. [21] they built a database with Italian emotional speech from the voices of up to 6 actors who played 14 sentences simulated the next emotional states: disgust, fear, anger, joy, surprise, sadness and neutral.

A Database with the participation of actors and non-actors was developed by Banotu et al. This database provides a potential resource to analyze emotions in the speech signal. From the design of drama situations to annotation, there are 5 stages involved in the data collection process. A different annotation procedure is adopted by the mixture of context-dependent and context-independent ways. There are some utterances in the database where there is an occurrence of multiple emotions. Perceptual and acoustic analyses are carried out to understand differences in the data among actors and non-actors. Perceptual studies indicate that the actors intend to convey emotions in speech without affecting the linguistic message much. It is observed that there is more jitter in non-actors data when compared to actors [24].

Lyatsko et al. designed "EmoChildRu" which is considered as the first database containing emotional speech material from 3–7 year old Russian children. The database includes 20.340 recordings (30 h) of 100 children growing in families [23].

3   Materials and Methods

This section deals with the process of converting the original analog sound waves into digital signals for storage and reproduce them later; snapshots of analog sounds are taken and are stored. The speed with which the device takes samples is called the Sample Rate (SR) and will be expressed in Hertz or Kilo Hertz (Hz, Khz). 1 Hz will be 1 sample per second and 10 kHz is 10,000 samples per second. Each of these samples will be assigned a value corresponding to the amplitude of that instant in the original signal (Quantization).

For the case study, only the emotions of: disgust, anger, afraid, happiness, and neutral (no emotion).

Figure 1 shows the methodology used for the classification and recognition of emotions through the parameterized voice signal.

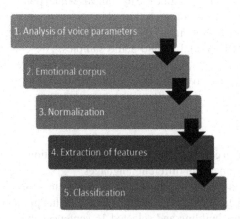

Fig. 1. Methodology implemented in recognition of emotional state.

3.1 Analysis of Voice Parameters

The voice is nothing but a sound and as such, it is characterized by a series of elements. The features that have been most recurrent in literature are the pitch, duration, voice quality, global pulse shape and vocal tract. García [12], divide his work into 13 features that have been used for emotion detection in the voice. These parameters are described in Table 1.

Table 1. Features used in Speech Emotion Recognition [12].

Features used	Description
Bandwidth	This range is measured in Hertz (Hz)
Vocal tract areas	Number of harmonics caused by non-linear airflow in the vocal tract that produces the voice signal
Spectral characteristics	Energy content of frequency bands divided by the sample length
Speech Activity Detection	This property is defined as the rhythmic profile of speech
Duration	Difference between the beginning and end time of a spoken sequence, obtaining a duration rate for emotional and neutral sentences
Energy	It is the value of the physical magnitude that expresses the greater or lesser amplitude of the sound waves
Formants	They are frequencies reinforced by resonance
Intensity	It is measured in Decibels (dB)
LPCs *(Linear Prediction Coefficients)*	A set of equivalent essential formulations for modeling a given waveform
MFCCs *(Mel Frequency Cepstrum Coefficients)*	Technique of fractioning the initial signal into a discrete set of spectral bands containing analogous information
Pitch	Represented as F0 (Fundamental Frequency)
Zero crossing rate	Represents how many times the signal changes sign passing through the abscissa axis
Speaking rate	The proportion of segmental units, syllables and pauses per unit of time produced by a speaker

Table 2 presents a summary of the relationships between emotions and the parameters of discourse. As is described, only five emotions appear. These correspond to the primary or basic emotions. Is known that there is a relationship between the prosodic information and the expression of emotions in speech; traits such as intensity, the fundamental frequency curvature and the speed of speech, are important characteristics of the discrimination of emotions in the voice [15–17].

Table 2. Comparison of emotions.

	Happiness	Anger	Disgust	Afraid	Sadness
Speed of the speaker	Slightly accelerated with increase	Slightly accelerated	Slow	Very accelerated	Paused
F_0	Increase in mean, variability	Increase in the mean, median and variability	-------	Increase in mean F_0, disturbance, variability of F_0 movement	Below the normal mean F_0
Articulation	Normal	Tense	Normal	Accurate	Dragged
Intensity	High	High	Slow	Normal	Slow
F_0 average	High	High	Slow	High	Slow
Spectrum	Increased high frequency energy	Raised at the midpoint	-------	Increased high frequency energy	Decrease in high frequency energy
Others	Irregular accent distribution	Speak cut off	------	Irregularity in the sound	Rhythm with irregular pauses

3.2 Emotional Corpus

The speech corpus consists of 880 Spanish sentences recorded by TISM (Technological Institute of San Marcos) students with a range in ages between 18 and 26. These sentences express 5 different emotional states: disgust, anger, happiness, fear and neutral with a total of 16 sentences for each of them. We have chosen sentences whose semantic content does not imply any particular emotion so the classification can be made on the basis of prosodic details [15]. Figure 2 shows the graphical interface used to create the emotional corpus.

As shown in Fig. 3, the audio recording was done in a closed classroom, located in the computer lab of the Technological Institute of San Marcos in the state of Guerrero, (TISM), in order to reduce noise and distractions.

There are two important factors during this process. For code development, parameters must be changed to determine what works best in the algorithm. Using a desktop program, audio is recorded with a sampling frequency of 44100 Hz and an audio rate of 16 bits. One channel (Mono) is used, resulting in a vector of thousands of data, from which non-significant data will be discriminated.

Fig. 2. Main interface of the voice recorder.

Fig. 3. TISM students in the recording process.

Table 3 includes some example sentences from the corpus used as a test to detect the corresponding emotion.

Table 3. Some example sentences from the corpus used.

No.	Phrases used
1	Times are not like before
2	What are you talking about?
3	Do you want some advice?
4	Homework is for tomorrow
5	He is the group leader
6	If true
7	I don't think so, don't be a gossip
8	You are always late
9	Can you keep quiet please?
10	If you don't like it, do it yourself
11	My mom's computer is broken
12	The school is painted blue
13	Would you live with me
14	My point of view is another
15	This activity does not correspond to me
16	There is a madman

3.3 Normalization

In general, it is understood that normalization is the operation by which a set of values of a given magnitude is transformed into others in such a way that the latter belong to a predetermined scale.

It is possible to normalize a set of values in the interval [0, 1] by applying for each value the transformation shown in Eq. 1.

$$v_i = \frac{a_i - min}{max - min} \tag{1}$$

Where a_i is the value to be transformed, *min* and *max* are the minimum and the maximum of the set of values and v_i is the normalized value.

The normalization consists of processing the acoustic signal and finding the optimal set of features that allow to perform the classification of emotions. The function algorithm that normalizes the data of a numerical vector, which it receives as a parameter, is as follows:

- Returns the maximum absolute value of the vector to transform
- Returns the number of elements of the vector to be transformed (Vector size = n)
- Returns a vector of zeros of n rows and 1 column
- A loop is made where the initial value of i is 1 and is increasing in 1 until it becomes the value of n
- The vector is divided at the position i between its absolute maximum values.

3.4 Feature Extraction

This module consists of grouping the spectral acoustic characteristics, as these describe the properties of a signal in frequency domain by means of harmonics and formants, prosodic information (volume, velocity, duration) is also extracted. The algorithm for feature extraction is the fast furrier transform (FFT) which performs the following:

- The first 60000 values of the vector are cut.
- The absolute value of the Fourier transform [18] of the recording is obtained.
- Multiply the result by the conjugate of the original vector.
- Accepts only frequencies above 150 Hz.
- Normalize the vector using the Euclidean norm.

The Euclidean norm (also called vector magnitude, Euclidean length, or 2-Norm) of a vector v with the elements of N is defined by Eq. 2.

$$||v|| = \sqrt{\sum_{k=1}^{N} |v_k|^2} \tag{2}$$

FFT is the usual abbreviation for Fast Fourier Transform, and is an efficient algorithm that allows to compute the discrete Fourier transform and its inverse given vectors of length N by Eq. 3.

$$X_k = \sum_{n=0}^{N-1} x_n e^{-j2\pi k\omega t \frac{n}{N}} \tag{3}$$

The FFTs of each section are obtained, containing 5 vectors for each emotion with the objective of generating a surface in which the frequencies and their variation in time can be observed. The FFTs of each section are averaged to obtain a pattern of the pronounced phrase.

3.5 Classification

Pearson's correlation coefficient is defined as an index that can be used to measure the degree of relationship of two variables as long as both are quantitative and continuous. Pearson's correlation coefficient is an easily performed index. In the first instance, its absolute values range from 0 to 1. If we have two variables X and Y, then we define Pearson's correlation coefficient between these two variables as $r_{x, y}$ as shown in Eq. 4.

$$px, y = \frac{\sigma xy}{\sigma x \sigma y} = \frac{E[(X - \mu x)(Y - \mu y)]}{\sigma x \sigma y} \tag{4}$$

3.6 Description of the System that was Developed

The development of the project was carried out in a period of 13. Figure 4, shows the general structure of the proposed system, starting with the capture of voices to have the emotional corpus. For the emotional corpus design, Students from the San Marcos Technological Institute in the state of Guerrero, Mexico, were invited to collaborate.

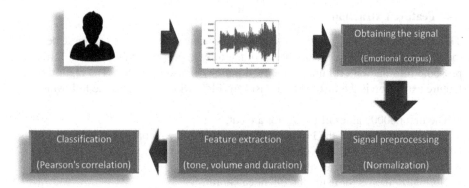

Fig. 4. Block diagram of the general structure of the proposed system.

4 Results

A Mexican emotional corpus has been created for the testing of the speech emotion recognition algorithm using a statistical method as a classifier. It is worth mentioning that more features are expected to be added to the vector to increase the efficiency of the recognizer using Machine Learning techniques.

Summary of results: In the processing stage, the audio signal was processed as shown in Fig. 5.

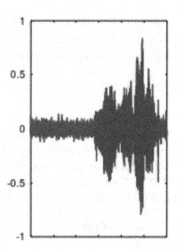

Fig. 5. The phrase: "You will live with me" recorded by TISM students.

In the feature extraction stage, we were able to obtain the frequency spectrum containing a vector with patterns necessary to detect the 5 emotions shown in Fig. 6.

In the classification stage we used the differences between the vector to be classified and the feature vectors stored in the database by means of Pearson's correlation, detecting the differences by means of the error coefficient. Table 4 shows the success in detecting

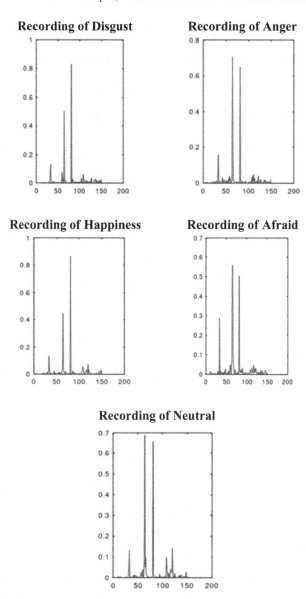

Fig. 6. Pattern of the sentence pronounced in each emotion.

the emotion "Disgust" by detecting the error coefficient which is the closest to 0 and thus pointing out the most significant similarity in the vector of features with emotion to be recognized.

Table 5 shows the confusion matrix of the algorithm used in this work where it can be observed that the neutral emotion has greater confusion than the other emotions, it is also worth mentioning that disgust and anger are emotions that are clearly identified with greater accuracy by this classifier.

Table 4. Recognition of "Disgust" using the sample correlation method.

PEARSON CORRELATION	**0.15327**
Error coefficient disgust	0.018317
Error coefficient anger	0.021492
Error coefficient happiness	0.022185
Error coefficient fear	0.020861
Error coefficient neutral	0.052955
Identified emotion:	**DISGUST**

Table 5. Confusion matrix for the classification algorithm using Pearson's correlation.

OBSERVATIONS	PREDICTION					
	Disgust	**Anger**	**Happiness**	**Afraid**	**Neutral**	**Totals**
Disgust	143	8	9	5	11	**176**
Anger	23	134	12	2	5	**176**
Happiness	25	13	116	4	18	**176**
Afraid	18	14	9	115	20	**176**
Neutral	39	34	21	2	80	**176**
Totals	**248**	**203**	**167**	**128**	**134**	**880**

5 Conclusions

A research of the acoustic parameters for the recognition of emotional states in the voice was carried out in the area of Intelligent Systems. It was achieved to have an algorithm capable of recognizing 80% of the sentences with emotion acted by TISM students. The results show the need for more parameters in the feature extraction step. It was necessary to creation a corpus due to the lack of standardization in the elicitation of emotions and the non-existence of norms that guarantee reproducibility. Although the initial results are satisfactory, we considered that, it is essential to use more classification methods and artificial learning techniques in order to have a higher classification efficiency.

1. References

1. Darwin, C.: The Expression of the Emotions in Man and Animals. University of Chicago Press (2015)
2. Carrera, M.J.M., Fernández, A.J.: El reconocimiento de emociones a través de la voz. Estud. Psicol. **9**(33–34), 31–52 (1988)

3. Scherer, K.: Speech and emotionnal states. Speech Evaluation in psychiatry. J. Darby. New York, Grune and Stratton (1981)
4. Scherer, K.R.: Methods of research on vocal communication: Paradigms and parameters. Handbook of methods in nonverbal behavior research, pp. 136–198 (1982)
5. Brown, B.L., Bradshaw, J.M.: Towards a social psychology of voice variations. In: Recent Advances in Language, Communication, and Social Psychology, pp. 144–181. Routledge, London (2018)
6. Zhao, M., Adib, F., Katabi, D.: Emotion recognition using wireless signals. In: Proceedings of the 22nd Annual International Conference on Mobile Computing and Networking, pp. 95–108, October 2016
7. Levenson, R.W.: Human emotion. a functional view. In: Ekman, P., Davidson, R.J. (eds.). The Nature of Emotions: Fundamental Questions, pp. 123–126. Oxford University Press, New York (1994)
8. Kim, E.H., Hyun, K.H., Kim, S.H., Kwak, Y.K.: Speech emotion recognition using eigen-fft in clean and noisy environments. In: The 16th IEEE International Symposium on Robot and Human interactive Communication. RO-MAN 2007, pp. 689–694. IEEE (2007)
9. Solís, V.J.F.: Modelo de procesamiento de voz para la clasificación de estados. PhD thesis, Instituto Politécnico Nacional. Centro de Investigación en Computación (2011)
10. Plutchik, R.: The nature of emotions: Human emotions have deep evolutionary roots, a fact that may explain their complexity and provide tools for clinical practice. Am. Sci. **89**(4), 344–350 (2001)
11. Fechner, E.H.: Children's understanding of the nonverbal communication of emotion in the visual, vocal and gestural (Doctoral dissertation, ProQuest Information & Learning) (1978)
12. García, M.J.V., Cobeta, I., Martín, G., Alonso-Navarro, H., Jimenez-Jimenez, F.J.: Acoustic analysis of voice in Huntington's disease patients. J. Voice **25**(2), 208–217 (2011)
13. Nwe, T.L., Foo, S.W., De Silva, L.C.: Speech emotion recognition using hidden Markov models. Speech Commun. **41**(4), 603–623 (2003)
14. Montero, J.M.: Estrategias para la mejora de la naturalidad y la incorporación de variedad emocional a la conversión texto a voz en castellano (Doctoral dissertation, Tesis Doctoral, ETSI Telecomunicación, UPD) (2003)
15. Ortego Resa, C.: Detección de emociones en voz espontánea (Bachelor's thesis) (2009)
16. Cowie, R., et al.: Emotion recognition in human computer interaction. IEEE Signal Process. Mag. **18**(1), 32–80 (2001)
17. Hasrul, M.N., Hariharan, M., Yaacob, S.: Human affective (Emotion) behaviour analysis using speech signals: a review. In: International Conference on Biomedical Engineering (ICoBE), vol. 27, p. 28, February 2012
18. Nussbaumer, H.J.: The fast Fourier transform. In: Fast Fourier Transform and Convolution Algorithms, pp. 80–111. Springer, Heidelberg (1981). https://doi.org/10.1007/978-3-642-818 97-4
19. Darwin, C.: 1965. The Expression of the Emotions in Man and Animals. John Marry, London (1872)
20. Ortego Resa, C. et al.: Detección de emociones en voz espontánea. B.S. thesis (2009)
21. Costantini, G., Iaderola, I., Paoloni, A., Todisco, M.: EMOVO corpus: an Italian emotional speech database. In: International Conference on Language Resources and Evaluation (LREC 2014), pp. 3501–3504. European Language Resources Association (ELRA) (2014)
22. Meftah, A., Alotaibi, Y., Selouani, S.A.: Designing, building, and analyzing an Arabic speech emotional corpus. In: Workshop on Free/Open-Source Arabic Corpora and Corpora Processing Tools Workshop Programme, p. 22, May 2014

23. Lyakso, E., et al.: EmoChildRu: emotional child Russian speech corpus. In: International Conference on Speech and Computer, pp. 144–152. Springer, Cham (2015). https://doi.org/10.1007/978-3-319-23132-7_18
24. Banothu, R., Botsa, K., Paidi, G., Suryakanth, V.: IIIT-H TEMD semi-natural emotional speech database from professional actors and non-actors. In: Proceedings of the 12th Conference on Language Resources and Evaluation (LREC 2020), pp. 1538–1545. European Language Resources Association (2020)

Importance of International R&D Collaboration Between Companies: The CollaborativeHealth Use Case

Oscar Apolinario-Arzube[1], José Antonio García-Díaz[2(✉)], Diego Roldán[3],
Lisardo Prieto-González[4], Germán Casal[5], and Rafael Valencia-García[2]

[1] VIAMATICA S.A., Edif. San Francisco 300, Córdova y Av. 9 de Octubre,
090313 Guayaquil, Ecuador
oapolinario@viamatica.com
[2] Facultad de Informática, Universidad de Murcia, Campus de Espinardo,
30100 Murcia, Spain
{joseantonio.garcia8,valencia}@um.es
[3] DANTIA Tecnología S.L., Parque Empresarial de Jerez 10, Calle de la Agricultura,
11407 Jerez de la Frontera, Cádiz, Spain
droldan@dantia.es
[4] Dpto. de Ciencias de la computación, Universidad Carlos III de Madrid,
Madrid, Spain
lpgonzal@inf.uc3m.es
[5] Oficina Española de Ciencia y Tecnología (SOST), Galileo 114, Polanco,
11550 Ciudad de México, Mexico
german.casal@cdti.es

Abstract. International R&D activities are strategical to provide solutions that can solve global problems by creating interdisciplinary and multicultural teams. One of the current challenges that international collaboration could solve is related to outbreaks of infectious diseases, which have a devastating impact on society. Influenza in Spain was responsible of 4000 deaths during 2019, despite having a vaccine. Tropical infectious diseases, such as Dengue or Zika, are transmitted through mosquitoes and proliferate in hot and humid conditions. Brazil reported more than 3 million cases and more than a thousand deaths during the dengue fever epidemic that started in 2019. New coronavirus have once again shown the consequences that infectious diseases have both for the society and for the economy, claiming thousands of lives and forcing many countries to take restrictive lockdowns. Preventive measures can mitigate the devastating consequences of outbreaks of infectious diseases. In this sense, infodemiological systems compile data regarding public-health concerns to forecast new outbreaks. In this manuscript we describe the CollaborativeHealth tool and we report three case-studies carried out with this tool: Influenza in Spain, Zika and Dengue in Ecuador, and COVID-2019 in Spanish-speaking countries.

Keywords: Infodemiology · Ontologies · Natural Language Processing · Progressive web apps

© Springer Nature Switzerland AG 2021
R. Valencia-García et al. (Eds.): CITI 2021, CCIS 1460, pp. 65–78, 2021.
https://doi.org/10.1007/978-3-030-88262-4_5

1 Introduction

Research & Development (R&D) activities from a knowledge transfer perspective allows to create robust solutions rooted in the idea of synergy, in which the abilities and experience of each member of the team is greater than the simple sum of its parts. Advances during last decades in communication strategies have reduced communication barriers between groups that are far geographically. Moreover, cultural and background differences can make a problem be seen from different points of view, reaching more robust and adaptable solutions.

CDTI is a Spanish public business entity, dependent on the Ministry of Science and Innovation, which promotes innovation and technological development in Spanish companies. One of its objectives is to promote the international R&D collaboration by providing R&D financing for Spanish companies. This paper presents a use case of an international collaboration project named CollaborativeHealth. This project has been developed by VIAMATICA and Universidad de Guayaquil (Ecuador); and DANTIA Tecnología S.L., Universidad de Murcia and Universidad Carlos III de Madrid (Spain). This project has been funded and supervised by CDTI.

1.1 Motivation

An outbreak of an infectious disease is when linked cases of the disease are observed in a specific region during a specific time interval. In case when the outbreak spreads globally, we refer to a pandemic. The consequences of outbreaks and pandemics are devastating for human life. On the one hand, they cost many human lives, collapse hospitals, and affect the physical and mental health of citizens. On the other hand, its containment requires drastic measures that have high costs for the economy, as the most effective measures require lockdown to prevent people to get infected and, thus, gradually release the hospital pressure.

Prevention is a key strategy to avoid outbreaks of infectious diseases. Prevention procedures have been explored from different point of views. For example, in [1] the authors explored risk mitigation in specific events than produced mass gatherings. When people from different parts of the world are meet, such as happens in sport events, there is a high chance for spreading an infectious disease. Other authors have focused on the study of preventive measures after natural disasters, such as the work presented in [15], since natural disasters change the environment and forces people to move to other areas. From a wider perspective, a novel approach concerning infectious diseases prevention is infodemiology [17], which can be defined as the science that compiles and analyses data from the Internet related to public health.

CollaborativeHealth is an online platform that surveys automatically data on the Internet from structured and non-structured sources [2,3]. CollaborativeHealth makes use of state-of-the-art technologies from Natural Language Processing, Information Retrieval, and Deep-Learning in order to create a set of smart and configurable Key Performance Indicators (aka KPIs) that healthcare professionals and organisations can adapt to survey infectious disease events in a temporal and spatial dimension.

The final stage of the development of CollaborativeHealth consisted in three case studies: The first case-study is based on compiling evidences of Influenza in Spain, the second one is based on Zika, Dengue and Chikungunya in Ecuador, and the third one is regarding Covid-2019 epidemic in Spanish-speaking countries. It is worth mentioning that the last case study was not originally scheduled in the development of the platform, since this disease did not show its effects until the end of 2019; however, the members of the consortium made an additional effort to consider this new disease.

In the rest of the paper the reader can find novel approaches concerning Infodemiology in Sect. 2, the system architecture in Sect. 3, the description of the three case-studies for validating the platform in Sect. 4 and, finally, the conclusions of this international collaboration as well as the following actions to be carried out with the tool in Sect. 5.

2   Background Information

According to [4], online health surveillance gathering can be used to schedule more effective strategies regarding public-health. Infodemiology is a novel field of research based in the use of public data from the Internet related to health. A survey regarding infodemiological approaches was conducted in [16], in which the authors indicate that the availability of performing real-time analysis is one of the key advantages over traditional surveillance methods. In the research evaluated in this survey, the most popular topics were related to diseases, outbreaks, epidemics, healthcare, drugs, and mental health. The study revealed that Twitter and the Google search engine were the most popular data sources representing, respectively, the 45% and the 24.4% of 338 publications. According to the authors, the major drawback of Twitter is that it is not widely used whereas search engines are most universal. Moreover, the analysis of queries in search engines ensures anonymity, as data seems to be more reliable.

One important limitation in infodemiology is the fact that their results are biased when there are few data to compile related to specific events. Moreover, fake-news and misinformation can also limit infodemiological approaches. In this sense, the authors of [23] analysed search queries to investigate search behaviours related to COVID-19 to find terms, queries, and hashtags that generates or feeds fake news. The authors identify topics related to Bill Gates, 5G-based technologies, laboratories, ozone, conspiracy, and tips regarding a cure of coronavirus based on the injection of disinfectant. Therefore, the usage of contextual feature engineering, that considers who transmits the information, along with Natural Language Understanding techniques, that considers how information is transmitted, could reduce the bias on the data.

In [9], the authors analysed mobile apps regarding collaborative systems focused on health reporting. In their report, the authors include tools focused on outbreaks of infectious diseases, most of them inspired by the 2009 H1N1 influenza pandemic. One of them is HealthMap [10], which is a tool that compiles evidences from unstructured data-sources. This tool is capable of classifying alerts from the disease that is being monitored within a location. From a technological point of view, HealthMap uses Natural Language Processing and web-based user interfaces. As far as our knowledge goes, HealthMap does not take into account information from social networks and based its reports on official sources. Moreover, HealthMap heavily relies on human process for the quality of the overall process. Outbreaks Near Me [9] is a tool focused on allowing citizens to contribute with reports based on their daily experiences through a web-app.

The analysis of surveillance platforms reveals two main challenges. On the one hand, the difficulty of verifying the quality and reliability of the submitted data. On the other hand, intentional or unintentional misinformation that it is present on the Internet. Therefore, to solve these drawbacks, CollaborativeHealth has a rule-based module focused on calculating the confidence of the reports based on several strategies, according to the source nature. This module boosts those reports that have been published from confidence sources, even in social media. More details regarding this module can be found in Sect. 3.

3   System Architecture

Figure 1 depicts the architecture of CollaborativeHealth. In a nutshell, CollaborativeHealth compiles evidences from several sources. For each evidence, a karma based on many factors is calculated and then stored in a distributed database based on blockchain. Next, evidences are annotated semantically with the use of a custom ontology and then its sentiment is extracted with an aspect-based sentiment analysis approach. Next, karma, semantic annotation, and the sentiment are used to build a bunch of smart KPIs that are available to health professionals by a final dashboard. Each module is described below.

The first module in the architecture is responsible of monitoring Internet for compiling evidences related to infectious diseases. Three sources are considered: (1) social networks, (2) official reports, and (3) direct citizen participation. For social networks, we focus on the micro-blogging social network Twitter, because its contents are public and free. Twitter has been widely adapted to conduct infodemiological studies [19,28]. Moreover, the length restriction of Twitter and its syndication mechanism by means of hashtags eases the identification of the information you are searching for. For the official reports, we rely on a custom web crawler. This crawler can filter relevant contents with regular expressions and can discard non-relevant parts of the documents, such as advertisements or asides. The last type of evidences are reported directly by the citizens. For this, we have developed a progressive web app that allows citizens to report a brief text, a geolocation, a photo, and a series of tags of any evidence they consider relevant.

The second module of the architecture is responsible to measure and rank the compiled evidences. To achieve this objective, we first calculate a confidence score (aka Karma) from a rule-based approach that takes into consideration multiple

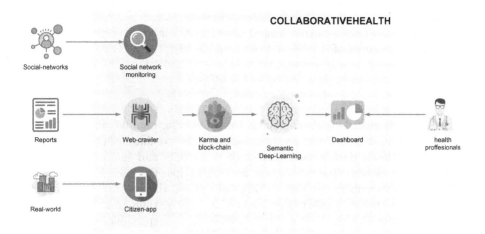

Fig. 1. System architecture of CollaborativeHealth

criteria. For example, in case of the evidences reported by citizens, the karma algorithm boosts those evidences that are reported by precise geolocation by GPS over those evidences reported from a WiFi connection, that have less precision. Next, those reports that exceed certain threshold of karma are stored in a distributed database based on blockchain technologies using BigchainDB [18]. The reasons of using blockchain in CollaborativeHealth are: (1) to ensure integrity of the data, (2) for reliable backup, and (3) to share securely data among instances of CollaborativeHealth.

The third module consists on the Information Retrieval (IR) module. For this, an ontology has been developed specifically for this tool. Ontologies are the backbone technology for the Semantic Web and have been applied successfully to different domains such as medicine [24,27], e-commerce [13] or hardware administration [5]. The foundations of the developed ontology are the Disease Ontology (DO) [25] and the Infectious Disease Ontology (IDO) [7]. From these two ontologies we have included terms such as SNOMED CT [8] for easing the interoperability with external systems. In addition, we have included other concepts such as regions, prevention mechanisms, or risk factors among others. For extracting the relationship between the evidences and the ontology we conduct semantic annotation approach. We annotate every concept of the ontology with a set of regular expressions and related words. Then, we apply an approach based on a extended version of TF—IDF. The main idea is to measure the relation of each topic with the ontology with the information that appears both explicitly and implicitly. The TF—IDF—e formula (see Eq. 1) measures the frequency of the concepts of the ontology but, at the same time, considers those concepts that are related to a specific concept based on their distance. This formula was inspired in the works described in [22]. In addition, we extract the sentiment of each evidence. For this, we train the evaluate different neural networks models based on sentence and word embeddings. These architectures include convolutional neural networks, recurrent neural networks, the usage of statistical features inspired in the works of [12,14] and the Spanish BERT, BETO [6].

$$\sum_{j=1}^{n} \frac{tf - idf}{e^{dist(i,j)}} \tag{1}$$

The fourth module is the Semantic Deep-Learning module, which objective is the creation of smart and configurable KPIs by combining all the previous information. Each KPI is independent of the others and has multiple views, such as word clouds, timelines, maps and heatmaps. For each KPI, the users can specify different filters than include the Karma, the geographical area, the concepts that appears explicitly and implicitly and by time area.

CollaborativeHealth platform is available as a responsible web interface, which core is based on the principles described in [20]. The dashboard allows users to configure the application, manage users, and access the data and the KPIs. Moreover, this dashboard can be used to send specific data and reports to the citizens that use the web app. It is worth mention that the development of the platform has been designed with scalability in mind. For this, some Docker containers encapsulate each module independently as well as there are other containers for the databases that can scale on demand.

4   Validation

The validation of the CollaborativeHealth platform has been carried out by three case studies: Influenza in Spain (see Sect. 4.1), Zika and Dengue in Ecuador (see Sect. 4.2), and COVID-2019 in Spanish-speaking countries (see Sect. 4.3).

4.1   Influenza in Spain

During 2017–2018, it was estimated that flu season affected in Spain to 800k people of which 15k people died[1]. Compared with previous years, there was an increase resulting in a significant number of hospitalisations with severe flu. Flu incidence in Spain is high even though there are annual vaccination campaigns.

From the beginning of the development of CollaborativeHealth, we started to compile tweets from Spain that include keywords such as *acatarrado* (cold), *constipado* (constipated), *influenza*, or *gripe* (flu). These tweets were used, on the one hand, to build the aspect-based sentiment analysis component and, on the other, to evaluate this case-study with past evidences. UMUCorpusClassifier [11] was used to compile the tweets and allow to the volunteers to annotate the tweets. A total of 13 volunteers evaluated the tweets in a five-scale of *very-positive*, *positive*, *neutral*, *negative*, and *very negative*. In addition, volunteers could also mark documents as unrelated. Volunteers performed a total of 9267

---

[1] https://www.redaccionmedica.com/secciones/sanidad-hoy/gripe-en-espana-casi-800-000-casos-52-000-ingresados-y-15-000-muertos-5427. Last accessed: 2021-06-18.

annotations achieving a Krippendorff's alpha inter-agreement [26] of 0.75711. Therefore, the same tweet could be annotated several times, which allows us to select those tweets with major agreement. Next, we configure the web crawler to compile evidences from Spanish newspapers such as *eldiario.es*[2] or *El Mundo*[3]. It is worth mentioning that news media in Spain is starting to adopt a sales strategy in which some articles are only available for premium users. However, many of the media left open those articles related to infectious diseases due to the COVID-2019 pandemic. We also extracted data from public organisations such as the WHO or press specialised in medicine such as *reacción médica*[4] and official organisms such as the Murcian health service[5]. Finally, the evidences from the citizens was performed by the members of the consortium as CollaborativeHealth was not released for public usage.

We show in Fig. 2 the relevance of the terms flu (gripe), fever (fiebre), and cold (resfriado) during the last year in Spain. We can observe that there were two peaks in September 2020 and March 2021. In case of September, it is when the balance of the season is made and when the return to school and professional activity after the holidays begins. In case of march, the high incidence of flu topics is related to COVID-2019 because it is one year after the COVID-2019 epidemic began.

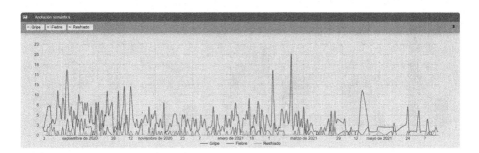

Fig. 2. Comparison of the terms flu (gripe), fever (fiebre), and cold (resfriado) during the last year in Spain in Twitter

Previous figure (see Fig. 2) gives health professionals a view of what are the relevant topics. Figure 3 (top) shows how the sentiments evolve from the same period. It can be noted that most of sentiments are mostly neutral and negative except during March 2021. As commented earlier, this fact is related to COVID-2019 as the forecasts were better, with the start of vaccination and the end of the fourth wave. As we can observe from this case-study, it is challenging to discern among two or more infectious diseases that coexist, as happens with the

[2] https://www.eldiario.es/.

[3] https://www.elmundo.es/.

[4] https://www.redaccionmedica.com.

[5] https://www.murciasalud.es.

flu and COVID-2019. Next, we can compare sentiments of several concepts as it is shown in Fig. 3 (bottom). This KPI uses three horizontal bar per concept (positive, neutral, and negative). It allows final users to see the impact of each concept and how their sentiment is distributed. We can observe that flu and COVID-2019 have almost identical distribution.

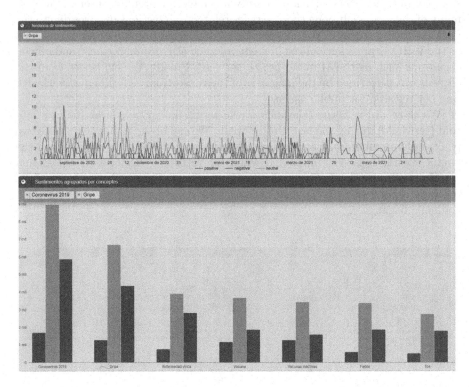

Fig. 3. Comparison of sentiment evolution of FLU during last year in Spain (top) and sentiments grouped by concepts to compare covid-2019 (coronavirus 2019), flu (gripe), viral disease (enfermedad vírica), vaccine (vacuna), fever (fiebre), cough (tos) (bottom)

4.2   Zika, Dengue, and Chikungunya in Ecuador

Zika, Dengue, and Chikungunya are infectious diseases that are transmitted by mosquitoes but also through fluids. Zika virus infection during pregnancy can cause microcephaly on newborns. Dengue is an endemic disease in certain regions of Latin America. Its symptoms are high fever and severe headache and eye pain (behind eyes) among others. Regarding Chikungunya, its most common symptoms are fever, pain, headache, or rash. There is currently no vaccine or medicine to treat chikungunya virus. Due to the high incidence, Ministry of Public Health of Ecuador is conducting activities to control these diseases by means of biolarvicides, intra- and extra-domiciliary fumigation, and communication campaigns.

Similar to the influenza use case in Spain, from the beginning of the development of CollaborativeHealth we started to compile evidences related to the infectious diseases Zika, Chikungunya, and Dengue in Ecuador. We have compiled a total of 105,064 tweets and 39,816 of them were rated in two periods of time four weeks. The first in 2017 and the second during 2019. Each period has a different set of 40 volunteers. Each annotator performed a average number of 3243 annotations with a standard deviation of 296.27138, achieving a Krippendorff's alpha of 0.68369. It is not surprising that the inter-annotator agreement was lower than the one achieved for the Spanish flu case study since there were more teams and more time periods.

In addition, we compiled data from reports of the 9 health coordination zones of Ecuador and some hospitals from Ecuador. Figure 4 shows a treemap of these zones in which the size of each area is proportional to the number of evidences compiled and its colour depends on the predominant sentiment of the area, from red colours (negative), to blue colours (positive). We can observe that zone 9, that coordinates the Quito Metropolitan District is the only one with positive sentiments whereas most of the evidences are from zone 8 (Guayaquil, Durán y Samborondón) with a predominant negative sentiment.

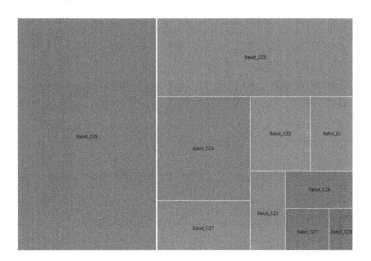

Fig. 4. Comparison of sentiments and number of topics in Ecuador by Health Coordination Zones (Color figure online)

CollaborativeHealth also contains KPIs that can be viewed as a map, as it is shown in Fig. 5, in which we can observe the number of evidences compiled. Next, an example of fine-grained details regarding specific evidences is shown in Fig. 6, in which the annotated concepts of the ontology identified in a evidence are highlighted.

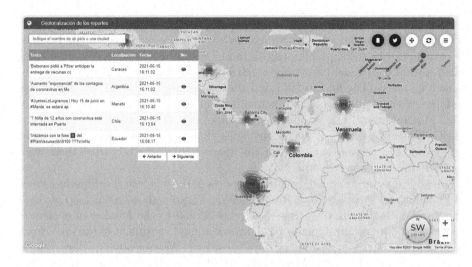

Fig. 5. Evidences compiled display in a map

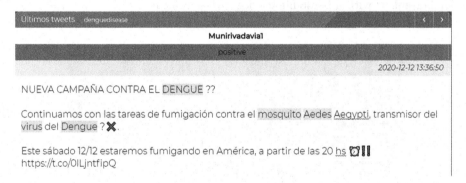

Fig. 6. Semantic annotation of a evidence compiled from social networks

4.3   COVID-2019 in Spanish Speaking Countries

COVID-19 is an *infectious disease caused by a newly discovered coronavirus*[6]. People infected by COVID-19 experience mild to moderate respiratory problems. COVID-19 has been extremely severe for older people, and those with health conditions such as chronic respiratory diseases, cancer, or diabetes. Due to its high propagation capacity and not having vaccines, governs over the world have been forced to take restrictive measures such as lockdown or the obligation to wear masks in open spaces to slow down transmission.

---

[6] https://www.who.int/health-topics/coronavirus1.

It is worth mentioning that COVID-19 epidemic started at the beginning of 2020, midway through development of CollaborativeHealth. Due to its relevance, we made a considerable effort to incorporate data from this new disease, such as symptoms, transmission methods, prevention measures, as well as news regarding vaccines and medications as soon as they were available. One of these efforts was the compilation and annotation of new tweets. We compile tweets related to COVID-19 in Spanish-speaking countries and prepare a set of volunteers that performed near 400k annotations, performing an average of annotations of 5k per annotator. The inter-annotator agreement, however, was lower than the previous case-studies, achieving a Krippendorff's alpha of 0.58073. However, due to the high number of tweets, we could select those tweets with major agreement to improve the aspect-based sentiment analysis models (described in Sect. 3).

Figure 7 shows a word cloud KPI regarding vaccination campaigns of COVID-19 during the last year. For example, it can be observed that the 9100-vaccination plan in Ecuador is a relevant topic[7].

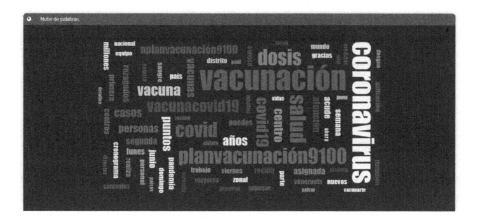

Fig. 7. KPI of a word cloud of vaccination campaigns regarding Covid-19 worldwide

A relevant feature of CollaborativeHealth is the ability of giving feedback regarding actual situation to citizens by means of the progressive web app. Figure 8 shows some KPIs related to COVID-19 that citizens can visualise on their mobiles. If the users grant geolocation permissions, the app automatically displays data in the nearby areas.

---

[7] https://www.salud.gob.ec/cronograma-semanal-y-preguntas-ciudadanas-plan-de-vacunacion-covid-19/.

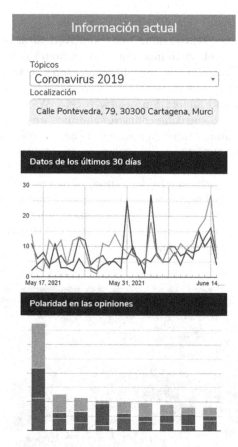

Fig. 8. Screen capture of the feedback that can visualise the citizens through Progressive Web App

5   Conclusions and Further Work

In this paper we have described the CollaborativeHealth platform, that has been the result of an international collaboration and knowledge transfer between companies and universities from Spain and Ecuador, and coordinated and funded by the CDTI. CollaborativeHealth contributes in surveillance tasks allowing health professionals to visualise evidences from different sources by a set of smart and configurable KPIs in a responsive web dashboard. The validation of the platform was carried out by performing three case studies regarding (1) Influenza in Spain; (2) Dengue, Zika, and Chikungunya in Ecuador; and (3) COVID-2019 in Spanish-speaking countries.

As further work we are planning to deploy the platform for commercial use and conversations with public administrations have been carried out for the implementation of pilot projects in real environments. In addition, we are adapting the platform to combine data from different languages apart of Spanish.

For this, we are evaluating the reliability of multilingual BERT [21] in order to adapt the aspect-based sentiment analysis module, as well as the development of tools to automatically translate the concepts of the ontology to another languages and cultures by means of SNOMED-CT codes and Disease Ontology Identifiers (DOI).

Acknowledgments. This work is being funded by CDTI and the European Regional Development Fund (FEDER/ERDF) through project CollaborativeHealth IDI-20180989.

References

1. Abubakar, I., et al.: Global perspectives for prevention of infectious diseases associated with mass gatherings. Lancet Infect. Dis. **12**(1), 66–74 (2012)
2. Apolinario, O., Medina-Moreira, J., Luna-Aveiga, H., García-Díaz, J.A., Valencia-García, R., Estrade-Cabrera, J.I.: Prevención de enfermedades infecciosas basada en el análisis inteligente en RRSS y participación ciudadana. Procesamiento del Lenguaje Nat. **63**, 163–166 (2019)
3. Apolinario-Arzube, Ó., et al.: CollaborativeHealth: smart technologies to surveil outbreaks of infectious diseases through direct and indirect citizen participation. In: Silhavy, R. (ed.) CSOC 2020. AISC, vol. 1226, pp. 177–190. Springer, Cham (2020). https://doi.org/10.1007/978-3-030-51974-2_15
4. Berkelman, R.L., Sullivan, P., Buehler, J.W., et al.: Public health surveillance. In: Oxford Textbook of Public Health, Volume 2: The Methods of Public Health 2, 5th edn, pp. 699–715 (2009)
5. Beydoun, G., Hoffmann, A.G., Fernández-Breis, J.T., Martínez-Béjar, R., Valencia-García, R., Aurum, A.: Cooperative modelling evaluated. Int. J. Coop. Inf. Syst. **14**(1), 45–71 (2005)
6. Cañete, J., Chaperon, G., Fuentes, R., Pérez, J.: Spanish pre-trained BERT model and evaluation data. In: PML4DC at ICLR 2020 (2020)
7. Cowell, L.G., Smith, B.: Infectious disease ontology. In: Sintchenko, V. (ed.) Infectious disease informatics, pp. 373–395. Springer, New York (2010). https://doi.org/10.1007/978-1-4419-1327-2_19
8. Donnelly, K., et al.: SNOMED-CT: the advanced terminology and coding system for eHealth. Stud. Health Technol. Inform. **121**, 279 (2006)
9. Freifeld, C.C., et al.: Participatory epidemiology: use of mobile phones for community-based health reporting. PLoS Med. **7**(12), e1000376 (2010)
10. Freifeld, C.C., Mandl, K.D., Reis, B.Y., Brownstein, J.S.: HealthMap: global infectious disease monitoring through automated classification and visualization of internet media reports. J. Am. Med. Inform. Assoc. **15**(2), 150–157 (2008)
11. García-Díaz, J.A., Almela, A., Alcaraz-Mármol, G., Valencia-García, R.: UMUCorpusClassifier: compilation and evaluation of linguistic corpus for Natural Language Processing tasks. Procesamiento del Lenguaje Nat. **65**, 139–142 (2020)
12. García-Díaz, J.A., Cánovas-García, M., Valencia-García, R.: Ontology-driven aspect-based sentiment analysis classification: an infodemiological case study regarding infectious diseases in Latin America. Future Gener. Comput. Syst. **112**, 614–657 (2020). https://doi.org/10.1016/j.future.2020.06.019

13. García-Sánchez, F., Valencia-García, R., Martínez-Béjar, R.: An integrated app-
    roach for developing e-commerce applications. Expert Syst. Appl. **28**(2), 223–235
    (2005)
14. García-Díaz, J.A., Cánovas-García, M., Colomo-Palacios, R., Valencia-García,
    R.: Detecting misogyny in Spanish tweets. An approach based on linguistics
    features and word embeddings. Future Gener. Comput. Syst. **114**, 506–518
    (2021). https://doi.org/10.1016/j.future.2020.08.032. http://www.sciencedirect.
    com/science/article/pii/S0167739X20301928
15. Kouadio, I.K., Aljunid, S., Kamigaki, T., Hammad, K., Oshitani, H.: Infectious
    diseases following natural disasters: prevention and control measures. Expert Rev.
    Anti-Infect. Ther. **10**(1), 95–104 (2012)
16. Mavragani, A.: Infodemiology and infoveillance: scoping review. J. Med. Internet
    Res. **22**(4), e16206 (2020)
17. Mavragani, A., Ochoa, G.: Google trends in infodemiology and infoveillance:
    methodology framework. JMIR Public Health Surveill. **5**(2), e13439 (2019)
18. McConaghy, T., et al.: BigchainDB: a scalable blockchain database. White paper,
    BigChainDB (2016)
19. Park, H.W., Park, S., Chong, M.: Conversations and medical news frames on Twit-
    ter: infodemiological study on COVID-19 in South Korea. J. Med. Internet Res.
    22(5), e18897 (2020)
20. del Pilar Salas-Zárate, M., Alor-Hernández, G., Valencia-García, R., Rodríguez-
    Mazahua, L., Rodríguez-González, A., López Cuadrado, J.L.: Analyzing best prac-
    tices on web development frameworks: the lift approach. Sci. Comput. Program.
    102, 1–19 (2015)
21. Pires, T., Schlinger, E., Garrette, D.: How multilingual is multilingual BERT?
    arXiv preprint arXiv:1906.01502 (2019)
22. Rodríguez-García, M.Á., Valencia-García, R., García-Sánchez, F., Zapater, J.J.S.:
   ˋ Creating a semantically-enhanced cloud services environment through ontology
    evolution. Future Gener. Comput. Syst. **32**, 295–306 (2014)
23. Rovetta, A., Bhagavathula, A.S.: Global infodemiology of COVID-19: analysis of
    Google web searches and Instagram hashtags. J. Med. Internet Res. **22**(8), e20673
    (2020)
24. Ruiz-Sánchez, J.M., Valencia-García, R., Fernández-Breis, J.T., Martínez-Béjar,
    R., Compton, P.: An approach for incremental knowledge acquisition from text.
    Expert Syst. Appl. **25**(1), 77–86 (2003)
25. Schriml, L.M., et al.: Disease ontology: a backbone for disease semantic integration.
    Nucleic Acids Res. **40**(D1), D940–D946 (2012)
26. Siegert, I., Böck, R., Wendemuth, A.: Inter-rater reliability for emotion annotation
    in human-computer interaction: comparison and methodological improvements. J.
    Multimodal User Interfaces **8**(1), 17–28 (2014). https://doi.org/10.1007/s12193-
    013-0129-9
27. Valencia-García, R., Ruiz-Sánchez, J.M., Vicente, P.J.V., Fernández-Breis, J.T.,
    Martínez-Béjar, R.: An incremental approach for discovering medical knowledge
    from texts. Expert Syst. Appl. **26**(3), 291–299 (2004)
28. Xue, J., et al.: Twitter discussions and emotions about the COVID-19 pandemic:
    machine learning approach. J. Med. Internet Res. **22**(11), e20550 (2020)

Evaluating Extractive Automatic Text Summarization Techniques in Spanish

Camilo Caparrós-Laiz🄳, José Antonio García-Díaz$^{(\boxtimes)}$🄳,
and Rafael Valencia-García🄳

Facultad de Informática, Universidad de Murcia, Campus de Espinardo,
30100 Murcia, Spain
{camilo.caparrosl,joseantonio.garcia8,valencia}@um.es

Abstract. Due to the large amount of data published on the Internet, the tasks related to the automatic generation of summaries from unstructured sources have gained enormous popularity in recent years. For instance, its applications are media monitoring, newsletter generation, legal document analysis, virtual assistants that can summarize email overload, e-learning, or patent research among others. One popular approach for generating the summaries is extractive summarization, that extracts the most meaningful keywords in a document and presents them to the reader comprehensively. To the best of our knowledge, there is a lack of studies that have evaluated extractive text summarization techniques in Spanish, specially novel techniques based on state-of-the-art transformers. Consequently, we perform a benchmark of traditional and recent approaches for conducting text summarization with the Corpus-TER dataset, that consists in 240 Mexican-Spanish news articles. Our preliminary results suggest that word embeddings from Word2Vec achieves the best results based on ROUGE-1, BLEU and edit distance metrics.

Keywords: Automatic text summarization · Extractive summarization · Transformers

1 Introduction

Since the beginning of the digital era, the amount of structured and unstructured data generated has not stopped growing. Newspapers, newsletters, emails, or technical reports are just examples of the large amount of data and information to which we are subscribed [12]. Handling such volume of information is impossible for human beings. Consequently, Natural Language Processing (NLP) together with Information Retrieval (IR) have focus on tasks that eases the shift between data and knowledge.

One task of IR is automatic summarization, which consists in shortening a set of documents keeping only the most relevant information [5]. It is not clear how humans summarize text as everyone has their own particular way of summarizing. However, there are two main approaches for automatic summarization

ⓒ Springer Nature Switzerland AG 2021
R. Valencia-García et al. (Eds.): CITI 2021, CCIS 1460, pp. 79–92, 2021.
https://doi.org/10.1007/978-3-030-88262-4_6

[4]. On the one hand, extractive summarization, focused on selecting the most valuable pieces of a text and presenting them to the final user in a comprehensive manner. On the other hand, abstractive summarization, focused on paraphrasing the document creating its own version, which can be adapted to audiences with special needs. It is worth noting that other research employs hybrid methods based on extractive and abstractive summarization.

One suited approach to solve the automatic generation of summaries is machine-learning by letting the models learn how to summarize specific domains or datasets. Specifically, extractive automatic text summarization is commonly approached as a supervised problem, in which new summaries are generated automatically and compared with summaries made by real people. Common approaches for generating the summaries are based on statistical features, such as Term Frequency—Inverse Document Frequency (TF—IDF), which encodes documents as the frequency of certain keywords but downplaying those terms that are too common in the rest of the documents. Recent advances in deep-learning and transformers have been a huge leap in NLP tasks such as Text Classification [8], Opinion Mining [14], or Name Entity Recognition [22], just to name a few.

In this paper we evaluate traditional and novel extractive automatic text summarization techniques in Spanish. Typically, summarization methods are tested on the corpus of Document Understanding Conference (DUC) [23] which contains only English texts. As a result of this, we use the Corpus-TER [19], a dataset compiled from Mexican-Spanish news websites. This dataset contains 240 news and two manual summaries for each article. In a nutshell, the main goals of this research are: (1) the selection and development of certain summarization methods, (2) the selection of a corpus on which we can test these methods, (3) the design of a concise and reusable interface, and (4) the evaluation of text summarization techniques.

The rest of the manuscript is organized as follows. First, in Sect. 2 we include a description of text summarization and analyze relevant bibliography concerning extractive summarization techniques. Second, in Sect. 3 we describe the architecture of our proposal, the techniques under analysis and a description of the Corpus-TER used for evaluation. Next, in Sect. 4 we compare and discuss the results achieved with each method and, finally, in Sect. 5 we summarize the main ideas of this research as well as we include promising future research lines.

2 Background Information

In this work we focus on automatic extractive summarization, which consist on reducing the size of a text while preserving the most relevant information by selecting a subset of the most relevant sentences. Accordingly, in this section we review novel approaches and datasets related to this field.

Luhn [18] was one of the first to propose a method to extract relevant sentences from text based on word frequencies and the density of relevant words contained. Since then, many other methods have emerged. Novel extractive summarization methods are based on transformer models such as BERT [3], which captures semantic relationships between words by taking into account their context. One method based on BERT is BERTSUM [16], which was evaluated on CNN/Daily Mail [10] and The New York Times (NYT)[1] datasets, achieving state-of-the-art results. BERTSUM works by inserting classification [CLS] tokens before each sentence. The embedding associated to each [CLS] represents the meaning of the entire sentence. Finally, the sentence embeddings are fed to a stack of transformer layers that captures relevant document features and a final classifier that scores each sentence. MATCHSUM [34] is another BERT-based method for automatic text summarization. Its core idea is that good summaries are the ones that are semantically similar to the original document. MATCHSUM relies on BERTSUM to score each sentence but uses a Siamese-BERT network to measure the similarity between the original document and the candidate summaries. This method outperformed previous state-of-the-art results with the CNN/Daily Mail dataset.

3   Materials and Methods

In this section we introduce the dataset and tools used to develop this project and we explain our proposed architecture in detail.

3.1   Corpus-TER Dataset

The dataset to evaluate the selected methods is Corpus-TER [19], which compiles 240 Mexican-Spanish news articles classified in 12 typical categories such as academia, well-being, culture or opinion among others. This corpus was extracted from online newspapers. The authors applied a process of cleaning and normalization and deployed the dataset in XML files containing the title and body of the news and two human generated summaries associated to each article. We divide this dataset into two parts, namely, training and testing, in a ratio of 80-20 applying a random sampling with a fixed seed.

Next, we show an example of a document from the Corpus-TER that is about a tightrope walker that crossed the Seine river in Paris at an altitude of 25 m.

---

[1] https://catalog.ldc.upenn.edu/LDC2008T19.

"Funambulista cruza el Sena por una cuerda a 25 metros de altura.
Un funambulista cruzó hoy el río Sena en París por un cable tendido
a 25 metros de altura por encima del nivel del agua en medio de una
gran expectación de barcos y público en tierra firme. Denis Josselin
estuvo en total 30 minutos esta tarde haciendo diversas figuras
en equilibrio sobre el cable de 150 metros que unía el muelle de la
Rapée, en la margen derecha del río, con el muelle de Austerlitz,
en la izquierda. Josselin, que atravesaba por segunda vez el Sena
caminando por una cuerda entre las dos orillas -la primera fue con
motivo del paso por la ciudad de la llama olímpica-, hizo una parte
del recorrido con los ojos vendados. Numerosos barcos de recreo y
de los que hacen recorridos turísticos por el centro de París se
concentraron en las alrededores, mientras cientos de personas seguían
las evoluciones del equilibrista desde el puente Charles de Gaulle.
El evento estuvo organizado por el organismo gestor de los Puertos
de París."

3.2 System Proposal

The scripts for evaluating[2] were developed using Python. We use the scikit-learn library for the overall machine-learning pipeline, as it contains methods for feature extraction such as TF—IDF, model selection, such as dataset split, cross-validation or parameter grid selection, and ML models like Latent Dirichlet allocation (LDA). NLTK [17] for BLEU metric and a list of Spanish stopwords. SpaCy [11] for tokenization and lemmatization. SciPy [33] and NumPy [9] are used for statistical computation and Singular Value Decomposition (SVD), which is used for Latent Semantic Analysis (LSA). Gensim for Word2Vec [21]. Transformers and PyTorch for BERT. And other packages for ROUGE and edit distance.

Our pipeline is depicted in Fig. 1. In a few words, we apply a tokenization step that consists into dividing each document into a list of sentences, and each sentence into a list of words. Next, we pre-process each document, calculate the score of each sentence and, finally, the best sentences are selected to compose the final summary.

Fig. 1. Architecture of our extractive summarization process

Next, each module is described in detail.

[2] Available at https://github.com/CamilUM/summarization.

1. **Tokenize:** It divides a text document into sentences and these sentences into words. The output of this process is first sent to *Clean* and next to *Extract*. It has to be done this way so that the summary includes the original sentences and not the cleaned ones.
2. **Clean:** It receives a text document and returns a normalized document. Pre-processing techniques include: (1) removing special characters, (2) removing stop-words, (3) removing duplicated spaces, (4) lowercase conversion, and (5) lemmatization to represent all derived words as their respective root word.
3. **Score:** It receives a text document and returns a score for each sentence and method of each document. This module accepts other parameters according to the method evaluated, as some methods need external assets such as other documents, pre-trained models or ontologies, among others.
4. **Filter:** It receives a list of scores and returns a list of indices indicating which sentences are selected. The basic idea is to select the best sentences that better summarize the texts.
5. **Extract:** It receives a list of indices and the tokens from the original document, that is, before pre-processing. The output is the resulting summary.

All modules are decoupled, so their implementation can be easily changed as long as they follow the interface. It is worth noting that the *Clean* stage is completely optional, although is recommended. *Filter* can also be optional as long as it is already integrated in the *Score* stage, as happens in SumBasic [32]. It is very important to separate *Score* and *Filter* as well as the use of indices to avoid that the evaluated methods filter the cleaned input rather than the original one. Besides, it reduces the complexity of the system as all methods share the same interface. Moreover, the usage of a list of integers, rather than an arbitrary data structure, simplifies the implementation of new methods. The design philosophy of this architecture is reusability and customization. We have identified clear stages that should be separated. We argue that letting users decide what kind of tokenization or preprocessing suits their summarization method would decrease the complexity of the system, resulting in more efficient code as the implementation does not have to do it again and can assume it was done by the user. In addition, the code is customizable as the use of common data structures such as lists of strings or lists of integers makes it easy to share compatible and interchangeable implementations.

3.3   Evaluation Methods

On the following paragraphs, we are going to focus on the core of the summarization process which are the *Score* and *Filter* stages, by describing the evaluated methods.

The first method is TF—IDF [29]. It measures the relevance of a word in certain document given a collection of documents. Equation 1 depicts the formula, in which w is a word, d is a document, D is a collection of documents, $f_d(w)$ is the frequency of a word in a document and $f_D(w)$ is the number of documents in which the word appears in. Understanding the formula, if we increase $f_d(w)$, the word is more relevant, but if we increase $f_D(w)$ the word becomes less relevant. In short, relevant words are the ones that repeat in certain document but not in the whole corpus. We can summarize by averaging the weights of the words that appear in each sentence.

$$TFIDF(w, d, D) = f_d(w) \cdot \log \left(\frac{|D|}{f_D(w)} \right) \tag{1}$$

The second method is Luhn [18] that is based on two ideas: (1) frequent words are significant, and (2) the more significant words a sentence has, the more relevance the sentence has. To determine what words are significant, we count them and set an upper bound C and a lower bound D. If a word is between the bounds, then it is significant. The formula can be seen on Eq. 2, in which f is the significance factor, s is the list of words of the sentence and w is the list of words which are significant in sentence s.

$$f(s) = \frac{|w|^2}{|s|} \tag{2}$$

The third method is SumBasic [32]. Its core idea is that the most probable words are the most eligible words to be in the summary. Its algorithm is depicted in Algorithm 1. Updating probabilities is a way to handle context and redundancy. It also gives the opportunity to unlikely words to appear in the summary [32]. To compute the desired length of the summary we use the formula from Eq. 3, in which n is the number of desired sentences, f is the number of sentences of the document, b is the base for the entropy, H is the entropy of the document, w is the number of words in the document. Therefore, b^H is the minimal number of words necessary in the document, $\frac{b^H}{w}$ is the proportion of minimal words. By multiplying f, we get the minimal number of sentences.

Algorithm 1: SumBasic's algorithm

---

(1) Work out the probabilities of each word $p(w)$.
(2) Score each sentence as the average of their word probabilities.
(3) Select the sentence with the highest score.
(4) Update probabilities of selected words so that $p_{new}(w) = p_{old}(w)$.
(5) If the summary has the desired length, halt. Otherwise, go to step 2.

$$n = f \cdot \frac{b^H}{w} \tag{3}$$

The forth method evaluated is LSA [31], which is based on the TF—IDF metric. LSA builds a matrix A with words-sentences where a_{ij} has the TF—IDF of the word i, if that word is in the sentence j. Otherwise, it is set to 0. Next, a SVD operation is applied over the matrix A, getting $A = U \Sigma V^T$ where U is the matrix with weights for words-topics, Σ is the diagonal matrix with weights for topics-topics, and V^T is the matrix with weights for topics-sentences. If we multiply $D = \Sigma V^T$ we get a new matrix with weights for topics-sentences. The computation of the weights of the sentences [31] are detailed in Eq. 4.

$$s_i = \sqrt{\sum_j d_{ij}^2} \tag{4}$$

The fifth method is LDA [1], which is a generative model that assumes that topics follow a Dirichlet distribution over documents, and words follow a Dirichlet distribution over topics. LDA has the following parameters that have to be estimated: α and β, which are the density factors of Dirichlet distribution and K, which is the number of topics. The parameters α and β have to be tuned to maximize logarithmic likelihood of data [1]. Thus, we can use Expectation–Maximization (EM) algorithm. The parameter K can be estimated with cross-validation. With LDA it is possible to obtain a words-topics matrix, that it is an association between words and topics. To get what are the most relevant sentences within a document, we compare each sentence vector with the document vector by using the cosine similarity. Both vectors (sentence and document) are calculated by averaging its word vectors. In addition, for LDA we conduct an hyperparameter optimization stage for obtaining the number of topics, achieving our best results with K = 15 (the evaluated values were from 8 to 16).

The sixth method is TextRank [20], which extends PageRank [24] by using weighted graphs. The idea is to score vertices according to the number of edges and their weights. Vertices represent the sentences and edges represent their relationships. The algorithm is similar to a voting system in which sentences cast votes (see Eq. 5). $WS(V_x)$ is the sentence weight. d is the damping factor between $[0, 1]$ which represents the probability to jump from one vertex to another. $In(V_x)$ are the sentences that point at V_x. $Out(V_x)$ are the sentences V_x is pointing at. Finally, w_{xy} is the weight of the edge from x to y. According to TextRank, a sentence is more relevant if more sentences point at it (first summation), but if those vertices point at a lot of other vertices, then their vote has less impact (second summation, at the denominator). Vertex scores $W(V_x)$ can be initialized arbitrarily. However, we initialize them with the average TF-IDF of its sentence. Edge weights are initialized as described in Eq. 6, in which S_x is a sentence. The algorithm halts when the weight differences between iterations fall under some threshold.

$$WS(V_i) = (1-d) + d \cdot \sum_{V_j \in In(V_i)} \frac{w_{ji}}{\sum_{V_k \in Out(V_j)} w_{jk}} WS(V_j) \tag{5}$$

$$Similarity(S_i, S_j) = \frac{|w_k| w_k \in S_i \wedge w_k \in S_j|}{\log(|S_i|) + \log(|S_j|)} \tag{6}$$

The seventh method is based on Word2Vec [21], which is a technique based on word embeddings that are capable of capturing relationships between words. One of the advantages of this technique is that is possible to obtain embeddings for other linguistic units, such as sentences and documents. Accordingly, we first obtain the embeddings for each word, and then the embeddings for each sentence by averaging their word embeddings. In a similar manner, the document embeddings are obtained by averaging all the word embeddings within the document.

Next, in order to get what are the most important sentences, we compare the distance of each sentence to the document embedding using cosine similarity. It is worth mentioning that there are two architectures to learn the word embeddings: Continuous Bag of Words (CBOW) and Skip-gram. On the one hand, CBOW tries to predict a word given its context and, on the other hand, Skip-gram tries to predict the context from a word. For this work, we conducted an hyperparameter selection stage using cross-validation in which the best results are achieved with CBOW, embeddings of length 140 (lengths of 100, 120, 140, 160, and 180 were evaluated), a window size of 5 (window size of 3, 5, and 7 were evaluated) during 2 epochs.

The final evaluated method is BERT, which is based also on word embeddings. However, the main difference is that BERT embeddings are contextual. That means that these embeddings take into account the context of each word, and solves issues related to homonym. Due to max-length restrictions of BERT, we can not calculate directly the documents embeddings. Therefore, we manually calculate the document embeddings by averaging their sentence embeddings. Finally, we rank each sentence in a similar manner as we do with Word2Vec. To obtain the sentence embeddings we rely on Sentence-BERT [28] and BETO, the Spanish pretrained BERT model [2].

It is worth mentioning that all the evaluated methods can be improved by taking into account the relative position of a sentence within the document. For this, we have included an heuristic that dismisses the importance of those sentences that are in the middle of the document, as we suppose that the beginning and the conclusions of a piece of news contains the most relevant sentences. To test this, we weight the score of each sentence based on the reverse of a Gaussian function, as it has a smooth curve and it is near zero in the middle (see Fig. 2). We observe that TF—IDF, Luhn and SumBasic improve their performance using this technique. In the rest of the evaluated methods, we observed that the results are similar or slightly worse. It is worth noting that it is possible to evaluate other functions that dismisses other parts of the documents.

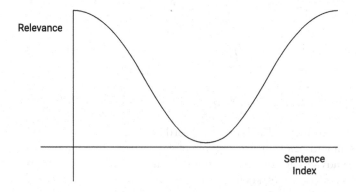

Fig. 2. Heuristic function based on a reverse Gaussian function

Finally, to obtain the final summary, there are multiple ways to do it.

1. **Mask:** a binary mask denoting which sentence go to the summary. It is the most generic way.
2. **Threshold:** where we select the sentences which exceed the threshold.
3. **k-top:** where we select the k best sentences, preserving their original order.
4. **p-top:** similar to *k-top* but indicating the percentage.

The last two options are the most intuitive for a user but using threshold gives us more freedom to select sentences as it adapts better to each document.

4 Results

The metrics used in this project to measure the quality of the summaries are: (1) Recall-Oriented Understudy for Gisting Evaluation (ROUGE) [15], which is a recall based measure, i.e. it measures the number of common n-grams between machine summary and human summary against the total n-gram in the human summary; and (2) Bilingual Evaluation Understudy (BLEU) [25] is precision based, i.e. it measures the number of common n-grams between machine summary and human summary against the total n-gram in the machine summary. In addition, we include the edit distance based on the Levenshtein distance [13], that measures the number of operations needed to convert the machine summary into the human summary, the size ratio between the summary and the original document, and the computation time.

First, we analyze the results on the training set (with no separation between training and validation set) in the Table 1.

Table 1. Results over training set

Method	ROUGE-1	BLEU	Edit	Ratio
TF—IDF	0.5598	0.5797	595	0.3098
Luhn	**0.6112**	**0.6628**	**519**	0.3102
SumBasic	0.4300	0.4459	608	**0.2006**
LSA	0.5454	0.5392	580	0.2946
LDA	0.5254	0.5080	600	0.2167
TextRank	0.5385	0.5209	572	0.2383
Word2Vec	0.5312	0.5142	607	0.2173
BERT	0.5477	0.5450	587	0.2329

Results in Table 1 are merely to compare them to the results on the test set in order to evaluate the capacity of generalizing of each method and observe whether they suffer from overfitting or underfitting. Nevertheless, it should be noted that Luhn approach got the best results in all its metrics while SumBasic

Table 2. Results over test set

Method	ROUGE-1	BLEU	Edit	Ratio
TF—IDF	0.5619	0.5896	864	0.4214
Luhn	0.5940	0.6190	929	0.3875
SumBasic	0.5075	0.5237	**642**	0.3143
LSA	0.5432	0.5488	651	**0.2799**
LDA	0.5704	0.6046	772	0.3143
TextRank	0.6052	0.6511	663	0.2980
Word2Vec	**0.6116**	**0.6590**	793	0.3143
BERT	0.6006	0.6337	802	0.3143

seems to be the worst. The remaining methods got decent results exceeding, at least, 0.5 both in ROUGE-1 and BLEU.

We can observe in the Table 2 the results over the test set. Word2Vec gives the best results with 0.6116 on ROUGE-1 and 0.6590 on BLEU. Again, SumBasic gets the worst results with 0.5075 on ROUGE-1 and 0.5237 on BLEU. All the methods increase their edit distance with respect to the training dataset. The increase difference ranges from 34 points for SumBasic to 410 points for Luhn. In addition, Luhn has lowered its results on ROUGE-1 and BLEU by 0.0172 and 0.4380 points, respectively. Therefore, it may suffer from overfitting. TextRank, Word2Vec and BERT offer the best performing results. However, Word2Vec had parameters to tune and, probably, it may have got the best results because it could adapt to the concrete dataset that we are using. We recall that word embeddings let us capture syntactical and semantic relationships between words. Therefore, they constitute a good tool to model related words. TextRank also lets us find relationships at the sentence level in a more efficient and simpler way. LSA and LDA find hidden topics in the documents. Although both LSA and LDA give good results, humans may not summarize around a mixture of a lot of topics but around the main topic or a small subset of topics. Hence, an heuristic that leverages the main topics of the document may benefit these methods. SumBasic is the one with the worst results but still has a good capacity of generalization and is the most stable in terms of its edit distance (34 points of difference between training and test set). In contrast, Luhn was the best on training set but got worse on test set and is quite unstable in terms of edit distance (410 points of difference). Luhn is probably the most intuitive method as it relies on the idea that the most dense sentences with the most important words are the most suitable sentences to be included in the summary. Besides, it is reinforced with to the TF—IDF matrix that puts more relevance to the words that repeat in the document but not in the corpus. However, SumBasic makes a fairer distribution of words by giving some opportunity to the least probable words.

It is obvious that similar summaries get 1 for ROUGE-1 and BLEU and 0 for edit distance. However, there are two possibilities to explain limited results: On the one hand, Machine summary is either too short or too long. In this case, if contents are still similar, then we still get some value in the result. On the other hand, the contents of the machine and human summaries are very different, so they will always get bad results. The first case is the one that boosts bad results for the edit distance as machine summaries that should have been longer or shorter need a lot of edit operations to be transformed into the human summary. For the second case, we could have very short summaries that are not similar. Therefore, the edit distance will report very few edit operations making us think that they are similar when they are not, so ROUGE and BLEU are more adequate in this sense.

It is worth noting that the data about size ratios is not an indicator of summary quality but rather an indicator of whether we are summarizing or not. For instance, if we have a summary which is a verbatim copy of the original document we would get 1 on ROUGE-1 and BLEU, and 0 on edit distance but we have the whole document not a reduced version of it, so we are not really summarizing in that case. Whether the size of the summary is more or less, is not really important. What is important is that we get the smallest summary with the highest results.

In order to observe the quality of the generated summaries, we show an example generated by the TF—IDF method:

"Funambulista cruza el Sena por una cuerda a 25 metros de altura.
Un funambulista cruzó hoy el río Sena en París por un cable tendido
a 25 metros de altura por encima del nivel del agua en medio de una
gran expectación de barcos y público en tierra firme."

Finally, we calculate the time to train the model and predict new data (see Table 3). There is a noticeable difference between Word2Vec and BERT methods with the rest. Word2Vec is based on neural networks and has to tune its parameters while BERT makes a lot of comparisons between sentence embeddings [28]. Other methods like LSA and LDA may take some time too as they are based on SVD and EM algorithm, respectively. The hardware used for this benchmark is an Intel i3-3110M CPU of 2.4 GHz and 2 cores and 8 GB of RAM. The software used in this project was the Python interpreter version 3.8.5.

Table 3. Computation time in seconds for training and predicting for each method

Method	Time (s)
TF-IDF	0.3906
Luhn	0.1093
SumBasic	0.3593
LSA	2.3946
LDA	2.8438
TextRank	0.3750
Word2Vec	12.0630
BERT	179.5665

5   Conclusions and Further Work

In this project we have put to the test a set of extractive summarization methods over a Spanish news corpus and analyzed their results using ROUGE-1, BLEU and edit distance metrics. Most of them present good results being Word2Vec the best with 0.6116 on ROUGE-1 and 0.6590 on BLEU. These are positive results but not enough. We can improve the results with a deeper understanding of the problem. The main limitation of our work is the limited size of the dataset. Consequently, we will evaluate larger Spanish corpora with a wider variety of texts such as scientific, encyclopedia or didactic articles. In this sense, we will evaluate the MultiLingual SUMmarization (MLSUM) dataset [30].

As future promising research directions we suggest to test new heuristics and comparing their results with existing methods. We will also evaluate methods that measure the degree of correctness of the summary. There is the possibility that certain combination of sentences are very informative but are not well linked or the expressed ideas have no relation or in the worst case scenario, grammatical errors. Therefore, it is interesting to have ways to measure coherence, adequacy and cohesion in a text. For this, we will use the UMUTextStats tool [6,7] in order to extract and compare the linguistic features for the original sentence and the original and automatized summaries. Moreover, as this tool extract linguistic features related to pragmatics and figurative language [26] we will explore the quality of the summaries for texts that use figurative language such as verbal irony [27].

Acknowledgments. This work has been supported by the Spanish National Research Agency (AEI) and the European Regional Development Fund (FEDER/ERDF) through projects KBS4FIA (TIN2016-76323-R) and LaTe4PSP (PID2019-107652RB-I00). In addition, José Antonio García-Díaz has been supported by Banco Santander and University of Murcia through the industrial doctorate programme.

References

1. Blei, D., Ng, A., Jordan, M.: Latent Dirichlet allocation. J. Mach. Learn. Res. **3**, 993–1022 (2003). https://doi.org/10.1162/jmlr.2003.3.4-5.993
2. Cañete, J., Chaperon, G., Fuentes, R., Ho, J.H., Kang, H., Pérez, J.: Spanish pre-trained BERT model and evaluation data. In: PML4DC at ICLR 2020 (2020)
3. Devlin, J., Chang, M.W., Lee, K., Toutanova, K.: BERT: pre-training of deep bidirectional transformers for language understanding. arXiv preprint arXiv:1810.04805 (2018)
4. El-Kassas, W.S., Salama, C.R., Rafea, A.A., Mohamed, H.K.: Automatic text summarization: a comprehensive survey. Expert Syst. Appl. **165**, 113679 (2021). https://doi.org/10.1016/j.eswa.2020.113679. https://www.sciencedirect.com/science/article/pii/S0957417420305030
5. Gambhir, M., Gupta, V.: Recent automatic text summarization techniques: a survey. Artif. Intell. Rev. **47**(1), 1–66 (2016). https://doi.org/10.1007/s10462-016-9475-9
6. García-Díaz, J.A., Cánovas-García, M., Valencia-García, R.: Ontology-driven aspect-based sentiment analysis classification: an infodemiological case study regarding infectious diseases in latin america. Futur. Gener. Comput. Syst. **112**, 614–657 (2020). https://doi.org/10.1016/j.future.2020.06.019
7. García-Díaz, J.A., Cánovas-García, M., Colomo-Palacios, R., Valencia-García, R.: Detecting misogyny in Spanish tweets. an approach based on linguistics features and word embeddings. Future Gener. Comput. Syst. **114**, 506–518 (2021). https://doi.org/10.1016/j.future.2020.08.032. http://www.sciencedirect.com/science/article/pii/S0167739X20301928
8. González-Carvajal, S., Garrido-Merchán, E.C.: Comparing BERT against traditional machine learning text classification. arXiv preprint arXiv:2005.13012 (2020)
9. Harris, C.R., et al.: Array programming with NumPy. Nature **585**, 357–362 (2020). https://doi.org/10.1038/s41586-020-2649-2
10. Hermann, K.M., et al.: Teaching machines to read and comprehend. In: NIPS, pp. 1693–1701 (2015). http://papers.nips.cc/paper/5945-teaching-machines-to-read-and-comprehend
11. Honnibal, M., Montani, I., Van Landeghem, S., Boyd, A.: spaCy: industrial-strength natural language processing in python (2020). https://doi.org/10.5281/zenodo.1212303
12. Kobayashi, M., Takeda, K.: Information retrieval on the web. ACM Comput. Surv. (CSUR) **32**(2), 144–173 (2000)
13. Levenshtein, V.I.: Binary codes capable of correcting deletions, insertions and reversals. Soviet Phys. Doklady **10**(8), 707–710 (1966). doklady Akademii Nauk SSSR, V163 No4 845–848 1965
14. Li, X., Bing, L., Zhang, W., Lam, W.: Exploiting BERT for end-to-end aspect-based sentiment analysis. arXiv preprint arXiv:1910.00883 (2019)
15. Lin, C.Y.: ROUGE: a package for automatic evaluation of summaries. In: Text Summarization Branches Out, pp. 74–81. Association for Computational Linguistics, Barcelona, July 2004. https://aclanthology.org/W04-1013
16. Liu, Y.: Fine-tune BERT for extractive summarization (2019)
17. Loper, E., Bird, S.: NLTK: the natural language toolkit. arXiv preprint cs/0205028 (2002)
18. Luhn, H.P.: The automatic creation of literature abstracts. IBM J. Res. Dev. **2**, 159–165 (1958)

19. Matias Mendoza, G.A., Ledeneva, Y., García Hernández, R.A., Alexandrov, M., Hernández Castañeda, Á.: Ground truth Spanish automatic extractive text summarization bounds. Computación y Sistemas **24**(3) (2020)
20. Mihalcea, R., Tarau, P.: TextRank: bringing order into text. In: Proceedings of the 2004 Conference on Empirical Methods in Natural Language Processing, pp. 404–411. Association for Computational Linguistics, Barcelona, July 2004. https://aclanthology.org/W04-3252
21. Mikolov, T., Chen, K., Corrado, G., Dean, J.: Efficient estimation of word representations in vector space. arXiv preprint arXiv:1301.3781 (2013)
22. Miranda-Escalada, A., Farré, E., Krallinger, M.: Named entity recognition, concept normalization and clinical coding: overview of the cantemist track for cancer text mining in Spanish, corpus, guidelines, methods and results. In: IberLEF@ SEPLN, pp. 303–323 (2020)
23. NIST: Document understanding conference (2001). https://duc.nist.gov/
24. Page, L., Brin, S., Motwani, R., Winograd, T.: The pagerank citation ranking: Bringing order to the web. Technical report 1999-66, Stanford InfoLab, November 1999. http://ilpubs.stanford.edu:8090/422/. Previous number = SIDL-WP-1999-0120
25. Papineni, K., Roukos, S., Ward, T., Zhu, W.J.: BLEU: a method for automatic evaluation of machine translation. In: Proceedings of the 40th Annual Meeting of the Association for Computational Linguistics, pp. 311–318. Association for Computational Linguistics, Philadelphia, July 2002. https://doi.org/10.3115/1073083.1073135. https://aclanthology.org/P02-1040
26. del Pilar Salas-Zárate, M., et al.: Review of English literature on figurative language applied to social networks. Knowl. Inf. Syst. **62**(6), 2105–2137 (2020). https://doi.org/10.1007/s10115-019-01425-3
27. del Pilar Salas-Zárate, M., et al.: Automatic detection of satire in twitter: a psycholinguistic-based approach. Knowl. Based Syst. **128**, 20–33 (2017). https://doi.org/10.1016/j.knosys.2017.04.009
28. Reimers, N., Gurevych, I.: Sentence-BERT: sentence embeddings using Siamese BERT-networks (2019)
29. Salton, G., Buckley, C.: Term-weighting approaches in automatic text retrieval. Inf. Process. Manage. **24**(5), 513–523 (1988). https://doi.org/10.1016/0306-4573(88)90021-0
30. Scialom, T., Dray, P.A., Lamprier, S., Piwowarski, B., Staiano, J.: MLSUM: the multilingual summarization corpus. arXiv preprint arXiv:2004.14900 (2020)
31. Steinberger, J., Jezek, K.: Using latent semantic analysis in text summarization and summary evaluation, January 2004
32. Vanderwende, L., Suzuki, H., Brockett, C., Nenkova, A.: Beyond sumbasic: task-focused summarization with sentence simplification and lexical expansion. Inf. Process. Manage. **43**, 1606–1618 (2007). https://doi.org/10.1016/j.ipm.2007.01.023
33. Virtanen, P., et al.: SciPy 1.0 contributors: SciPy 1.0: fundamental algorithms for scientific computing in Python. Nature Methods **17**, 261–272 (2020). https://doi.org/10.1038/s41592-019-0686-2
34. Zhong, M., Liu, P., Chen, Y., Wang, D., Qiu, X., Huang, X.: Extractive summarization as text matching (2020)

Mobile and Collaborative Technologies

Gamification Tools as a Learning Strategy in Virtual Classes in University Students: Elemental Education Major Case Study

Cristina Páez-Quinde[1]([⊠]) [iD], Daniel Morocho-Lara[1] [iD],
Angela Chasipanta-Nieves[2] [iD], and Xavier Sulca-Guale[1] [iD]

[1] Facultad de Ciencias Humanas y de La Educación, Grupos de Investigación Research in Language and Education and Marketing C.S, Universidad Técnica de Ambato, Ambato, Ecuador
{mc.paez,hd.morocho,manuelxsulcag}@uta.edu.ec
[2] Empresa Capacitaciones Integrales en Recursos Organizacionales – CIRORESOURCES, Ambato, Ecuador

Abstract. This research work focuses on the use of gamification as strategy learning tool for university students of the Elemental Education Major of Universidad Técnica de Ambato. Several resources were applied within the classroom online for one semester as an alternative to traditional strategies in online education. Education has taken an abysmal turn as a result of the pandemic throughout this year, so that teachers and students had to adapt to new educational models, the educational model was the application of flipped classroom, also use of synchronous and asynchronous tools, and use of digital grading rubrics, video conferences Tools, and multimedia materials developed by teachers, among others. The authors applied ADDIE methodology to develop these tools which propose the generation of more effective resources in educational innovation. The statistic that was applied to test the hypothesis was Wilcoxon due to the fact it was an experimental-exploratory research. Finally, the results of this research allowed to identify the difference in the academic performance of the students when using resources based on gamification developed by the Professors, these results show that there is better attention to online classes when direct gamification tools are used. Thus, teachers promote better participation active when they use synchronous tools within online classes and not just common everyday tools.

Keywords: ICT · Gamification · Higher education · Learning · Serious games

1 Introduction

Normally, gaming is considered a trivial activity, associated with entertainment and leisure. However, what happens when it becomes a tool to build the future of Higher Education? It is undeniable that with the introduction of new technologies to education, teachers face new roles and challenges, including using the necessary techniques to motivate and generate students' commitment [1].

© Springer Nature Switzerland AG 2021
R. Valencia-García et al. (Eds.): CITI 2021, CCIS 1460, pp. 95–106, 2021.
https://doi.org/10.1007/978-3-030-88262-4_7

In the educational context of the Elemental Education Major of the Universidad Técnica de Ambato, there is the need to implement new learning strategies based on the development of new resources created by the Professors, so that these resources are part of new learning. They will be identified by a more intuitive, creative, and based on gaming [2]. This also will be a very important aspect for the students to feel motivated. Thus, they become the active participatory entities of the class, especially the authors of knowledge.

These strategies allowed students to adapt to a process to respond to a need where they seek to work educational content by providing experiences. In general, a need, dynamics, mechanics, etc. are defined. but this can also vary. Zichermann and Cunningham (2011) suggest categorizing the elements of a game into 3 groups: mechanics, dynamics, and aesthetics. Mechanics often define how games convert specific inputs into specific outputs. They tend to have a direct connection with the learning content, and when working with educational content which also include the use of challenges. The dynamics, on the other hand, indicate the needs that have to be satisfied [3].

Maintaining learners' interest and attention in the classroom is a difficult task; it is even more in an online environment due to the given the conditions that it presents. When a subject is not very stimulating or the methodology is not interesting for the student, this may be a reason to promote dropping out. Experts in different fields are testing the effectiveness of gaming to promote dynamic and proactive participation in actions that generally require good will effort [4].

Although gaming's use in non-recreational environments remains stigmatized, especially in advanced ages, gamification increasingly achieves a great adherence in the military field, in business, in industry and in education now.

Gamification can not only be used at the educational levels of younger students, but it is also appropriate for higher education classrooms. The games, designed efficiently, favor a significant increase of students' productivity and creativity. An interface that offers experiences, the opportunity to connect and build an online reputation, through achievements that are rewarded, is a valuable tool for professional construction [5].

A growing number of institutions are experimenting with video games, transforming homework into exciting challenges that reward student performance, so that they naturally promote the emergence of leader figures.

It is possible to capture students' attention through different gamification activities that transfer the functioning and mechanics of the game to an educational context to motivate learning [6]. In this sense, it works as a tool to increase motivation, encourage interactivity and socialization among students.

However, it is important to mention that gamification provides motivation only when it is executed correctly. For gamification to work properly, you need three critical elements:

- Context: The gamification element of your educational program should relate to a very specific topic.
- Value: participants should feel that they get value from the activity. Do not gamify just for the sake of it.

- Success - If you make a gamification strategy too complex, no one will be able to complete the challenge. Instead of creating commitment, it will generate frustration. The goals or objectives of the game must be achievable.

Gamification in higher education can be a valuable didactic tool that allows combining various aspects that are important in students training such as the cognitive, the social and the emotional parts. Cognitive because it has to do directly with their learning even more with meaningful learning; social because it represents an opportunity for discussion and exchange of learning while promoting attitudes and values; emotional because this component influences motivation, i.e. it maintains student's attention for a longer periods of time. However, it is important that the design of challenge-based gamified activities is creative and interesting to all students. Also, they have to be achievable, if not, a wrong design can significantly affect the purpose of the activity [7].

2 State of the Art

In the university context, authors such as [8] have found in gamification an opportunity to motivate, improve group dynamics, attention, reflective criticism and meaningful student learning. In addition, among the advantages to the teaching role; they improve and motivate learning using different dynamics [9]. However, it is necessary to take care of the established game mechanics when implementing this type of strategy in universities because success or failure depends on them. For instance, in the gamification strategy called "JOCS Creation Workshop" at the University of Barcelona, it was identified that students lowered their academic level and even considered the level of demand of the subject minimal [5]. In this sense, it is recommended to take special care in the design, planning and implementation of the strategy [2]. Therefore, [10] consider that to implement a successful gamification strategy it is necessary to take into account 6 elements, they are described with direct application in education:

1. Clearly define the educational objectives to be achieved in the classroom, so that gamification strategies are designed with coherence and efficiency.
2. Define the behaviors that we want to promote in students such as knowledge, attitudes, and skills, among others.
3. Establish who the players are, identify traits and characteristics to design activities relevant to their real interests.
4. Establish the activity cycles, defining the gamification system (game mechanics, order of events, interaction, among others).
5. Fun (it is the basis of every game), the events of this type that are included in the strategy must be described.
6. Resources, includes the tools that will be used for the development of the strategy (measurement, monitoring, indicators, etc.) [11].

The potential of video games as an educational tool was highlighted more than a decade ago by the visionary and technologist Marc Prensky. Since then, there has been a gradual increase in the use of video games and game mechanics in the context of teaching both at the primary and secondary level and in the context of higher education. This use of video games occurs in a more general context of culture gamification [12].

Serious games, alternative reality games, augmented reality games or serious toys are some examples of gamification in areas such as advertising, business, teaching or entertainment. Specifically in the area of education and training, numerous proposals based on gamification have been developed in recent years: from cases such as Virtoonomics (perhaps one of the most complete and complex business management simulators that can be found in the market) to platforms like Scratch, which allow students to develop their own educational video games.

However, despite the growing interest in the gamification of teaching, there are still few analysis tools that help to understand how the incorporation of the different elements of the games takes place (such as rules, game controls or rewards) as well such as the use of narrative elements used to convey the teaching-learning process through gamification.

The concept of gamification is a recent concept, documented for the first time in 2008 [7], which overlaps with other related concepts such as serious games or game-based learning. Although the concept of game-based learning has a long tradition and is clearly limited to the field of education [13] as its name indicates (game-based learning), both the concept of serious Games such as gamification are more ambiguous terms that can be found both in academic literature and in commercial practice linked to areas that are not strictly educational.

Gamification has elements of great value in the comprehensive training of students. [3] and [14] agree that playing constitutes a unique opportunity to integrate cognitive, affective, and social aspects. Undoubtedly, these aspects must be considered in the design of all gamified activity. The cognitive aspect occurs when the student receives immediate feedback and is given several attempts in such a way that it leads to a metacognitive process or when faced with a challenge [15].

The emotional aspect occurs when the student receives recognition for their achievement [6] and the social aspect occurs when the achievements are socialized through a leadership board or when students work collaboratively to achieve a challenge or mission. Thus, serious games have been linked both to the field of education and training in business management as well as to the military field and even to the field of marketing and advertising; as executing strategies of innovation, creativity and interaction between users, motivating mental exercise, abstract reasoning and above all based on games, gamification as a fundamental basis for the cognitive development of users.

Therefore, serious games have been defined as "any type of interactive computer game, for one or multiple players, to be used on any platform and that has been developed with the intention of being more than entertainment" [18].

Two things deserve to be highlighted from this definition: serious games are video games and that they are used not only as a form of entertainment. On the other hand, gamification has been defined as "the use of game design elements in contexts that are not games" [19]. This definition encompasses a more general scope considering not only video games but also the elements of game design in Educational innovation has gained strength in recent decades. Likewise, it has given rise to conflicting opinions. It is not about changing for changing, i.e. introducing a novel technology or some didactic strategy to the teaching-learning process will not always result in an educational innovation [20]. For this innovation to take place, the changes must be based on teaching, the purpose is to improve learning. In addition, this innovation must be evaluated in order to verify that the teaching-learning process was improved [21].

In order to evaluate innovations in higher education, [22] established four criteria: a) there is research on the innovation that is adopted; b) the innovations have been universally adopted in the institution; c) there is evidence of its effect on student learning or retention; and d) the innovation is distinguished from other innovations. [4] argue that there are three essential elements in the development of an innovation: openness, updating and improving quality. Openness is the ability to adapt, as well as the development or improvement of attitudes, knowledge, skills, and resources.

Updating consists of keeping up to date with the latest advances related to implemented innovation, while quality improvement consists of evaluating the extent to which the innovation improves the process. These criteria are interesting and can be useful to evaluate various educational innovations in any area of knowledge.

3 Methodology

This research was an experimental-exploratory type. It was possible to measure the differences between the academic performance of a sample of the students of the Elemental Education Major by applying gamification tools in the subject of Convergence of Educational Media (CEM).

This experimentation and exploration of the data was developed for a semester in all the online sessions of the subject.

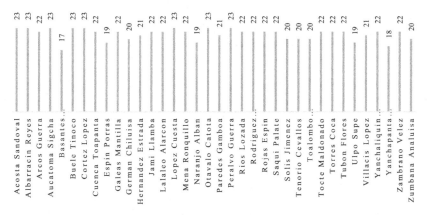

Fig. 1. Number of sessions per student

The implemented gamification strategy presented in this research article aimed to motivate students to actively participate in class to stimulate the development of thematic content and improve some recurring negative behaviors in the classroom. The following elements were established to achieve these features (Table 1):

Table 1. Elements of the strategy

1. Educational objectives	- Motivate students to actively participate in online classes - Encourage the development of thematic content in the online classroom - Improve some recurring negative behaviors of students
2. Behaviors (negative)	- Lack of participation in class - Failure to hand in assignments - Low quality in handing in assignments
3. Players (traits and characteristics)	- Digital natives [1], young people between the ages of 18 and 22 who constantly use technology (mobile devices). In addition, they want to obtain high marks to maintain GPA above 8.0
4. Activity cycles (game mechanics)	- At the beginning of the semester: presentation of the game and its mechanics - In each online class: carrying out activities to assign points - At the end of the academic school year: exchange of student points for defined prizes
5. Fun	- For each thematic content, dynamic activities (interactive maps, quizzes, word search, crossword, among others) were developed on the Kahoot and Educaplay platforms
6. Resources	Select the appropriate resources for gamification in the subject of Convergence of Educational Media and evaluate their acceptability

Source: Mullins, Jeffrey K.; Sabherwal, Rajiv (2020)

To know the evaluation of the students of the gamification strategy, the research approach was quantitative and the design descriptive. This allowed the orderly and methodical record of data collection according to the variables established in the research.

50 undergraduate students from the Faculty of Human Sciences and Education of the Universidad Técnica de Ambato participated in the gamification strategy. According to [1] digital natives with ages ranging from 18 to 22 years. The research was carried out in the Elemental Education Major with a sex distribution of 66% (33) were females and 34% (17) were males.

An ad hoc questionnaire was developed to find out the students' assessment of the strategy used. The instrument had a total of 7 questions; 2 dichotomous, 4 with a Likert scale with 5 response options (0 = None; 1 = Little; 2 = Somewhat; 3 = a lot and 4 = a great deal), and one open question to know the opinion about the awards and the application used in the gamification strategy.

The gamification strategy was carried out in 3 groups (group 1, 20 students; group 2, 12 students; group 3, 18 students). These students belong to the ICT class of the above mentioned Major. The implementation was carried out in 3 moments; thus: First, interaction, dynamics and mechanics characteristics of the game were presented at the beginning of the semester, emphasizing how to accumulate points. For instance, attendance to all classes −2 points- (assigned at the end of each academic cutoff for students without absences in the class); participation −1 point- (subject to the coherence and relevance of the response and / or intervention of each student in class), submissions −1 point- (students who submit their work first), quality of the work presented −2 points- (for assignments with a grade of 5). In addition, awards and an exchange scale were socialized (Table 2).

Table 2. Points of activities

Points	Awards
4	Book separator
6	1 (0.1) tenth in the lowest grade
8	Delete 1 absence (One hour of absence from class)
10	2 (0.2) tenths in the lowest grade
12	Delete 2 absences (Two hours of absence from class)
14	5 (0.5) tenths in the lowest grade

Then ClassDojo registration and monitoring platform (https://www.classdojo.com) was introduced to the players, the students in this case. ClassDojo was created in 2011 with the aim of innovating education by connecting teachers, students, and parents. The application allows teachers to create interactive spaces called personalized classrooms with the skills and feedback for each group.

On their part, students have a user code to access and consult progress, weaknesses, and communication with the teacher. In addition, each parent receives an account where they can interact with the teacher and immediately receive reports on the abilities (positive and negative) of the participants. To develop the strategy, each student installed the application on their mobile device and registered with the code assigned by the teacher.

Also, the skills were created with their respective points on the platform (Fig. 1). On the other hand, at the beginning of each class, the teacher presented the status of points on the screen to extrinsically motivate students to get more points in the activities that were to be developed in class.

Fig. 2. Interface ClassDojo

Finally, both group and individual game dynamics were developed around thematic contents that were being developed in the ICT class. These included questions about the teacher's knowledge and activities such as videoquiz, quiz, word search, crossword, matching, among others; In the Kahoot and Educaplay platforms, interaction and play were generated within the framework of the competition. These activities became the main motivating agent for the students.

In each academic cutoff of units and terms, the teacher made the exchange of points with each student, therefore, the player (student) selected their favorite award or did not exchange with the intention of continuing to accumulate points for the next academic cutoff or term.

Finally, both group and individual game dynamics were developed around thematic contents that were being developed in the ICT class. These included questions about the teacher's knowledge and activities such as videoquiz, quiz, word search, crossword, matching, among others; In the Kahoot and Educaplay platforms, interaction and play were generated within the framework of the competition. These activities became the main motivating agent for the students.

In each academic cutoff of units and terms, the teacher made the exchange of points with each student, therefore, the player (student) selected their favorite award or did not exchange with the intention of continuing to accumulate points for the next academic cutoff or term.

4 Results

Regarding the usefulness of the strategy for the development of thematic content in class (Fig. 2), 90% of the students consider that it is useful, while 5% consider that it is not useful. In relation to the evaluation of the strategy, the acceptance of the students is high, 89% qualified positively with a score $> = 3$ and 11% as low. Females were the ones with the highest approval (Fig. 3). In this sense, when investigating motivation in students generated by the strategy for the development of the thematic contents of the class, 88% indicated that it is motivating and 12% that it is not motivating (Fig. 4). According to these results, it is confirmed that this type of strategy fosters a favorable environment to motivate students learning in the classroom (Fig. 5).

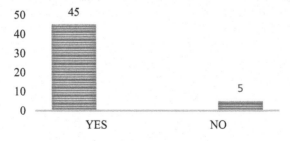

Fig. 3. Usefulness of the strategy based on gamification

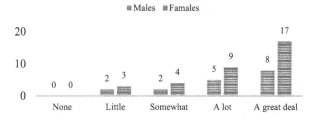

Fig. 4. Assessment of the usefulness of the gamification strategy

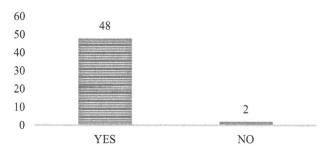

Fig. 5. Motivation of the students regarding the gamification tool

Another aspect that the students evaluated was the relevance of the awards. In this sense, 88% of the students considered the convenience of the awards within the strategy as quite very favorable. Males were the ones with the greatest agreement. Consequently, the effectiveness of the mechanical gamification in education using points and awards documented by authors such as [6] is validated; [22, 18].

Regarding the information presented above, students were asked what other prizes and/or incentives could be part of the gamification strategy. The largest number of responses focused on increasing the exchange options for grades. In addition, they propose the elimination of the finals and bonus marks in the classroom project.

Finally, the students were asked to rate the ClassDojo app, 88% rated it fairly and very good. It should be clarified that the platform has academic management tools such as attendance record, communication with parents, among others. However, in the implemented strategy was only used for the registration and exchange of points.

For the validation of the hypothesis, the statistic of ranks with Wilcoxon signs was applied because it was an experimental type of research. The hypothesis could be corroborated because gamification tools improve these college students learning in the Media Convergence subject (Table 3).

By having a p (value) less than 0.05, the alternative hypothesis is accepted where tools such as Kahoot and Educaplay improved the learning of the Media Convergence subject. Consequently, the academic performance of the students improved notably; The use of these gamification tools was taken into consideration because they allow the development of products generated by the Professor and meet the learning outcomes.

Table 3. Contrast statistics

	Kahoot App Ratings - Educaplay App Ratings
Z	−4,425[b]
Sig. asintót. (bilateral)	,000

a. Wilcoxon signed rank test, b. Based in the positives ranks

5 Discussion

The classical model of education in universities limits the interaction between students, teachers, and content. In this sense, gamification emerges as a relevant tool to motivate the development of content and the participation of students in the classroom.

The success of a gamification strategy in higher education lies in the design, the Werbach and Hunter model [23] is convenient and practical because it establishes a general planning, implementation and monitoring framework. However, in the observations of the players (students) elements emerge that a priori were not taken into account but that are of great importance to improve the gaming experience such as; prizes (include more percentages in grades and a higher prize for not taking a final exam), resources (diversify the way to obtain points with elements such as tests, challenges, among others) and establish levels of difficulty (determine a minimum number of points to be able to continue in the game in each academic cut-off).

The level of evaluation of the strategy was high (89%). Females were the ones with the highest approval. However, in the evaluation of the awards, the approval of this group was low, and men were the ones with the highest approval. This indicates that the female students felt more satisfied with the game mechanics and males with the prizes.

The results support the effectiveness of the mechanics of points and prizes in gamification strategies in education as indicated by [20]. Furthermore, it allows extrinsic motivation to change the negative behaviors of students who are encouraged to compete for prizes.

The ICT tools used in interaction, measurement, monitoring and control of the gamification strategy facilitate and optimize teacher management. In this sense, the use of the ClassDojo application was limited to the registration and control of points and players. However, it has more functions (attendance record, messages, quiz, etc.) that can be of great help for students and teachers. Also, within the strategy, limitations were identified since student-type accounts do not allow customizing the avatar or observing the total accumulated points.

6 Conclusions and Future Work

The limitations of this research were the restriction at the time of connection that the students had for the correct development of the activities; in the same way, students do not have adequate technological devices for the correct development of virtual classes, thus limiting the lack of continuity in activities based on gamification; consequently, the use of these types of tools, as they are hosted on the web, restrict continuity in learning outcomes.

As future work it is planned to develop some mobile applications by teachers, to evaluate the impact of mobile learning in higher education such as the works presented in [22, 23].

Acknowledgment. Thanks to the Technical University of Ambato, to the Directorate of Research and Development (DIDE acronym in Spanish) for supporting our research project Development of Web 3.0 Tools in education as support in collaborative learning and being part of the research groups: Research in Language and Education and Marketing Consumption and Society.

1. References

1. Gentina, E., Chen, R.: Digital natives' coping with loneliness: Facebook or face-to-face? Inf. Manage. **56**(6), 103138 (2019)
2. Mishra, S., Malhotra, G.: The gamification of in-game advertising: examining the role of psychological ownership and advertisement intrusiveness. Int. J. Inf. Manage. 102245 (2020). in press, Corrected Proof
3. Mullins, J.K., Sabherwal, R.: Gamification: a cognitive-emotional view. J. Bus. Res. **106**, 304–314 (2020)
4. Blanchard, K.: Innovation and strategy: does it make a difference! A linear study of micro & SMEs. Int. J. Innov. Stud. **4**(4), 105–115 (2020)
5. Xi, N., Hamari, J.: Does gamification affect brand engagement and equity? A study in online brand communities. J. Business Res. **109**, 449–460 (2020)
6. Cho, V.: The past and future technology in classroom management and school discipline: a systematic review. Teach. Teacher Educ. **90**, 103037 (2020)
7. Argilés, M., Jurado, L.A., Junyent, L.Q.: Gamification, serious games and action video games in optometry practice. J. Optometry **13**(3), 210–211 (2020)
8. Gerdenitsch, C., et al.: Work gamification: effects on enjoyment, productivity and the role of leadership. Electron. Commerce Res. Appl. 100994 (2020)
9. Ulmer, J., Braun, S., Cheng, C.-T., Dowey, S., Wollert, J.: Human-centered gamification framework for manufacturing systems. Proc. CIRP **93**, 670–675 (2020)
10. Whittaker, L., Mulcahy, R., Russell-Bennett, R.: Go with the flow' for gamification and sustainability marketing. Int. J. Inf. Manage. 102305 (2021). in press, Corrected Proof
11. Sanchez, D.R., Langer, M., Kaur, R.: Gamification in the classroom: examining the impact of gamified quizzes on student learning. Comput. Educ. **144**, 103666 (2020)
12. Tobon, S., Ruiz-Alba, J.L., García-Madariaga, J.: Gamification and online consumer decisions: is the game over? Decis. Support Syst. **128**, 113167 (2020)
13. Fleming, T., Sutcliffe, K., Lucassen, M., Pine, R., Donkin, L.: Serious games and gamification in clinical psychology. Ref. Module Neurosci. Biobehav. Psychol. (2020)
14. Chow, C.Y., Riantiningtyas, R.R., Kanstrup, M.B., Papavasileiou, M., Liem, G.D., Olsen, A.: Can games change children's eating behaviour? A review of gamification and serious games. Food Qual. Preference **80**, 103823 (2020)
15. Mitchell, R., Schuster, L., Jin, H.S.: Gamification and the impact of extrinsic motivation on needs satisfaction: making work fun? J. Bus. Res. **106**, 323–330 (2020)
16. Quintas, A., Bustamante, J.-C., Pradas, F., Castellar, C.: Psychological effects of gamified didactics with exergames in physical education at primary schools: results from a natural experiment. Comput. Educ. **152**, 103874 (2020)

17. Mishra, L., Gupta, T., Shree, A.: Online teaching-learning in higher education during lockdown period of COVID-19 pandemic. Int. J. Educ. Res. Open **1**, 100012 (2020)
18. Pâquet, L.: Gamified identification: gamification and identification in indigenous Australian interactive documentaries. Comput. Composit. **56**, 102571 (2020)
19. Sokal, L., Trudel, L.E., Babb, J.: Canadian teachers' attitudes toward change, efficacy, and burnout during the COVID-19 pandemic. Int. J. Educ. Res. Open **1**, 100016, (2020)
20. Guan, C., Mou, J., Jiang, Z.: Artificial intelligence innovation in education: a twenty-year data-driven historical analysis. Int. J. Innovat. Stud. **4**(4), 134–147 (2020)
21. Werbach, K., Hunter, D.: How Game Thin-King can Revolutionize your Business. Wharton Digital Press, Philadelphia (2012)
22. Furió, D., Seguít, I., Vivó, R.: Mobile learning vs. traditional classroom lessons: a comparative study. J. Comput. Assisted Learn. 13 (2014)
23. Dashtestani, R.: Moving Bravely Towards Mobile Learning: Iranian Students' use of Mobile Devices for Learning English as a Foreign Language, p. 20. Routledge, London (2015)

Visualization Tools for Collaborative Systems: A Systematic Review

Mitchell Vásquez-Bermúdez[1,4](✉) ⓘ, Cecilia Sanz[2,3] ⓘ, María Alejandra Zangara[2] ⓘ, and Jorge Hidalgo[1] ⓘ

[1] Facultad de Ciencias Agrarias, Universidad Agraria del Ecuador, Avenida 25 de Julio y Pio Jaramillo, Guayaquil, Ecuador
{mvasquez,jhidalgo}@uagraria.edu.ec
[2] Instituto de Investigación en Informática LIDI, Facultad de Informática, Universidad Nacional de La Plata, La Plata, Argentina
{csanz,azangara}@lidi.info.unlp.edu.ar
[3] Investigador Asociado de La Comisión de Investigaciones Científicas de La Prov. de Buenos Aires, Buenos Aires, Argentina
[4] Facultad de Ciencias Matemáticas y Físicas, Universidad de Guayaquil, Cdla. Salvador Allende, Guayaquil, Ecuador
mitchell.vasquezb@ug.edu.ec

Abstract. Visualization tools have become a fundamental technique in the process of collaborative work, and they have become even more relevant when it comes to monitoring an educational task. The need to carry out proposals mediated by digital technologies has led to the emergence of new tools that allow visualizing the collaborative activity of the participants. This makes it possible to develop an educational review and monitoring approach in which information is presented graphically to the students who participate in a group activity, based on interaction indicators during their online work. Having this type of tools makes it possible to carry out collaborative work in a participatory and self-regulated way. This work will focus on conducting a systematic literature review process, from which studies that will be analysed are the ones which propose or design indicator visualization tools that can be used during educational collaborative activities. The results of the systematic review show that visualization tools give support to collaborative activities and also improve the participation and detail of the activities progress. Improving at the same time, the knowledge of the user about the interactions that arise in the collaboration of the participants, leading to a better way of actions coordination for correct decision making.

Keywords: Visualization tools · Collaborative activities · Higher education

1 Introduction

Due to the great involvement of people making use of information technologies, nowadays we can evidence the ability that they have acquire to solve a large number of problems in different areas of knowledge [1]. For this reason, today online learning

© Springer Nature Switzerland AG 2021
R. Valencia-García et al. (Eds.): CITI 2021, CCIS 1460, pp. 107–122, 2021.
https://doi.org/10.1007/978-3-030-88262-4_8

systems are opening up to implement technological tools that allow dynamic and fluid collaboration in the educational environment in order to encourage students to join others and also to complement projects or develop them together. The problem with today's learning systems is they do not allow a visualization of collaborative relationships and effect, in fact few studies have been carried out to university groups on visualization tools of their collaborative work [2]. [3] The main function of visualization in collaborative groups is to promote a clear and complete understanding of the relationships that arise in collaborative teams from a project, task or activity, which is an effective mean to coordinate and analyze collaborative relationships. Just as it indicates [3] and [4], this visualization helps track participants' progress to increase collaboration, reinforce findings, and provide an analysis of how the task is progressing. On [5] it is mentioned that different types of collaborative activities such as writing, information search, collaborative design, among others, can be also be developed. In addition, the authors highlight the importance of analyzing patterns of participation or factors that might affect individual or group collaborations, so that interventions could be carried out and the dynamics of the group is not affected. In such a way that motivation of learning in a digital environment can be stimulated in students, allowing the traditional study system to be transformed into modern systems with visualization approaches for the interactions between teacher and students in groups, therefore the necessity to explore the technological impact on collaborative learning [6].

The possibility of visualizing indicators about a collaborative activity can make it possible for participants to develop critical thinking and discussion among them about the strategies to be addressed during the group work. In addition, depending on the type of collaboration, it encourages analysis and questioning about the incorporation of the new ideas [7]. In accordance with [8], *mirroring tools*[1] are part of the tools for visualizing the activity of a work group. Through indicators these tools make it possible to monitor collaborative work. This work focuses on the study of these tools that are of special relevance today, since they allow the monitoring, self-reflection and analysis of the group and can contribute to its self-regulation.

This article is organized as follows: Sect. 2 shows the applied methodology, later Sect. 3 discusses the results of the research. In Sect. 4, the discussion of the results of the various tools is proposed. Finally, Sect. 5 sets out the conclusions and future work.

2   Methodology

To research and learn about the use and design of visualization tools for collaborative participation in Higher Education, which, due to the aforementioned, is an actual and important issue, it is carried out a systematic review (SR) of literature. The present work is focused on a type of scientific research whose objective is to identify, evaluate and synthesize all relevant studies on a given topic [9]. The stages of the SR are: (1) definition of the research questions; (2) specification of the types of studies; (3) conducting a comprehensive literature research; (4) evaluation of the research results and selection

---

[1] Mirroring consists of systems that reflect actions, they are also called replication systems. They collect raw data in log files and display it to collaborators [17] y [18].

of articles; (5) analysis of included studies; (6) synthesis; and (7) dissemination of the findings.

In particular, for this work, the proposal by Petticrew and Roberts is used [9]. Thus, a review of the last 5 years is carried out, focused mainly on the visualization tools of collaborative work and the uses that they contribute to the educational setting. From this, the following research questions are established:

P1. Which are the tools that enable the visualization of group and individual indicators during collaborative activities?

P2. Which characteristics and functionalities do the tools have?

P3. What are the ways of monitoring activities that the tools allow?

P4. What contributions do visualization tools have in the framework of these investigations?

2.1 Types of Studies

To carry out the search planning, the recommendation proposed in [9] was used. And in order to obtain more reliable results, just original published articles were taken into consideration.

Therefore, for the protocol of the proposed methodology, once the key questions that the review proposes to answer have been defined, the second stage is to define the types of studies that allow the research to be directed to the answers of the questions under study. This work will be limited to:

- Studies written in English and Spanish.
- Publications in peer-reviewed scientific journals, or conferences and congresses that have been peer-reviewed.
- Articles published or accepted for publication between January 2015 until April 2021.

2.2 Inclusion and Exclusion Criteria

To include the most relevant works, selection criteria were applied to titles and abstracts with the following characteristics:

- Empirical studies that consider as a population of interest collaborative work visualization tools with Higher Education students.
- Empirical studies that inquire about the use of visualization strategies of collaborative work in scenarios mediated by digital technology in higher education.

Criteria for excluding papers were the following:

- Empirical studies that do not investigate visualization strategies of collaborative works on the population of interest.
- Studies that address strategies and visualization tools with an instrumental, formative, reflective, or theoretical approach.

- Empirical studies that inquire about the use of collaborative work visualization strategies in educational contexts mediated by digital technology in higher education, but do not analyse their relationship with specific tools.
- Empirical studies that investigate the relationship between the use of visualization strategies of collaborative works in educational contexts that are not mediated by digital technology in higher education and this type of mediation is not specified.
- Empirical studies that do not include Higher Education students within the population of interest.
- Studies not accessible in full text.

2.3 Search Strategy

Once the particularities of the articles to be included or excluded have been raised, the databases and search chain are selected to carry out an exhaustive bibliographic investigation corresponding to stage 3 of the proposed systematic review.

As part of the search strategy, the following databases, digital libraries, and journal portals are selected: ACM Digital Library, Directory of Open Access Journals (DOAJ), Education Resources Information Center (ERIC), IEEE Xplore Digital Library, JSTOR Journals, Scientific Electronic Library Online (ScieLO), Scopus, ScienceDirect. Additionally, in order to identify relevant articles a manual search will be used on the tables of contents of the journals: Journal of New Approaches in Educational Research (NAER), American Journal of Distance Education, Revista Iberoamericana de Tecnología en Educación y Educación en Tecnología (TE&ET). As well as the searches in spanish of the Electronic Library of Science and Technology (Secretariat of Scientific-Technological Articulation; Ministry of Science, Technology, and Productive Innovation; Argentine Republic), and the RedALyC portal (Network of Scientific Journals of Latin America and the Caribbean, Spain and Portugal), since it is interesting to learn about IberoAmerican works on these topics.

Table 1 shows the string of terms used in the search process, a set of 12 search terms in Spanish and English will be used.

Table 1. Search terms

	Spanish	English
A1	Herramientas de visibilización	Visibility tools
A2	Herramientas de visualización	Visualization tools
A3	Herramienta de espejo	Mirroring tool
A4	Software de visibilización	Visibility software
A5	Software de visualización	Visualization software
A6	Plugin de visibilización	Visibility plugin
A7	Plugin de visualización	Visualization plugin

(continued)

Table 1. (*continued*)

	Spanish	English
B1	Actividades colaborativas	Collaborative activities
B2	Trabajos colaborativos	Collaborative work
B3	Trabajo online	Work online
C1	Educación Superior	Higher Education
C2	Universidad	University

The search strings used corresponded to the Boolean expression (A1 OR A2 OR A3 OR A4 OR A5 OR A6 OR A7) AND (B1 OR B2 OR B3) AND (C1 OR C2).

According to the search carried out with the established conditions, the following results were obtained, which are shown in Table 2.

Table 2. Number of results per database

Database	Search
ACM – DIGITAL LIBRARY	1999 results
IEEE	207 results
SCOPUS (SCIENCEDIRECT)	50 results
Other databases	0 results

3   Search Result

3.1   Analysis and Selection Process

Once the search strategy described in Subsect. 3.4 had been proposed, the documents obtained in the search were analyzed and selected (stage 4 corresponding to the methodology).

The results obtained according to the search with conditions were 2256, after that the include and exclude method was applied, such as: eliminating duplicate articles, quick reading of the abstract, flash exclusion sampling, reading of the full text, review of excluded publications, as shown in Fig. 1.

3.2   Search Posts

Table 3 shows the studies selected based on the focus of this review. According to the searches carried out in the different databases, a favorable result has been obtained in the ACM journals due to the greater number of publications about tools related to collaborative monitoring. The results are shown in Fig. 2.

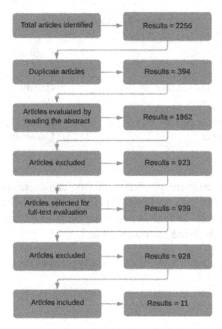

Fig. 1. Number of articles included and excluded in the process

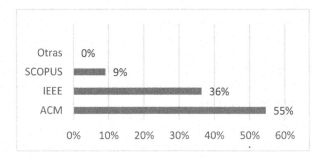

Fig. 2. Search result by databases

3.3 Analysis of Results

In the preliminary search in the databases, 2256 preselected articles were obtained, of which 11 met the inclusion criteria considered in the present work. From the results obtained, it was decided to group the criteria into three categories:

1. Visualization tool
2. Monitoring virtual activities
3. Contributions of visualization tools

Table 3. Search relevant posts

Relevant results			
Authors	Data base	Visualization tool	Objective
Freitas et al. [10]	Acm	StarQuest, Navi Badgeboard-Navi Surface and Curtin Challenge	Analyse three game dashboards where StarQuest provides information on levels of cooperation, competition, and contextual variables. Navi Badgeboard supports the awareness and reflection of each student and collaboration measured through badges and Curtin Challenge incorporates information on challenges that support the design and resolution of team problems, obtaining visualized percentages of activities achieved in collaboration
Qiang et al. [3]	Acm	StoryLine	The purpose of the StoryLine tool is to monitor or explore the participation of the actors in an activity
Athukorala et al. [4]	Acm	SAT	The purpose of the SAT (Search Activity Traces) system with CIS (Collaborative Information Search) interface is to visualize three types of traces or traces: keyword traces, query traces, and bookmark traces to support collaborative literature search tasks. with an explicit visualization of the activities of other collaborators through a timeline
Yim et al. [5]	Acm	DocuViz	This study presents the tool DocuViz, that has as objective a general-purpose interactive display system for Google Docs. It allows to visualize who did what and when
Torres, García y Peláez [7]	IEEE	D3 sunburst	An analytical framework is described for the quantitative and qualitative visualization of the contribution of students in an interactive web tool for collaborative writing, which gives teachers a presentation of the work done by each of the students while collaborative writing

(continued)

Table 3. (*continued*)

Relevant results			
Authors	Data base	Visualization tool	Objective
Muñoz-Alcántara et al. [11]	Acm	ALICE	The ALICE web tool is proposed because it stands out for its online collaboration that integrates various commercial cloud storage services and reconfigures the interactions of team members in a representation that considers the time
Coelho y Braga [12]	Acm	ColMiner	This study presents the ColMiner tool whose purpose is the automated analysis of communications in software projects. It gives the possibility of calculating the relevance of the comments published by the participants and establishing a relationship with other factors of the project, in order to support the management of communications
Papanikolaou [13]	IEEE	INSPIREus	The study proposes a model applied to INSPIRE us to visualize specific indicators on the behavior of student interactions. Where users make up an online community having one or more roles: learners, tutors, authors, reviewers
Schwab et al. [14]	IEEE	VisConnect	The VisConnect tool is presented as a web-based distributed collaborative visualization system, supports simultaneous interaction with a locking system that gives each collaborator control over specific elements of a Document Object Model, simplifying the creation of collaborative visualizations
Agredo et al. [15]	SCOPUS	MEPAC	Presents the MEPAC computer tool (Monitoring and Evaluation of the Collaborative Learning Process). Take advantage of the functionality provided by Moodle. It allows the monitoring and evaluation of activities of the collaborative learning process. It allows the creation of forms to manage the phases of the process

(*continued*)

Table 3. (*continued*)

Relevant results			
Authors	Data base	Visualization tool	Objective
Claros, Echeverria y Cobos [16]	IEEE	PABEC	Presents PABEC (Learning Platform Based on Collaborative Scenarios) is composed of three services, from *plugins* developed and integrated in the LMS Moodle: SAE, SGN and SGM

The evaluation criteria are presented and described below:

1. Visualization tool.
- Type of application. For this criterion, 3 types of application are considered: Web, Mobile and Desktop.
- Display type. This criterion focuses on identifying the way in which the monitoring of collaborative activity is made visible. 6 categories are considered: timeline, social network chart, histogram, bar chart, pie chart, and polar area chart.
- Type of Communication. This criterion considers whether the display of the indicators is synchronous and/or asynchronous.
2. Monitoring of Collaborative Activities.
- Tracking provided by the collaborative tool. This criterion refers to what type of activities the tool tracks. For this, 7 types are considered: Workshop, Forum, Editors, Task, Wiki, Chat, Essays.
- Visualization of group interaction indicators. This criterion refers to what types of indicators the tool considers. They are analyzed if they are: Quantitative and/or Qualitative.
- Development of the Collaborative Activity. Consider the indicators by phase of the activity. 3 aspects are considered: Phases of the activity, Type of participation (Individual or Group), delivery of activity (online or on file).
3. Contributions of visualization tools
- Student. This criterion refers to the benefits reported from the point of view of the students in the use of visualization tools. 3 types are considered linked to: improving student participation, self-regulation, and social awareness.
- Teacher. This criterion refers to the benefits reported from the teachers' point of view in the use of visualization tools. 3 aspects are considered such as: progress of groups in collaboration, visualizing group performance and levels of participation.

Table 4 summarizes the information from the studies of the visualization tools of collaborative activities, their monitoring and the contributions generated, based on the criteria. From the analysis it is possible to show that more than three articles use time-lines and bar graphs for the visualizations [3–5, 10–14], indicators such as time of access to the activity, presence of structuring in phases for collaborative activity and visualization with affective qualitative indicator are presented in 45% of the cases studied. In addition, compared to the use of collaborative work of visualization tools, 73% of articles refer to the improvement of student participation, adding to this that 45% reflect the visualization of group performance that the teacher can obtain as a benefit. Within the category of visualization tools, 91% of articles use web applications, while 9% use mobile applications and no desktop. The timeline and bar charts are highlighted as the most used type of visualization in articles.

Regarding the type of activities, they follow up, 90% of the articles focus on activities with editors, workshops, and essays. In turn, in the visualization with qualitative indicators, those oriented to the content and the affective component are highlighted. In relation to the quantitative ones, they focus on the quantity and percentage of interaction messages. Another important indicator mentioned is access time. In addition, interactions are analysed through social media analysis tools.

The contributions of the visualization tools are multiple and among them the improvement in self-regulation, in the progress of groups, and the levels of participation are mentioned. It should be clarified that 77% of the articles highlight the improvement of student participation, social awareness, and the visualization of group performance.

Table 4. Analysis of relevant publications

| | | | Relevant publications | | | | | | | | | | |
			[3]	[4]	[5]	[7]	[10]	[11]	[12]	[13]	[14]	[15]	[16]
VISUALIZATION TOOLS	Application functionality	Web	X	X	X	X	X	X	X		X	X	X
		Mobile					X						
		Desk											
	Type of visualization	Timeline	X	X	X			X					
		Social network graphic		X			X						
		Histogram			X						X		
		Bars chart					X		X	X			
		Circular chart					X		X	X			
		Polar area chart				X							
	Type of communication	Synchronous		X	X	X	X	X				X	X
		Asynchronous	X	X	X	X		X	X	X	X	X	X

		Relevant publications	[3]	[4]	[5]	[7]	[10]	[11]	[12]	[13]	[14]	[15]	[16]
MONITORING OF VIRTUAL ACTIVITIES — Tracking of the usage of the collaborative tool		Workshop						X			X	X	X
		Forum								X		X	
		Editors	X		X			X	X				
		Task									X	X	
		Wikis				X						X	
		Chat										X	
		Essays		X	X				X				
Visualization with interaction indicators — Qualitative		Organizational	X						X		X	X	X
		Affective			X		X			X		X	X
		Content	X	X	X	X			X	X	X		
		#Cualitative messages			X					X			
		#Cuantitative messages			X					X	X	X		
Quantitative		Social network											
		Self-regulation		X	X			X				X	X
		Time of acces to the activity					X	X	X		X	X	
Development of collaborative activity		Phases of the activity	X	X		X						X	X
	Type of participation	Individual		X		X	X	X	X	X	X	X	X
		Group	X	X	X		X	X	X			X	X
	Activity delivery	Online		X	X	X	X			X		X	X	X
		File				X		X	X			X	X
CONTRIBUTION OF TOOLS — Student		Improves the student participation		X	X	X			X	X	X	X	X
		Self-regulation					X	X			X	X	X
		Social awareness	X		X		X	X			X		X
Teacher		Group progress		X			X			X			
		Group performance		X	X	X	X		X				
		Levels of participation			X			X			X		

4 Results of Analysis: Discussion

Collaboration is becoming a competence key in educational society. The constant evolution of technology and the speed of change with which students interact with technology today, forces researchers and professionals to generate strategies to improve its impact on learning. Thus, collaborative work in educational processes is increasingly popular, few are the studies that focus on the visualization of indicators throughout the process of these collaborative activities, instead of measuring the performance of the group, the progress of its members, and the support they can give for the decision-making of teachers or students.

According to the results obtained from the systematic review proposed in this research, the visualization tools of collaborative activities currently serve to improve participation and social awareness. It allows the teacher to maintain knowledge about the performance and progress of the group, through interactive visualizations. Many of these tools provide synchronous or asynchronous communication, and based on their indicators, they help the actors to self-regulate the progress of the activity.

In studies such as the one carried out by Freitas et al. [10] the use of three dashboards in different game applications is compared (StarQuest-Navi Badgeboard y Navi Surface-Curtin Challenge), where the StarQuest *dashboard* reports about collective efforts, specific subject areas and the performance page provides benchmark scores for participants. *Navi Badgeboard and Navi Surface dashboard*s implement an interactive visualization supporting not just collaboration, but social awareness and reflection by assigning badges that reflect that the student has collaborated with the participants. The authors indicate that there is an increase in student engagement. The Curtin *dashboard* reflects the progress of activities through a percentage figure, achieving real-time monitoring of social collaboration. It also enables active exploration of efforts and results, visualization of multi-user interactions, and challenge-based learning. All these are characteristics that are identified in applications that focus on an interactive visualization to support students in the effective reach of their goals.

In another study by Alcántara et al. [11], a web prototype for online collaboration is presented which integrates the monitoring of shared documents and, through a timeline, reveals the levels of work of the design team; Therefore, by making possible the visualization of the work carried out in its different interactions, it has helped designers to coordinate actions, track progress, issue feedback on the work that is carried out and generate team discussions about the activities carried out.

In this sense, Qiang et al. [3], proposes a visualization model based on StoryLine (timelines), to effectively represent the changing process that arises from dynamic relationships in group collaboration and thus provide users with an intuitive means of analysis. At the same time, this method includes the mapping of basic elements, implementation of design algorithms, addition of visual metaphors, means of interaction and view of results.

In the same way Athukorala et al. [4], implemented a prototype that visualizes the follow-up of three types of activities (written queries, bookmarked articles and interested keywords) on a search system, in order to design new follow-up visualizations that is complemented with *social network* graphics and timelines to serve the collaborative search. From the visualization based on the content that the researchers can contribute in the search using keywords, the system calculates the performance in the search through indicators such as: the article is marked by the collaborators, the article is marked by me, the article is bookmarked by me and contributors, and the article is not bookmarked by anyone, providing traces of all the actions carried out by all the collaborators of the group identified by colours that optimize an optimal visualization, increasing the opportunity to see effective activity traces.

The approach proposed by the authors of [5] and [7] of a collaborative synchronous and asynchronous collaboration, indicates the contribution has multiple benefits, among them, the improvement of productivity, the quality of writing and the usage of e-learning approaches to motivate students to join in collaboration. Likewise, the metrics raised in the three articles focus on the semantic data of content that collaborators can contribute together and the visualization that allows identifying the amount of writing, interactions in the reviews, number of comments published and number of questions that the author made or participated in. It is also highlighted that the delivery of the activities is carried out online to facilitate the automated analysis of the communication. Thus, through indicators, the interactions proposed by the application or model are calculated.

Papanikolaou [13], affirms that collaborative visualizations in interactive systems have led to the novel proposal of instructional strategies that adapt to the learning style preferences of students. It also indicates that the interaction data can be used to analyse its effectiveness and guide the system's recommendations to strengthen decision-making, where the displayed indicators determine the effort of the students, progress, work style, the control that reflects the individual student activity, and the contribution of each one of them. The relevance of the proposed indicators is highlighted, which can be used to analyse individual and group data and the participation/intervention of tutors. In the same way, Agredo et al. [15] and Claros et al. [16] mention the lack of technological tools that guarantees effective collaboration with visible results that allow a compendium of mechanisms to support the collaborative learning process and identify the key points of the interactions. Agredo et al. [15] implements a technological tool named MEPAC (Monitoring and Evaluation of the Collaborative Learning Process), where the indicators established to calculate the utility include: the average range of students must be between 80% and 100%, average range of favourable responses by part of the teacher between 80% and 100%, the average range of students who pass the activity must be between 80% and 100%. In addition, to determine applicability: the effort to develop a collaborative activity with MEPAC considering the time of the teacher and the student within the three phases of the process should be an average of 10 to 12 h. In this way, the indicators help to determine, monitor, and evaluate in each phase of the process (Pre-process, Process and Post-Process), the appropriate interventions of the teacher in the proposed activities. At the same time, Claros et al. [16] make a review of the PABEC platform (Platform for Learning Based on Collaborative Scenarios) made up of three services: SAE-Teaching Assistant System, SGN-Notification Management Service and SGM-Motivation Management Service, where the proposed indicators (added documents, comments made and ratings made) in the case study, yielded positive results by strengthening support in collaborative activities for teachers and students. There it is indicated that the proposed metrics become relevant when they provide valuable interaction data, motivating students and teachers to get involved in collaborative activities, and in this way the teacher supports students to achieve learning goals.

Schwab et al. [14], confirms that the collaborative visualization system proposed in his article adapts to many collaborators with simultaneous interactions with the ability to respond to a satisfactory user experience, by having a timeline and *social network* graphics.

In this sense, visualization tools of collaborative activities can be applied in universities, to have a wide set of data on progress and both individual and group participation in collaborations. In this way, it can be achieved that both the teacher and the student have knowledge of the interactions that arise in collaboration, and support decision-making in these processes.

In order to address the research question P1, 11 collaborative tools were found that contain visualization of collaborative activities [3, 4, 5, 7, 10, 11, 12, 13, 14, 15 16]. In response to the research question P2, among the characteristics found, the Star-Quest, Navi Badgeboard and Curtin Challenge *dashboards* support awareness, student reflection, social collaboration and collaborative visualization; StoryLine is based on the monitoring or exploration of the participation of the actors of an activity; SAT supports collaborative literature search tasks with explicit visualization of the activities of other collaborators; DocuViz enables interactive viewing for Google Doc revision histories; ALICE reconfigures team member interactions in a time-oriented visualization; D3 sunburst is a quantitative and qualitative visualization framework for collaborative writing contribution. For its part, ColMiner offers monitoring of communications in software projects, INSPIREus supports visualization of interactions meaningfully for students and tutors; VisConnect synchronized visualizations of concurrent interactions; MEPAC supports collaboration times between teacher and students as part of indicators to determine, monitor and evaluate timely teacher interventions in proposed activities and PABEC supports collaborative learning services in the Moodle system. 91% of the functionality of these tools is based on the web. As an answer to the research question P3, in 84% of the tools found, their form of follow-up is based on tasks, wikis, chat and editors; where 73% are group type and the delivery of the activities is online. Regarding the research question P4, among the contributions it is found that 73% of the tools give relevance to the improvement of participation, 45% support self-regulation and 55% favor the social awareness of the students; while 27% contribute to the teacher in the progress of collaboration groups, 45% support the visualization of group performance and 27% improve the levels of participation.

5   Conclusion and Future Work

This work presents a systematic review that managed to identify and analyze several studies of visualization tools for collaborative activities. The visualization tools observed in collaborative activities positively influence both teachers and students, and at the same time they become a challenge for researchers on the subject, to continue improving and implementing new functionalities, indicators, and strategies in the visualizations. Most of the tools have been developed for the web and with interactive visualizations predominantly timelines, social networks, bar, and pie charts. In reviewed studies it was shown that visualization tools allow students to improve their participation, examine their progress, review individual and group performance to improve self-regulation in group work, and generate social awareness of the participants who are working and interacting. In addition, these tools provide teachers with the control of the group work that students carry out online, diverting unnecessary attention and helping in decision-making and interventions.

References

1. Vásquez-Bermúdez, M., Hidalgo, J., Crespo-León, K., Cadena-Iturralde, J.: Citizen science in agriculture through ICTs. a systematic review. In: Valencia-García, R., Alcaraz-Mármol, G., Cioppo-Morstadt, J.D., Vera-Lucio, N., Bucaram-Leverone, M. (eds.) CITAMA 2019. AISC, vol. 901, pp. 111–121. Springer, Cham (2019). https://doi.org/10.1007/978-3-030-10728-4_12
2. Korhonen, A., Vivitsou, M.: Digital Storytelling and Group Work, pp. 140–146 (2019)
3. Qiang, L., Bingjie, C., Longlong, M., GaoFeng, Z., Xun, L.: Dynamic collaboration modeling and visualization. In: ACM Internatioanl Conference Proceeding Ser., vol. Part F1311, pp. 93–100 (2017). https://doi.org/10.1145/3127404.3127415
4. Athukorala, K., et al.: Visualizing activity traces to support collaborative literature searching. In: ACM Internatioanl Conference Proceeding Ser., vol. Part F1301, pp. 45–52 (2017). https://doi.org/10.1145/3105971.3105981
5. Yim, S., Wang, D., Olson, J., Vu, V., Warschauer, M.: Synchronous writing in the classroom: Undergraduates' collaborative practices and their impact on text quality, quantity, and style. In: Proceedings ACM Conference Computer Support Coop Work. CSCW, pp. 468–479 (2017). https://doi.org/10.1145/2998181.2998356
6. Islam Sarker, M.N., Wu, M., Cao, Q., Alam, G.M.M., Li, D.: Leveraging digital technology for better learning and education: a systematic literature review. Int. J. Inf. Educ. Technol. 9(7), 453–461 (2019). https://doi.org/10.18178/ijiet.2019.9.7.1246
7. Torres, J., García, S., Peláez, E.: Visualizing authorship and contribution of collaborative writing in e-learning environments. In: International Conference Intelligent User Interfaces, Proc. IUI, vol. Part F1476, pp. 324–328 (2019). https://doi.org/10.1145/3301275.3302328
8. Vásquez-Bermúdez, M., Sanz, C., Zangara, M.A., Hidalgo, J.: Mirroring tools and interaction indicators in collaborative work: a systematic review. In: Valencia-García, R., Alcaraz-Marmol, G., Del Cioppo-Morstadt, J., Vera-Lucio, N., Bucaram-Leverone, M. (eds.) CITI 2020. CCIS, vol. 1309, pp. 179–192. Springer, Cham (2020). https://doi.org/10.1007/978-3-030-62015-8_14
9. Terms, F., Petticrew, M., Roberts, H.: Systematic reviews in the social sciences: a practical guide. Oxford: Blackwell 2006. 352, pp. ISBN 1 4051 2110 6. £29.99, Couns. Psychother. Res., vol. 6, no. 4, pp. 304–305 (2006). https://doi.org/10.1080/14733140600986250
10. De Freitas, S., et al.: How to use gamified dashboards and learning analytics for providing immediate student feedback and performance tracking in higher education. In: 26th International World Wide Web Conf. 2017, WWW 2017 Companion, pp. 429–434 (2017). https://doi.org/10.1145/3041021.3054175
11. Muñoz-Alcántara, J., Kreymer, R., Markopoulos, P., Funk, M.: Alice: design of a time-oriented collaboration service for design teams. In: Proceedings ACM SIGCHI Symposium Engineering Interact. Comput. Syst. EICS 2018 (2018). https://doi.org/10.1145/3220134.3220143

12. Neto, L.E.C., Braga E Silva, G.: ColMiner: a tool to support communications management in an issue tracking environment [ColMiner: Uma ferramenta de apoio ao gerenciamento das comunicações em um ambiente de issue tracking], ACM Int. Conf. Proceeding Ser., pp. 392–399 (2018). https://www.scopus.com/inward/record.uri?eid=2-s2.0-85060056171&doi=10.1145%2F3229345.3229398&partnerID=40&md5=3964f48e09d86de2d91dd236d9f46694

13. Papanikolaou, K.A.: Constructing interpretative views of learners' interaction behavior in an open learner model. IEEE Trans. Learn. Technol. **8**(2), 201–214 (2015). https://doi.org/10.1109/TLT.2014.2363663

14. Schwab, M., et al.: VisConnect: distributed event synchronization for collaborative visualization. IEEE Trans. Vis. Comput. Graph. **27**(2), 347–357 (2021). https://doi.org/10.1109/TVCG.2020.3030366

15. Agredo Delgado, V., Ruiz, P.H., Collazos, C.A., Fardoun, H.M., Noaman, A.Y.: Software tool to support the improvement of the collaborative learning process. In: Solano, A., Ordoñez, H. (eds.) CCC 2017. CCIS, vol. 735, pp. 442–454. Springer, Cham (2017). https://doi.org/10.1007/978-3-319-66562-7_32

16. Claros, I., Echeverria, L., Cobos, R.: Towards MOOCs scenarios based on collaborative learning approaches. In: IEEE Global Engineering Education Conference, EDUCON, vol. 2015, pp. 989–992, April 2015. https://doi.org/10.1109/EDUCON.2015.7096093

17. Jermann, P., Soller, A., Muehlenbrock, M.: From mirroring to guiding: a review of the state of art technology for supporting collaborative learning from mirroring to guiding: a review of state of the art technology for supporting collaborative learning (2001). https://telearn.archives-ouvertes.fr/hal-00197377. Accessed 04 May 2021

18. Soller, A., Martínez, A., Jermann, P., Muehlenbrock, M.: From mirroring to guiding: a review of state of the art technology for supporting collaborative learning. Int. J. Artif. Intell. Educ. **15**(4), 261–290 (2005)

Networks and IoT Technologies

Design and Implementation of Traffic Balancer over Overlay Networks with Vxlan Tunneling

Eduardo Antonio Alvarado-Unamuno$^{(\boxtimes)}$ (iD) and Jenny Elizabeth Arizaga-Gamboa

Universidad de Guayaquil, Cdla. Universitaria Salvador Allende, Guayaquil, Ecuador
{eduardo.alvaradou,jenny.arizagag}@ug.edu.ec

Abstract. These days networks are and important characteristic in the daily life and this makes users experience a goal that must be reached in order to keep this in complete operation. Load balancing methods help improve performance, availabitlity, reduce delays and avoid congestions as well. In the present work, the use of overlay networks with Vxlan tunnels is proposed to balance traffic between them, the load balancing is carried out through an SDN network in the data plane. This type of proposal represents an alternative with routing problems which the routing protocols are not efficient enough at the moment of balancing traffic through several links, software-defined networks represent an economical and efficient system, they proceed to achieve maximum resource utilization and reduced transfer times with results that show load balancing with overlay networks decreases access times. The main contribution of this work is the application of a load balancer in overlay networks based on SDN to decrease latency.

Keywords: Software defined network · Overlay network · VxLAN · Traffic balancer

1 Introduction

Communication over the Internet is based on interactions between a set of endpoint systems. The location of software components, such as servers and databases in relation to a customer endpoint, can have a significant impact on the latency experienced by a user when accessing an application, as data must travel across multiple of communication networks, latency is the time it takes a bit to reach the destination, measured from the moment it was required for the first time [1], therefore, the search to minimize this problem is a priority, since applications Critical use such as health, transactions or purchases, cannot maintain high response times.

Load balancing is a method of managing incoming traffic by distributing and sharing the load equally among available network resources, improving network availability, reducing latency and bandwidth utilization [2].

In the Internet, the Border Gateway Protocol (BGP) is used for routing between domains, when a BGP router learns multiple routes to a destination IP prefix, it applies a classification algorithm to select the best route, BGP allows network operators define their own policies on how to select the best routes, which means that the border routers

© Springer Nature Switzerland AG 2021
R. Valencia-García et al. (Eds.): CITI 2021, CCIS 1460, pp. 125–139, 2021.
https://doi.org/10.1007/978-3-030-88262-4_9

of each operator can apply different and independent route policies [3], while the policy-based routing of BGP allows A flexible selection of routes makes it difficult to predict routing decisions, which makes load balancing difficult.

The success and development of the Internet in the last five decades was made possible by the basic principle of keeping it simple in the middle and smart on the edge. However, new applications bring new demands and for many of them the principle of the Internet presents limitations, among these applications we can mention the transport of video. For these applications and others in this new generation of Internet services, structured overlay networks offer a powerful framework [4]. In a simple definition, overlay networks are logical networks on top of physical networks. the way to experiment with new Internet protocols, to expand its functionalities and characteristics, among these protocols we can mention Virtual Extensible LAN (VXLAN) [5], VXLAN is an overlay method that extends layer 2 network traffic over an IP-based Layer 3 network.

Software Defined Networking (SDN) is a new network paradigm [1, 6, 7], which separates the control and data plane, this functional separation and the implementation of the control plane functions in platforms. Centralized systems have been of great interest due to the various operational benefits, it also facilitates the control plane to have a global vision of the state of the network. For example, Google has implemented SDN to interconnect its data centers, in which it expects an improvement in network utilization of 20–30%, as well as better performance in delays [8], the fact that the controller can view network resources globally together with application knowledge make it suitable for load balancing with SDN, as a result, SDN offers new possibilities to improve conventional network load balancing technology [4].

In the present work, an overlay network with VXLAN tunnels will be implemented to balance load between them, the round robin method will be used for load balancing due to its easy and simple implementation in the data plane of an SDN network, using an overlay network based SDN, given the programmability of SDN, allows the study and experimentation with new methods for load balancing different from the traditional ones. The main contribution of this research is the use of overlay networks combined with SDN to provide flexibility and geographic availability, allowing the ability to communicate devices at the layer 2 level, with the only requirement of a transport network that guarantees IP connectivity. As an alternative to reduce latency, this implementation is a research contribution to the project FCI 011 - TEMONET phase II of the University of Guayaquil.

2   Related Work

The following tasks in the overlay SDN networks give a starting point for the present investigation. In [5] the dynamic flow balance is studied in order to improve performance and reduce network response time. The flow balance is applied on the data plane of an Open-Flow SDN network with a controller Open Daylight. The results show that the balance of the flow can improve the net general performance and reduce delays. In [9] a solution is proposed about flow balance for multiple routes based on software defined networks operated by commuters Open-Flow, where the rules of flow management are installed by the SDN controller, the routes can be automatically adjusted, the experimental outcome verify that the solution can balance the flow efficiently. In [10] overlay networks based on SDN are proposed with algorithm about the balance flow. The proposed algorithm allows to trace the present state of the network and answer to the changes in real time. This way, the application of the proposed algorithm avoids the overcharge of the channel.

3   Software Defined Networking (SDN)

According to the Open Foundation Networking (ONF), SDN is an emergent network architecture where the net control is disengaged from the forward stage and it's programmed directly. This control migration which was previously laced tightly to individual network devices, to data devices, allows to abstract the underlying infrastructure for applications and network services that can handle the network as a logical or virtual [11].

The objective of the SDN is to facilitate the implementation of new characteristics in network architecture and protocol design. Figure 1 represents a logical view of the SDN architecture. The network intelligence is centered in SDN controllers based on software that keep a network global vision. As a result, applications think the network is the only logic switch. With SDN, there is control on all the network from a standard logic point of view which simplifies a large measurement of the design and network operations [11].

In the data Plane layer there are data processing devices, the data packets are managed based on the actions given by the network controller to the devices. Openflow is the standard protocol that is used for the communication between the network controller and the network devices in order to install data processing rules. The network devices supported by SDN can be in hardware or software mode. One of the options to implement a SDN network with software switches which executes in an operating system Linux switching between virtualized nodes. This is commonly used in cloud computing to connect many VM on the same host to the external layer two networks. Open vSwitch [12], is an open source multilayer switch for soft switching in a virtualized environment.

In the Control Plane layer, the network control is found and therefore it is dominated the network controller that communicates with other data forward devices to install, update and eliminate open flow rules based on logic defined by running applications, there are many SDN controllers with Open Source that intake different Openflow versions, programming interfaces and provide different executing application services too.

3.1   SDN Controller

The Controller is a unique entity that manages all other forward devices in the network. The SDN controller utilizes an open protocol or a proprietor in order to control all the network elements and data flow. This controller also takes information about the elements condition in the network, including statistics and events that are in motion. Only one controller cannot be enough to administer a network handling a great amount of elements in the data plane; therefore, there are two other ways of centralized and distributed implementation.

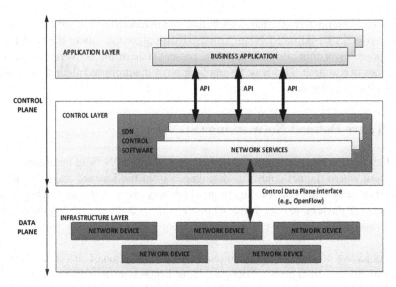

Fig. 1. Software defined network architecture.

Centralized Controllers like NOX, Maestro, Beacon and Floodlight have been designed as highly concurrent systems in order to achieve the required performance by companies networks and data center. Other centralized controllers like Trema, Ryu, NOS, Meridian are directed in specific surroundings like data center, cloud infrastructures and operating value networks [7]. A SDN controller can be described in a general manner as a software system or a collection of systems that handle the behavior in general of any network from the application requirements. The following is a chart about some of the characteristics supported by SDN Open Source controller.

SDN Ryu Controller
Its name comes from the Japanese word which means flow. The Ryu Controller is of open code and is under Apache 2.0 license, based on Python. The main source code can be found in GitHub, proported and backed up by the Open Ryu community. It's compatible with NETCONF administrative protocols and OF-config. Just like OpenFlow, which has a compatibility of the 1.5 latest version. Ryu puts out software components with a well define API that facilitates the development of the new created applications about management and network control [14].

Just like other SDN controllers, Ryu manages events related to incoming and outgoing packages, working with protocols like XFlow (Netflow and Sflow), OF-Config, NETCONF, Open vSwitch Database Management Protocol (OVSDB), etc. The RYU applications are entities of only one subprocessor that implements many functions, the functional architecture of an application Ryu which is shown in Fig. 2.

In [15] it is mentioned that Ryu showed it best results about latency by making a lot more adequate for delayed sensible applications.

Table 1. Features supported by Open Source SDN [13].

	BEACON	FLOODLIGHT	NOX	POX	TREMA	RYU	ODL
Openflow support	OF v1.0	OF v1.0	OF v1.0	OF v1.0	OF v1.3	OF v1.0 v1.2, v1.3 and Nicira extensions	OF v1.0
Virtualization	Mininet and Open Vswitch	Mininet and Open Vswitch	Mininet and Open Vswitch	Mininet and Open Vswitch	Construction of a virtual simulation tool	Mininet and Open Vswitch	Mininet and Open Vswitch
development language	Java	Java	C++	Python	Rudy/C	Python	Java
Provide REST API	Not	Yes	Not	Not	Yes(Basic)	Yes(Basic)	Yes
Graphic interface	Web	Web	Python+, Qt4	Python+, Qt4, Web	Not	Web	Web
Supported platforms	Linux, Mac OS, Windows and Android for mobiles	Linux, Mac OS, Windows	Linux	Linux, Mac OS, Windows	Linux	Linux	Linux, Mac OS, Windows
OpenStack support	Not	Yes	Not	Not	Yes	Yes	Yes
Multiprocess	yes	yes	yes	Not	Yes	Not	Yes
Open Source	Yes	Yes	Yes	Yes	Yes	Yes	Yes

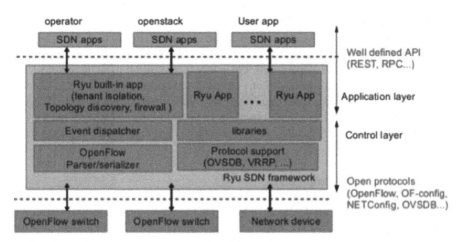

Fig. 2. Ryu SDN controller architecture [14]

3.2 OpenvSwitch (OVS)

It's a open source software based switch, which has as objective a switch platform that interfaces standard administration and allows forward functions and control while programming. This software works as a virtual switch. It exposes control interfaces and standard visibility of the virtual network cover. OVS is compatible with the Linux systems and it is developing the program language C. This provides the platform independency where it wants to be used at. The version that is most compatible are the following functions [16]:

- 802.1q vlan standard with access portals
- NIC link with or without LACP in the ascendent switch
- NetFlow, sFlow and duplication for a major visibility
- QoS configuration and more vigilance
- Tunnels GRE, VXLAN, STT and LISP
- Connection failure management 802.1ag
- OpenFlow 1.0 plus numerous extensions
- Data transactional base with C and Python links
- The Linux kernel model is compatible with Linux 3.10 and superior

In Fig. 3, it shows that the main components of this distribution are [16]

- ovs-vswitchd, a demon that is implemented by the switch joined with a Linux kernel module complementing communication based on flow.
- ovsdb-server is a light data base server which relates to ovs-vswitchd in order to obtain its configurations.
- ovs-dpctl is a tool to change the settings in the switch kernel module.
- Scripts and specifications to create RPM for Citrix XenServer and Red Hat Enterprise Linux. The RPM of XenServer allow Open vSwitch to install in a Citrix XenServer host as a direct substitute in its switch and completely operational.
- ovs-vsctl is an utility to consult and update the ovs-vswichd settings.
- ovs-appctl is an utility that sends commands in order to execute Open vSwitch
- ovs-ofctl is an utility to consult and control switches and OpenFlow controllers.

Load Balancing in the Data Plane
This technique is used to achieve load balancing (LB) with low latency network performance, additionally it is used to resolve load imbalance on routes and servers to avoid bottlenecks in an SDN network. The LB in the data plane can be classified into LB for servers and LB for links. In a multi-path SDN network, different approaches have been reported for the LB in the data plane, most of these techniques are aimed at optimizing the load by decreasing the network latency, selecting the least loaded route to overcome the congestion in the data plane, according to [4] the LB techniques for links can be classified into: metaheuristic algorithms, Machine Learning algorithms and other algorithms.

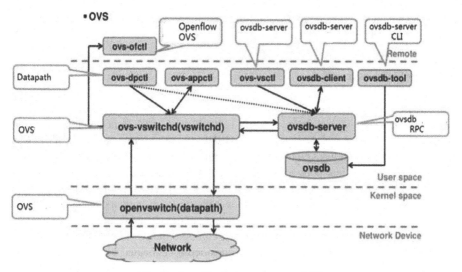

Fig. 3. OpenVswitch components [17]

Metaheuristic Algorithms [4]

For this type of algorithms SDN offers a perfect architecture for the optimization of the entire network using artificial intelligence (AI) to create an open, scalable, programmable and manageable network.

Machine Learning Algorithms [4]

This type of algorithms together with the SDN architecture allow to improve the routing performance, in SDN, the network operators can place certain centralized logic in the control plane, which facilitates obtaining a global view of the network with the Machine Learning algorithms.

Other Algorithms [4]

We found three different types of controllers, spanning tree protocol (STP) -based controller, LB based controller, and hub-type controller, these algorithms are used to improve network performance and enhance its ability to meet the needs of the network. QoS needs.

One of the algorithms used in LB for its simplicity and efficiency is round ro-bin, which allows requests to be passed to each server in our case to each route consecutively, this algorithm has proven and continues to be useful as a way from LB [18] in [19] a data plane LB is used to balance traffic to servers in a layer 2 switch network, based on the round robin algorithm.

All these techniques start from the fact of having the administration of an entire SDN network, but if we wanted to apply these techniques in a network such as the Internet that is made up of networks of different operators, each one applying different network administration policies, we would not are applicable. This is where the overlay networks give us a starting point [20] since the implementation of SDN as an overlay network is based on switches connected by logical links and allows to separate the virtual network topology from the physical one.

4 Overlay Networks

Many SDN architecture solutions are based on network overlay principles, the implementation of SDN as an overlay network is based on virtual switches and tunneling protocols such as VXLAN, NVGRE, LISP, GENEVE... The implementation of SDN as An overlay network allows you to separate the virtual network topology and the configuration from the physical network topology. The virtual network creates the route and forwards data between virtual components, the physical network only delivers packets to the destination node. This approach allows the physical network to be rebuilt and modernized as needed, without changing anything at the virtual level [10].

According to [21] an overlay network is a computer network that is built on top of another, the nodes in this network can be considered connected by virtual or logical links, each of which corresponds to a path, these virtual links can be achieved perhaps through many physical links in the underlying network.

Overlay networks do not require or cause changes to the underlying network, consequently, overlays have been used for a long time and are relatively easy and inexpensive to implement new functions and arrangements on the Internet, many applications have been proposed using overlay designs of layers in recent years to address various issues such as internet routing, denial of service (DoS) attack protection, content distribution, and file-sharing services [22].

The links between the overlay nodes are implemented through tunneling, this provides a mechanism for delivering packets from one end to the other, the overlay networks pave the way to experiment with new Internet protocols, to expand the functionality and characteristics of the Internet.

4.1 Virtual Extensible LAN (VXLAN)

VXLAN is a layer 2 overlay schemes in a layer 3 network. Each superposition dominates a VXLAN segment. Only the nods that are inside the same segment of VXLAN can communicate among themselves. Each segment of VXLAN is identified by a 24 bits segment ID, named "VXLAN Network Identifier (VNI) [22]. The VNI is on an external heading which encloses the MAC interior plot originated by a node due to the encapsulation. VXLAN can also denominate itself as a tunneling scheme to overlay layer 2 networks over layer 3 networks. The tunnels are stateless so each frame is encapsulated according to the set of rules [23]. The final stage of the tunnel denominates VXLAN Tunnel End Point (VTEP), in Fig. 4; the format of a Vxlan frame is described.

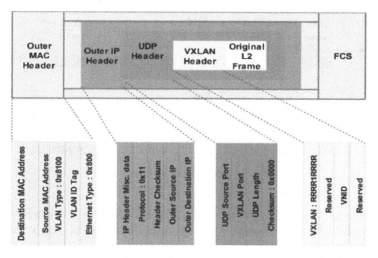

Fig. 4. VXLAN frame format [24]

5 Design and Implementation

For this proposal an overlay network is designed to perform load balancing using Vxlan tunnels, based on SDN, it was used as controller SDN to Ryu and SDN switch to Open Vswitch, these were installed on laptops with Core I5 processor and operating system Ubuntu 18.04, 4 Cisco 2801 routers with static routing were used for the wan connection, the filezilla [25] application was used for the download tests. Figure 5 shows the underlying network implementation diagram and Fig. 6 shows the overlay network.

Given the programmability of SDN networks, the code to perform load balancing was developed with the round robin method, this code is executed in the RIU controller, for the development part of SimpleSwitch13 was used as a base, which is a Ryu class that implements a switch, this class consists of several methods, two of which stand out, which are executed in child threads of the main program execution. Figure 7 shows these methods.

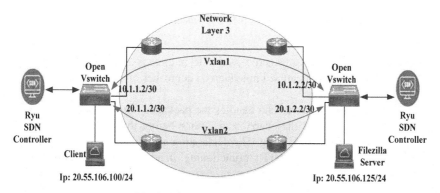

Fig. 5. Underlying network diagram

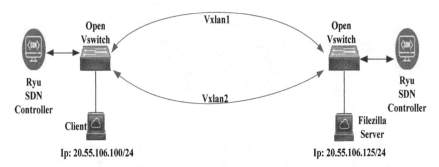

Fig. 6. Overlay network diagram

switch_features_handler(): This method is executed when a new switch is registered in the controller which also creates the Vxlan with the functioning of _add_vxlan_port().

_packet_in_handler(): This method is executed when a package is sent to the controller which takes charge of selecting the portal which will receive the package using RoundRobin() so later such action can be done using packagessent(). To do a delivery, a specific portal can be used or can be distributed to many other portals. In this case, a RoundRobin load balance will be done only among Vxlan interface.

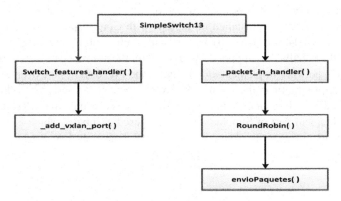

Fig. 7. Class SimpleSwitch13 implemented in Ryu controller

When an OpenFlow message is received in Ryu, there is an event corresponding to the message. The Ryu application implements a controller of events corresponding to the message that it receives.

_packet_in_handler receives and handles the packages. The methods interact with OVS. These recognize that they carry a decorator before their declaration which is necessary for the proper functioning. The declaration is done which it will have all the methods that are necessary for the Ryu functioning. In addition, the OpenFlow version is also mentioned that it will be used.

The class constructor implementation creates a list of the variables that will be used. This is a detail from the most meaningful ones:

self.remoteIP1: First remote link IP address.

self.remoteIP2: Second remote link IP address.

self.localIP1: First local link IP address.

self.localIP2: Second local link IP address.

self.ifaces: List that has interfaces names which allow communication among OVS equipment and others.

self.countPkt: Variable that has packages that are sent through a link. It is used to control the relationship for package delivery.

self.limitPkt: Variable which shows the maximum package deliverance that will be sent for each link before changing the interface for the balance at hand.

6 Results

Using defined networks for software, it is possible to create an implementation of load balance in cover 2, having some packages delivered through a link and by another link. These are the two testing scenes:

1. Transferring files of different sizes through only one link.
2. Transferring files of different sizes through two links.

The transferring timing is taken from the Filezilla client.

Table 2. Transferring time according to the size of the file

File size (bytes)	Transferring time one link (seg)	Transferring time two links (seg)	Time transferring reduction percentage
18.973.696	15	13	13,33%
79.986.688	75	70	6,67%
148.065.861	138	126	8,70%
160.327.680	148	136	8,11%
236.189.495	221	209	5,43%
296.345.020	283	253	10,60%
310.410.203	293	272	7,17%
397.379.065	359	336	6,41%
447.601.003	415	390	6,02%
492.830.720	475	436	8,21%

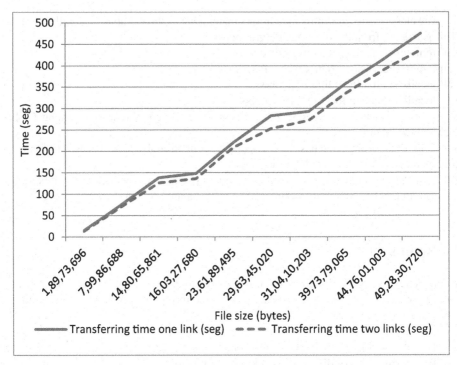

Fig. 8. Transferring time vs file size with one and two links.

The following is a percentage of the reduction in the download timing using two links (Fig. 8).

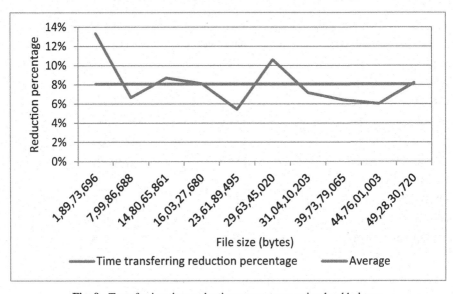

Fig. 9. Transferring time reduction percentages using load balance.

In Table 2 and in Fig. 9, the reduction in transferring time is appreciated. The load balances between both links according to the obtained values are reduced with an 8.06%.

While in [26] the round robin algorithm and a dynamic load balancing algorithm are compared in an SDN-based LAN, the experimental analysis shows that the dynamic load balancing algorithm gives better results than the round robin algorithm to balance traffic within the network.

In the work presented, the round robin algorithm allows us to balance traffic in an easy and simple way, over two virtual links as if we were inside a layer 2 LAN network obtaining satisfactory results, but the same works as [26] open the field for further testing with other dynamic algorithms and comparing their performance in overlay network environments.

7 Conclusions

Overlay networks based on a software-defined network allows network administrators to control, manage and dynamically change the behavior of the network, in this work the problem of balancing traffic in an overlay network based on SDN was addressed, it is concluded that the use of networks superimposed on an underlying network based on SDN, solves connectivity problems, generally in layer 3 environments in which the routing protocols are not efficient when balancing traffic over several links, the networks defined by software represent an economical and efficient system, given their programmability they allow new developments to achieve maximum use of resources and reduce latency.

Based on this work, it is proposed in the future to design a dynamic algorithm for load balancing in the data plane using overlay networks and to evaluate the performance of the proposed solution in a suitable simulation environment.

References

1. Mousa, M., Bahaa-ElDin, A.M., Sobh, M.: Software defined networking concepts and challenges. In: Proceedings 2016 11th International Conference Computer Engineering System, ICCES 2016, pp. 79–90 (2017). https://doi.org/10.1109/ICCES.2016.7821979
2. Bhandarkar, S., Khan, K.A.: Load balancing in software-defined network (SDN) based on traffic volume. Adv. Comput. Sci. Inf. Technol. 2(7), 72–76 (2015)
3. Rekhter, Y., Li, T., Hares, S.: A border gateway protocol 4 (BGP-4), Ietf Rfc4271, no. S, pp. 1–104 (2006)
4. Hamdan, M., et al.: A comprehensive survey of load balancing techniques in software-defined network. J. Netw. Comput. Appl. **174**, 102856 (2021). https://doi.org/10.1016/j.jnca.2020.102856
5. Nkosi, M.C., Lysko, A.A., Dlamini, S.: Multi-path load balancing for SDN data plane. In: 2018 International Conference Intelligence Innovation Computer Applications, ICONIC 2018 (2019). https://doi.org/10.1109/ICONIC.2018.8601241
6. Feamster, N., Rexford, J., Zegura, E.: The road to SDN. ACM SIGCOMM Comput. Commun. Rev. **44**(2), 87–98 (2014). https://doi.org/10.1145/2602204.2602219
7. Ieee, F., et al.: Software-defined networking : a comprehensive survey, vol. 103, no. 1 (2015)

8. Agarwal, S., Kodialam, M., Lakshman, T.V.: Traffic engineering in software defined networks. In: Proceedings IEEE INFOCOM, pp. 2211–2219 (2013). https://doi.org/10.1109/INFCOM.2013.6567024
9. Li, J., Chang, X., Ren, Y., Zhang, Z., Wang, G.: An effective path load balancing mechanism based on SDN. In: Proceedinds 2014 IEEE 13th International Conference Trusting Security Private Computer Communication Trusting 2014, pp. 527–533 (2015). https://doi.org/10.1109/TrustCom.2014.67
10. Tkachova, O., Yahya, A.R., Muhi-Aldeen, H.M.: A network load balancing algorithm for overlay-based SDN solutions. In: 2016 3rd International Science Conference Problems Infocommunications Science Technology PIC S T 2016 – Proceedings, pp. 139–141 (2017). https://doi.org/10.1109/INFOCOMMST.2016.7905360
11. Open Networking Foundation, "Software-defined networking: the new norm for networks [white paper]," ONF White Pap., pp. 1–12 (2012)
12. Pfaff, B., et al.: The design and implementation of open vSwitch. In: Proceedings 12th USENIX Symposium Networked System Design Implementation, NSDI 2015, pp. 117–130 (2015)
13. Centeno, A.G., Manuel, C., Vergel, R., Calderón, C.A.: Controladores SDN, elementos para su selección y evaluación, no. November 2014 (2017)
14. Asadollahi, S., Sameer, M.: Ryu Controller's scalability experiment on software defined networks
15. Mamushiane, L., Lysko, A., Dlamini, S.: A comparative evaluation of the performance of popular SDN controllers. IFIP Wirel. Days, vol. 2018-April, pp. 54–59 (2018). https://doi.org/10.1109/WD.2018.8361694
16. What Is Open vSwitch? — Open vSwitch 2.15.90 documentation. https://docs.openvswitch.org/en/latest/intro/what-is-ovs/. Accessed 08 May 2021
17. Análisis de la arquitectura OpenvSwitch y práctica funcional - programador clic. https://programmerclick.com/article/33321925977/. Accessed 08 May 2021
18. O'Loughlin, F., Chambers, D.: The measurement of an optimum load balancing algorithm in a master/slave architecture. In: Laganá, A., Gavrilova, M.L., Kumar, V., Mun, Y., Tan, C.J.K., Gervasi, O. (eds.) ICCSA 2004. LNCS, vol. 3044, pp. 136–145. Springer, Heidelberg (2004). https://doi.org/10.1007/978-3-540-24709-8_15
19. Chahlaoui, F., Raiss El-Fenni, M., Dahmouni, H.: Performance analysis of load balancing mechanisms in SDN networks. In: ACM International Conference Proceeding Serving, vol. Part F1481 (2019). https://doi.org/10.1145/3320326.3320368
20. Briscoe, B., et al.: Reducing internet latency: a survey of techniques and their merits. IEEE Commun. Surv. Tutorials 18(3), 2149–2196 (2016). https://doi.org/10.1109/COMST.2014.2375213
21. Ding, J., Balasingham, I., Bouvry, P.: Management of overlay networks: a survey. In: 3rd International Conference Mobile Ubiquitous Computer System Serving Technology, UBICOMM 2009, pp. 249–255 (2009). https://doi.org/10.1109/UBICOMM.2009.49
22. Naranjo, E.F., Salazar Ch., G.D.: Underlay and overlay networks: the approach to solve addressing and segmentation problems in the new networking era: VXLAN encapsulation with Cisco and open source networks. In: 2017 IEEE 2nd Ecuador Technology Chapters Meeting ETCM 2017, vol. 2017-Janua, pp. 1–6 (2018). https://doi.org/10.1109/ETCM.2017.8247505
23. Mahalingam, M., et al.: VXLAN: a framework for overlaying virtualized layer 2 networks over layer 3 networks. Ietf Rfc 7348, no. October, pp. 1–23 (2014). https://doi.org/10.17487/RFC7348
24. Nadeem, M.A., Karamat, T.: A survey of cloud network overlay protocols. In: 2016 6th International Conference Digital Information Communication Technology its Application DICTAP 2016, pp. 177–182 (2016). https://doi.org/10.1109/DICTAP.2016.7544023

25. FileZilla - The free FTP solution. https://filezilla-project.org/. Accessed 08 May 2021
26. Shrivastava, G., Kaushik, P., Pateriya, R.K.: Load balancing strategies in software defined networks. Int. J. Eng. Technol. **7**(3), 1854–1857 (2018). https://doi.org/10.14419/ijet.v7i3.14017

Relationships of Compression Ratio and Error in Trajectory Simplification Algorithms

Gary Reyes[1] (✉) ⓘ, Víctor Maquilón[1] ⓘ, and Vivian Estrada[2]

[1] Facultad de Ciencias Matemáticas y Físicas, Universidad de Guayaquil, Cdla. Universitaria Salvador Allende, Guayaquil 090514, Ecuador
{gary.reyesz,victor.maquilonc}@ug.edu.ec
[2] Universidad de las Ciencias Informáticas, Carretera a San Antonio de los Baños km 2 1/2, La Habana, Cuba
vivian@uci.cu

Abstract. GPS trajectory simplification algorithms are of great importance for GPS data analysis and processing. The correct selection of these algorithms in accordance with the type of trajectory to be analyzed facilitates the reduction of storage and processing space in data analysis. This paper analyzes the correlation between the compression ratio of GPS trajectory simplification algorithms and their margin of error. These metrics measure the effectiveness of simplification algorithms in general and this work focuses specifically on batch simplification. For this purpose, coordinates in GPS trajectories of different sets of data are used and the algorithms are executed on them, taking into account that the analysis performed for the simplification process takes into account the beginning and the end of each trajectory. Finally, the data obtained from the experiments are presented in tables and figures. The experiments show that TD-TR has better performance than Douglas-Peucker algorithm due to the selected variables.

Keywords: Trajectory simplification · GPS trajectories · Compression ratio

1 Introduction

A trajectory is represented as a discrete sequence of geographic coordinate points [1]. An example of trajectories are vehicular trajectories that are composed of thousands of points, since the stretches traveled in cities are usually long and with many stops, which implies a greater emission of coordinates generated from GPS devices. There are currently active research areas related to GPS trajectories. Among these is the area of trajectory pre-processing, which studies trajectory simplification techniques and algorithms. The trajectory simplification algorithms eliminate some sub traces of the original route [2]; which decreases the data storage space and data transfer time. A framework where these areas are observed is proposed in [3].

Reducing the data size of a trajectory facilitates the acceleration of the information extraction process [4]. There are several path simplification methods that are suitable for different types of data and yield different results; but they all have the same principle

© Springer Nature Switzerland AG 2021
R. Valencia-García et al. (Eds.): CITI 2021, CCIS 1460, pp. 140–155, 2021.
https://doi.org/10.1007/978-3-030-88262-4_10

in common: compressing the data by removing the redundancy of the data in the source file [5–7]. GPS trajectory simplification algorithms can be classified into [8]:

- Online algorithms
- Batch algorithms

Online algorithms do not need to have the entire trajectory ready before starting simplification, and are suitable for compressing trajectories in mobile device sensors [9, 10]. Online algorithms not only have good compression ratios and deterministic error bounds, but also are easy to implement. They are widely used in practice, even for freely moving objects without the constraint of road networks [9, 11]. Batch algorithms require all points in the trajectory before starting the simplification. Batch algorithms have all the points in the trajectory before starting the simplification process, which allows them to perform better processing and analysis of these [12]. Among the most commonly used batch GPS trajectory simplification algorithms according to the analyzed literature [13–16] are:

- Douglas-Peucker algorithm.
- TD-TR algorithm.

From the documentary analysis performed, a set of common deficiencies were identified in the aforementioned batch GPS trajectory simplification algorithms [17]. These deficiencies attempt against the efficiency of batch simplification algorithms, the efficiency in these algorithms is given by the compression ratio and the error (margin of error).

This work is focused in the GPS trajectory simplification algorithms to address the problem of storage space optimization in order to face of the large volumes of data that are generated today from GPS trajectories. For this purpose, we analyze the compression levels originated by the use of simplification algorithms, but it is also important to analyze the relationship between these compression levels and the quality of the resulting trajectory denoted by the margin of error. The values obtained from the correlation of these two variables are analyzed according to the elimination of points considered nonsignificant. The analysis of the results allows the use of the appropriate algorithms according to their compression levels and the data characteristics to be processed.

The present work identifies the relation between the compression ratio and the margin of error, and is organized as follows: in the previous work session, a description of the algorithms to be experimented is given. In the experimentation session, the experiments performed and the data sets used are described. In the discussion session, the results obtained are described briefly and concisely.

2 Previous Work

GPS trajectory simplification is an active field of research, especially in recent years with the increasing use of this technology [18]. In the present work, it is considered important to analyze the Douglas-Peucker and TD-TR algorithms in order to compare their performance in terms of the selected metrics.

2.1 Douglas-Peucker Algorithm

Douglas-Peucker (DP) is a GPS trajectory simplification algorithm that uses the top-down method for data analysis. It is used to remove a series of line segments from a curve, which reduces the amount of data present in a GPS trajectory [19]. The selection of points is performed recursively and on the original series [9, 20–22].

Douglas-Peucker implements a divide and conquer strategy and is composed of several steps which are listed below [23, 24]:

1. The first and last nodes of a polygonal chain are taken as endpoints of a line.
2. For all intermediate points, the distances less than this line are determined. If it is greater than any distance, the polygonal chain is separated with the point having the greater distance, forming two new segments.
3. The new segments formed are analyzed by performing the same procedure.
4. It ends when it does not exceed any point line distance.

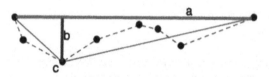

Fig. 1. Douglas-Peucker algorithm

As shown in Fig. 1 the algorithm starts with an initial data set formed by n points, where we start from the initial point (x_1, y_1) drawing a straight line towards the final point of the data set (x_n, y_n), in the graph it is represented with the letter a.

Obtaining the straight line we proceed to take the following points (x_2, y_2), (x_3, y_3).....(x_n, y_n) and it is verified if its perpendicular distance (letter b) with respect to the line is greater than the tolerance entered, once the farthest point is obtained, this is taken as a reference to repeat the process, that is, straight lines are drawn from (x_1, y_1) to the farthest point found (x_3, y_3) and from (x_3, y_3) to (x_n, y_n), repeating the process of obtaining the point with the tolerance greater than the one entered.

2.2 TD-TR Algorithm

This algorithm is a modification of the Douglas-Peucker algorithm where the time variable is added. For this, the coordinates of point P_i' in time are calculated by the ratio of two time intervals. The difference between the time of the end point and the time of the initial point is calculated using the formula 1

$$\Delta_e = t_e - t_s. \tag{1}$$

The difference between the time of the point to be analyzed and the time of the starting point is calculated using the formula 2:

$$\Delta_i = t_i - t_s \tag{2}$$

To obtain the coordinates of P_i' formulas 3 and 4 are applied:

$$x_i' = x_s + \frac{\Delta_i}{\Delta_e}(x_e - x_s) \tag{3}$$

$$y_i' = y_s + \frac{\Delta_i}{\Delta_e}(y_e - y_s) \tag{4}$$

After obtaining the coordinates, the synchronous Euclidean distance between P_i' and P_i, is calculated. If the distance is greater than the tolerance, that reference point is taken and the calculation of the intervals is performed again. The worst-case computational complexity of TD-TR is $O(n^2)$, since it extends the original Douglas-Peucker algorithm. The improved implementation of $O(n\log_n)$ for Douglas-Peucker that takes advantage of geometric properties cannot be applied to TD-TR [25]. In Fig. 2 the TD-TR algorithm is shown.

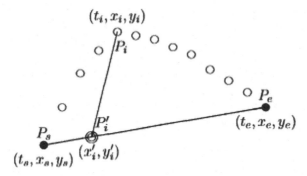

Fig. 2. Process of trajectory simplification using TD-TR algorithm

3 Methodology

The methodology applied in this work is composed by the following steps:

- Literature review and identification of main characteristics of the algorithms to be analyzed.
- Implementation of the Douglas Peucker and TD-TR algorithms in R language.
- Adaptation for the algorithms to process the three Datasets used in the experimentation.
- Implementation of the calculations of the compression ratio and error metrics to the results of the execution of the algorithms.
- Generation of log files for analysis and application of descriptive statistics measures to the compression ratio and error metrics.
- Application of a Correlation Test to the compression ratio and error metrics.

It is important to mention that part of the methodology is the final visualization of the processed trajectories before and after simplification, which for the purpose of this work was not necessary.

4 Experimentation and Results

This session describes the experiments carried out and presents the results achieved for the compression ratio and margin of error metrics with both the Douglas Peucker algorithm and the TD-TR algorithm.

The experimentation process was carried out by implementing the Douglas Peucker and Top Down Time Ratio (TD-TR) algorithms in R language. For the execution of the experiments, a laptop PC with an Intel core i5-8250 CPU @ 1.60 GHz, 8 GB RAM memory and 64bit architecture was used. As data sets were used:

- Guayaquil city dataset[1]
- Beijing city dataset[2]
- Aracaju city dataset.[3]

The Guayaquil-Ecuador trajectories dataset corresponding to the trips made by 218 university students in some means of transportation such as cab, motorcycle, metro-via, collected in the city of Guayaquil, Ecuador. It contains GPS coordinates collected in the northern and central sectors of Guayaquil during October 28, 2017. The locations in this dataset were collected by smartphones with an average time interval between two consecutive locations of 5 s. The file format for each mobility trajectory is as follows: Each record contains id trajectory, latitude, longitude, time, username, email, and time. The data were pre-processed and after filtering by time 30557 records were obtained representing 206 trajectories from the entire dataset.

The Beijing dataset was collected from cab routes in the city of Beijing, China. The dataset comes from the t-drive project and contains GPS coordinates of 10,357 cabs collected in Beijing during February 02, 2008. The locations in this dataset were collected by GPS devices from taxis with average devices with an average time interval between two consecutive locations of 177 s. The file format of each trajectory is as follows: Each record contains. id trajectory, date-time, longitude, latitude. The data were pre-processed and after filtering by time 62138 records were obtained representing 630 trajectories from the whole dataset.

The Aracaju dataset used within the experiments is formed by user paths in cars or buses through the Go! Track application in the city of Aracaju, Brazil. The dataset comes from trajectories collected in Aracaju during September 13, 2014 and January 19, 2016. The locations in this dataset were collected with high time variability between two consecutive locations.

The file format for each trajectory contains a series of records. Each record has id, latitude, longitude, track id, time. The data were pre-processed and filtered by time. In this database are 14096 records which represent 137 trajectories.

The formulas for the compression ratio and error indicators were implemented so that they can be calculated once each of the algorithms processes different samples from the three data sets. For this purpose, the sample size calculation for finite populations

---

[1] https://github.com/gary-reyes-zambrano/Guayaquil-DataSet.git.

[2] https://www.microsoft.com/en-us/research/publication/tdrive-trajectory-data-sample.

[3] https://archive.ics.uci.edu/ml/machine-learning-databases/00354/.

was performed. The sampling method used was simple random. Compression ratio: It is defined as the size of the original trajectory divided by the size of the compressed representation of that trajectory. For example, a compression ratio of 50 indicates that only 2% of the original points remain in the compressed representation of the trajectory [4]. Formula 5 is used to calculate the compression ratio where n represents the total number of points and x represents the number of resulting points after applying the corresponding compression technique.

$$r(x) = \frac{n - x}{n} * 100 \tag{5}$$

Margin of Error: Where SED (Synchronized Euclidean Distance) is defined in Equation 2.1 as the synchronous Euclidean distance and the distortion units between a point on the original trajectory and its corresponding synchronous point on the approximate trajectory are calculated [26]. The maximum of the distances is selected to evaluate the point acceptance condition.

$$SED(pti, pti) = \sqrt{\left(x_{ti} - x'_{ti}\right)^2 + \left(y_{ti} - y'_{ti}\right)^2} \tag{6}$$

To evaluate the distortion of the whole trajectory, the maximum synchronized Euclidean distance is used, which is defined as:

$$SED(P, P') = MAX(SED(pti, pti')) \tag{7}$$

4.1 Douglas Peucker Algorithm Evaluation Result

The descriptive statistics measured for the compression ratio and error variables are shown in Table 1.

Table 1. Descriptive Statistics for Compression Ratio and Margin of Error (SED) - Douglas Peucker Algorithm

	Aracaju		Beijing		Guayaquil	
	Compression ratio	SED	Compression ratio	SED	Compression ratio	SED
Valid	101	101	230	230	134	134
Missing	0	0	0	0	0	0
Mean	75.085	0.746	62.412	0.419	89.107	0.787
Std deviation	31.559	1.349	19.885	0.804	15.462	0.964
Skewness	−1.721	3.208	−0.927	6.370	−4.766	2.508
Std. Error of Skewness	0.240	0.240	0.160	0.160	0.209	0.209

(*continued*)

Table 1. (*continued*)

	Aracaju		Beijing		Guayaquil	
	Compression ratio	SED	Compression ratio	SED	Compression ratio	SED
Kurtosis	1.486	12.697	0.976	55.367	24.391	7.121
Std. Error of Kurtosis	0.476	0.476	0.320	0.320	0.416	0.416
Range	99.342	8.070	99.558	8.752	98.802	5.454
Minimum	0.000	0.000	0.000	0.000	0.000	0.000
Maximum	99.342	8.070	99.558	8.752	98.802	5.454

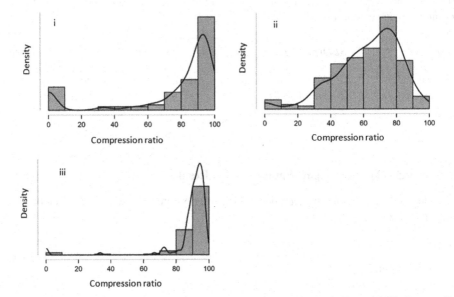

Fig. 3. Compression Ratio Distribution in the data sets (i) Aracaju (ii) Beijing and (iii) Guayaquil - Douglas Peucker Algorithm

The compression ratio distribution plot evidences negative skewness (Skewness < 0) with leptokurtic kurtosis (Kurtosis > 0). The curves for the three data sets are shown in Fig. 3.

The SED plot shows a positive skewness (Skewness > 0) with leptokurtic kurtosis (Kurtosis > 0). The curves for the three sets of data are shown in Fig. 4.

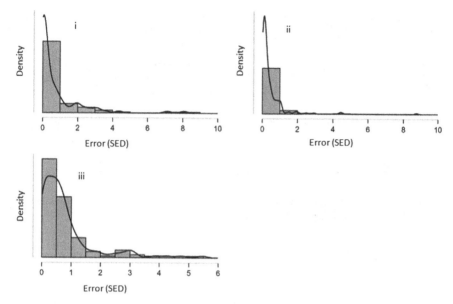

Fig. 4. Error Distribution (SED) (margin error) in the data sets (i) Aracaju (ii) Beijing and (iii) Guayaquil - Douglas Peucker Algorithm.

Pearson's correlation test between compression ratio and margin error (SED) for the Aracaju dataset, shows a significantly positive correlation with r = 0.313 and p-value = 0.001, as shown in Table 2.

Table 2. Pearson's Correlation for Compression Ratio and Error (SED) in the Aracaju data set - Douglas Peucker Algorithm

Variable		Compression ratio	SED
Compression ratio	Pearson's r	n/a	
	p-value	n/a	
SED	Pearson's r	0.313	n/a
	p-value	0.001	n/a

Pearson's correlation test between compression ratio and error margin for the Beijing data set evidences a significantly positive correlation with r = 0.376 and p-value < 0.001, as shown in Table 3.

Pearson's correlation test between the compression ratio and the margin error (SED) for the Guayaquil data set shows a significantly positive correlation with r = 0.248 and p-value = 0.004, as shown in the Table 4.

A visual inspection of the scatter plot, showed in Fig. 5, for the three data sets shows the correlation between compression ratio and margin of error.

Table 3. Pearson's Correlation for Compression Ratio and Error (SED) on Beijing data set - Douglas Peucker Algorithm

Variable		Compression ratio	SED
Compression ratio	Pearson's r	n/a	
	p-value	n/a	
SED	Pearson's r	0.376	n/a
	p-value	<.001	n/a

Table 4. Pearson's Correlation for Compression Ratio and Error (SED) on Guayaquil data set - Douglas Peucker Algorithm

Variable		Compression ratio	SED
Compression ratio	Pearson's r	n/a	
	p-value	n/a	
SED	Pearson's r	0.248	n/a
	p-value	0.004	n/a

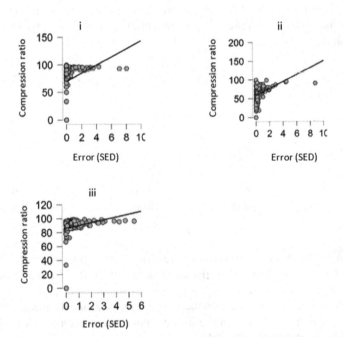

Fig. 5. Dispersion of the Correlation between Compression Ratio and Error (SED) (margin error) in the data sets (i) Aracaju (ii) Beijing and (iii) Guayaquil - Douglas Peucker Algorithm.

4.2 Top Down – Time Ratio (TD-TR) Algorithm Results

The descriptive statistics measured for the compression ratio and margin error variables are shown in Table 5.

Table 5. Descriptive Statistics for the Compression Ratio and Error (SED) - TD-TR Algorithm

	Aracaju		Beijing		Guayaquil	
	Compression ratio	SED	Compression ratio	SED	Compression ratio	SED
Valid	101	101	230	230	134	134
Missing	0	0	0	0	0	0
Mean	72.126	0.726	47.357	0.341	88.052	0.778
Std deviation	31.190	1.335	25.786	0.779	15.036	0.946
Skewness	−1.602	3.309	−0.259	6.767	−4.981	2.455
Std. error of skewness	0.240	0.240	0.160	0.160	0.209	0.209
Kurtosis	1.089	13.535	−0.965	61.041	26.133	6.769
Std. error of kurtosis	0.476	0.476	0.320	0.320	0.416	0.416
Range	99.342	8.103	99.558	8.613	97.305	5.289
Minimum	0.000	0.000	0.000	0.000	0.000	0.000
Maximum	99.342	8.103	99.558	8.613	97.305	5.289

The compression ratio distribution plot evidences a negative skewness (Skewness < 0) with leptokurtic kurtosis (Kurtosis > 0) except for the Beijing data where the kurtosis is slightly platykurtic (Kurtosis < 0). The curves for the three data sets are seen in Fig. 6.

The Skewness Error Distribution (SED) plot evidences a positive skewness (Skewness > 0) with leptokurtic kurtosis (Kurtosis > 0). The curves for the three data sets are shown in Fig. 7.

Pearson's correlation test between the compression ratio and the margin error (SED) for the Aracaju data set, shows a significantly positive correlation with $r = 0.322$ and p-value $= 0.001$, as shown in Table 6.

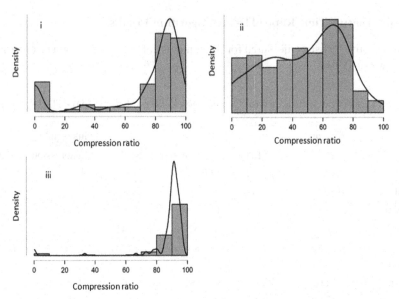

Fig. 6. Compression Ratio Distribution in the data sets (i) Aracaju (ii) Beijing and (iii) Guayaquil - Algorithm TD-TR

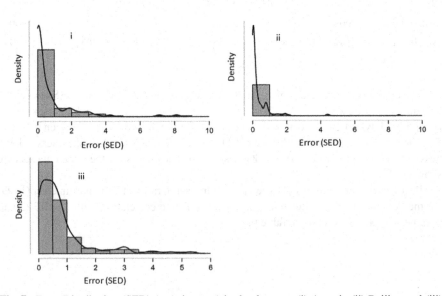

Fig. 7. Error Distribution (SED) (margin error) in the data sets (i) Aracaju (ii) Beijing and (iii) Guayaquil - Algorithm TD-TR

Table 6. Pearson's Correlation for Compression Ratio and Error (SED) in the Aracaju data set - TD-TR Algorithm

Variable		Compression ratio	SED
Compression ratio	Pearson's r	n/a	
	p-value	n/a	
SED	Pearson's r	0.322	n/a
	p-value	0.001	n/a

Pearson's correlation test between compression ratio and error (SED) for the Beijing data set evidenced a significantly positive correlation with r = 0.424 and p-value < 0.001, as shown in Table 7.

Table 7. Pearson's Correlation for Compression Ratio and Error (SED) on the Beijing data set - TD-TR Algorithm

Variable		Compression ratio	SED
Compression ratio	Pearson's r	n/a	
	p-value	n/a	
SED	Pearson's r	0.424	n/a
	p-value	<.001	n/a

Pearson's correlation test between the compression ratio and the margin error (SED) for the Guayaquil data set, shows a significantly positive correlation with r = 0.241 and p-value = 0.005, as shown in Table 8.

Table 8. Pearson's Correlation for the Compression Ratio and Error (SED) in the Guayaquil data set - TD-TR algorithm

Variable		Compression ratio	SED
Compression ratio	Pearson's r	n/a	
	p-value	n/a	
SED	Pearson's r	0.241	n/a
	p-value	0.005	n/a

A visual inspection of the scatter plot, showed in Fig. 8, for the three data sets shows the correlation between compression ratio and margin of error.

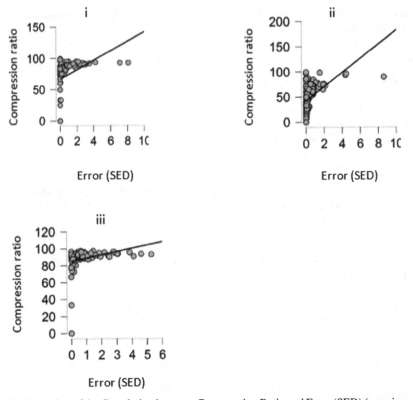

Fig. 8. Dispersion of the Correlation between Compression Ratio and Error (SED) (margin error) in the data sets (i) Aracaju (ii) Beijing and (iii) Guayaquil - Algorithm TD-TR

5   Analysis and Discussion

The results of this work reveal a significant positive correlation between compression ratio and error (SED) suggesting that the higher the compression ratio, the higher the error (SED). Three different data sets (obtaining different sample sizes randomly from different populations) were used on the two algorithms identified as relevant in the literature in order to provide sufficient and robust conclusions. After the experiments for the r indicator in Pearson's correlation, a mean of 0.312 for the Douglas Peucker algorithm and 0.329 for the TD-TR algorithm and a significant p-value level between 0.001 and 0.005 were obtained for both algorithms.

It is argued that the existing relationship between compression ratio and error (SED) when a point simplification algorithm processes a GPS trajectory is based on the fact that the results depend on the characteristic of the trajectory to be processed, so studies as in [27] use different simplification techniques on different datasets to make their studies consistent. On the other hand, removing points from an original trajectory implies an affectation in the quality of this and this is why multiple researches study how to improve the error levels when the compression ratio is improved [28].

The compression ratio by eliminating points from the trajectory to be simplified is decreasing the quality of the trajectory, therefore affecting its margin of error; the impact it causes on the quality will depend on whether the eliminated points are relevant or not. For certain data sets the simplification algorithms will remove relevant points which affects the margin of error. The main reason for the correlation between the two variables, in the authors' opinion, depends on the analysis of the data. In the case of the Douglas-Peucker algorithm, it performs a spatial analysis, while the TD-TR algorithm performs a spatio-temporal analysis, which allows simplifying points according to both their spatial and temporal location.

The main purpose of this work is to analyze the correlation between the compression ratio and margin of error metrics in the selected path simplification algorithms. As a result, it can be evidenced that the compression levels are given according to the characteristic of the data to be processed, so the compression levels vary from one dataset to another.

6 Conclusions and Future Work

The purpose of this work was to identify the relation between the compression ratio and the margin of error, which are indicators used by GPS trajectory simplification algorithms. The findings show a positive correlation between these two variables when trajectories are simplified, the value of the correlation should be interpreted depending on the level of compression of the algorithm when eliminating points considered not significant in a given context; likewise, the incidence of the margin of error and its effect when changing the compression ratio will depend on how significant the eliminated points are. GPS trajectory simplification algorithms seek to reduce the size of the trajectory to optimize storage space. In this sense, future studies can address mechanisms for these simplification algorithms to improve their compression ratio without affecting the error, i.e. that the correlation between these two variables is maintained or lower, demonstrating that the quality of the original trajectory would not be affected. Another important aspect would be to introduce a new variable to the correlational analysis such as the processing time of the algorithms.

References

1. Corcoran, P., Mooney, P., Huang, G.: Unsupervised trajectory compression. In: Proceedings - IEEE International Conference on Robotics and Automation, vol. 2016, pp. 3126–3132, June 2016. https://doi.org/10.1109/ICRA.2016.7487479
2. Ji, Y., Liu, H. , Liu, X., Ding, Y., Luo, W.: A comparison of road-network-constrained trajectory compression methods. In: Proceedings of the International Conference on Parallel and Distributed Systems - ICPADS, pp. 256–263 (2017). https://doi.org/10.1109/ICPADS.2016.0042
3. Zheng, Y.: Trajectory data mining: an overview. ACM Trans. Intell. Syst. Technol. **6**(3), 1–41 (2015)
4. Muckell, J., Olsen, P.W., Hwang, J.H., Ravi, S.S., Lawson, C.T.: A framework for efficient and convenient evaluation of trajectory compression algorithms. In: Proceedings - 2013 4th International Conference on Computing for Geospatial Research and Application, COM.Geo 2013, pp. 24–31 (2013). https://doi.org/10.1109/COMGEO.2013.5

5. Salomon, D.: Data Compression: The Complete Reference. Springer, London (2007). https://doi.org/10.1007/978-1-84628-603-2
6. Gudmundsson, T.W.J., Katajainen, J., Merrick, D., Ong, C.: Compressing spatio-temporal trajectories. Comput. Geom. Theory Appl. **42**(9), 825–841 (2009)
7. Lv, C., Chen, F., Xu, Y., Song, J., Lv, P.: A trajectory compression algorithm based on non-uniform quantization. In: 2015 12th International Conference on Fuzzy Systems and Knowledge Discovery, FSKD 2015, pp. 2469–2474 (2016). https://doi.org/10.1109/FSKD.2015.738 2342
8. Zheng, Y., Zhou, X.: Computing with Spatial Trajectories. Springer (2011). https://doi.org/10.1007/978-1-4614-1629-6
9. Lin, X., Ma, S., Zhang, H., Wo, T., Huai, J.: One-pass error bounded trajectory simplification. Proc. VLDB Endow. **10**(7), 841–852 (2017). https://doi.org/10.14778/3067421.3067432
10. Feldman, D., Sugaya, A., Rus, D.: An effective coreset compression algorithm for large scale sensor networks. In: IPSN'12 - Proceedings of the 11th International Conference on Information Processing in Sensor Networks, pp. 257–268 (2012). https://doi.org/10.1145/218 5677.2185739
11. Hendawi, A.M., Khot, A., Rustum, A., Basalamah, A., Teredesai, A., Ali, M.: A map-matching aware framework for road network compression. In: Proceedings - IEEE International Conference on Mobile Data Management, vol. 1, pp. 307–310 (2015). https://doi.org/10.1109/MDM.2015.78
12. Song, R., Sun, W., Zheng, B., Zheng, Y.: A novel framework of trajectory compression in road networks. In: 40th International Conference on Very Large Data Bases, pp. 661–672 (2014). https://doi.org/10.14778/2732939.2732940
13. Van Hunnik, R.: Extensive comparison of trajectory simplification algorithms (2017)
14. Asif, M.T., Kannan, S., Dauwels, J., Jaillet, P.: Data compression techniques for urban traffic data. In: Proceedings of the 2013 IEEE Symposium on Computational Intelligence in Vehicles and Transportation Systems, CIVTS 2013 - 2013 IEEE Symposium Series on Computational Intelligence, SSCI 2013, pp. 44–49 (2013). https://doi.org/10.1109/CIVTS.2013.6612288
15. Meratnia, N., de By, R.A.: Spatiotemporal compression techniques for moving point objects. In: Bertino, E., et al. (eds.) EDBT 2004. LNCS, vol. 2992, pp. 765–782. Springer, Heidelberg (2004). https://doi.org/10.1007/978-3-540-24741-8_44
16. Lawson, C.T.: Compression and Mining of GPS Trace Data: New Techniques and Applications, New York (2011). http://www.utrc2.org/research/assets/202/Compression_and_Min ing_of_GPS1.pdf
17. Reyes, G.: Algoritmo de compresión de trayectorias GPS basado en el algoritmo Top Down Time Ratio (TD-TR). In: 5to Congreso Científico Internacional Tecnología universidad sociedad, pp. 194–204 (2017)
18. de Vries, G.K.: Trajectory Compresion. University of Amsterdam (2011)
19. Sim, M., Kwak, J.-H., Lee, C.-H.: Fast shape matching algorithm based on the improved Douglas-Peucker algorithm. KIPS Trans. Softw. Data Eng. **5**(10), 497–502 (2016). https://doi.org/10.3745/ktsde.2016.5.10.497
20. Wu, S., Silva, A.C.G., Márquez, M.R.G.: The Douglas-Peucker algorithm : sufficiency conditions for non-self-intersections. J. Brazilian Comput. Soc. **9**, 1–17 (2004)
21. Wang, H.: Shark DB: An In-Memory Storage System for Large Scale Trajectory Data Management. The University of Queensland (2016)
22. Visvalingam, M., Whyatt, J.D.: Line generalisation by repeated elimination of the smallest area. In: Cartographic Information Systems Research Group, July 1992
23. Koegel, M., Baselt, D., Mauve, M., Scheuermann, B.: A comparison of vehicular trajectory encoding techniques. In: 2011 the 10th IFIP Annual Mediterranean Ad Hoc Networking Workshop, Med-Hoc-Net 2011, pp. 87–94 (2011). https://doi.org/10.1109/Med-Hoc-Net.2011.597 0498

24. Zhang, S.K., Liu, Z.J., Cai, Y., Wu, Z.L., Shi, G.Y.: AIS trajectories simplification and threshold determination. J. Navig. **69**(4), 729–744 (2016). https://doi.org/10.1017/S03734633150 00831

25. Hershberger, J., Snoeyink, J.: Speeding up the Douglas-Peucker line-simplification algorithm. ACM (1992)

26. Chen, M., Xu, M., Franti, P.: Compression of GPS trajectories. In: Data Compression Conference Proceedings, no. 61072146, pp. 62–71 (2012). https://doi.org/10.1109/DCC.201 2.14

27. Zhang, D., Ding, M., Yang, D., Liu, Y., Fan, J., Shen, H.T.: Trajectory simplification: an experimental study and quality analysis. Proc. VLDB Endow., 934–946 (2018)

28. Muckell, J., Patil, V., Ping, F., Hwang, J.-H., Lawson, C.T., Ravi, S.S.: SQUISH: an online approach for GPS trajectory compression. In: Proceedings of the 2nd International Conference on Computing for Geospatial Research & Applications, 1–8 (2011)

Sensor Network Prototypes for Environmental Noise Monitoring Based on Free Software

Maria Fernanda Molina-Miranda$^{(\boxtimes)}$ ⓘ, Ximena Acaro ⓘ,
and Miguel Giovanny Molina Villacís ⓘ

Facultad de Ciencias Matemáticas y Físicas, Universidad de Guayaquil, Ciudadela
Universitaria "Salvador Allende", Av. Delta y Av. Kennedy, Casilla Postal 471,
Guayaquil, Ecuador
maria.molinam@ug.edu.ec

Abstract. At present we are exposed to various polluting phenomena, one of these is environmental noise. In general, the environmental noise is not being monitored or controlled by the authorities in Ecuador, this led to this contribution to the ICF (Internal Competitive Fund) project "Noise pollution measurement systems in learning environments" in University of Guayaquil. In this article, a review is made of the studies carried out in countries such as Mexico, Peru and Chile on noise pollution that affects people's health. Several works related to ours that have been developed under various platforms are also disclosed. The methodologies used have been descriptive research and PPDIOO (PPDIOO stands for Prepare, Plan, Design, Implement, Operate, and Optimize) for the implementation of two prototypes of environmental noise sensors. This hardware and free software monitor in real time the noise levels measured in decibels to which students and teachers of the Faculty of Mathematical and Physical Sciences of the University of Guayaquil are exposed. It will demonstrate the noise levels to which the academic community is exposed and make the authorities aware of it. Laws can then be generated to reduce this pollution that affects the health and well-being of the population. In the results, values greater than 50 dB were obtained during the working day.

Keywords: IoT · Environmental noise · Open source · Sensor network

1 Introduction

Environmental noise has become one of the main pollutants in society caused by the increase in population, large construction projects, vehicular and pedestrian traffic. Actions of a society in the process of modernization that mainly affects the quality of life of the population and with consequences on health [1] is and additional contributor.

© Springer Nature Switzerland AG 2021
R. Valencia-García et al. (Eds.): CITI 2021, CCIS 1460, pp. 156–169, 2021.
https://doi.org/10.1007/978-3-030-88262-4_11

The unit of measurement of sound is the decibel (dB) and the instrument used to measure the noise is the sound level meter. The indicator for measuring environmental noise is the sound pressure level (SPL) expressed in dB and corrected by the A-weighting filter.

The World Health Organization (WHO) indicates that approximately 1.1 billion people around the world are exposed to harmful sounds that lead to a partial impairment of their hearing. Among them are 43 million people who range from 12 and 35 years of age in underdeveloped countries who suffer hearing impairments [2].

In countries such as Mexico and Peru, studies [3] y [4] have been carried out on the evaluation of environmental noise, also known as acoustic pollution. These studies showed that the population is exposed to higher levels than those established by the environmental standard. This is due mostly to the lack of awareness and ignorance about the seriousness of the risks of its effects on health and well-being in the population.

According to [5] the environmental noise report carried out in Europe in 2020 describes that 20% of the European population lives in harmful noise levels. In cities of the European continent such as: Valencia, Madrid, and Barcelona the noise level exceeds 75 dBA. Only 1% of their populations are within the moderate range established by the WHO of 65 dBA, these cities are considered to have the largest source of noise pollution.

In the Organic Environmental Code [6] it mentions that, in the future, regulations will be issued to control environmental pollution. Based on past history, it is highly unlikely the regulations will be followed in Ecuador. Noise pollution does not receive the attention of regulatory bodies that guarantee the health of the population. This is the direct cause of several syndromes or conditions in the individuals that impact the development of their daily activities such as: study or work.

In the city of Quito, a project to create noise maps in urban areas was carried out by the University of the Americas (UDLA) [7], which yielded values greater than 65 dB for more than 25% of the Quito's population. In the city of Guayaquil, some sectors of the city are recognized as bustling, where it has reached 70 to 80 dBA, especially during peak hours [8]. The WHO suggests a noise value of 55 dBA as the desirable upper limit outdoors and 35 dBA in schools.

Two integrated prototypes with noise sensors and real-time monitoring based on free software are proposed to measure the noise levels. According to all the above, the objectives of this study focused on: (i) gathering information on the study area, concepts, elements, and entities that are part of the problem, (ii) proposing network prototypes with noise sensor nodes, controller nodes and communication protocols, (iii) carry out prototype tests and monitor the study area and (iv) visualize the data obtained.

2 Related Works

Unlike traditional noise measurement methods which are expensive, systems based on the Internet of Things (IoT) have been developed to monitor noise pollution through mobile phones or cell phones, integrating of free software platforms, GPS, and sensors [9,10]. In addition, systems based on various types of sensors and microcontrollers have been implemented nationwide, such as:

In the study [11] the IoT model is applied to guarantee system aspects such as data collection, control, and storage. The hardware used in this prototype corresponds to the MAX98 family of amplifiers, specifically the MAX9814 module and a GSM module terminal for cellular communication in conjunction with Claro telephone Company. The study was performed by the placement of the prototype at strategic points of the commercial area of city of Ambato. The monitoring was carried out several hours of the day, with an error range of 3% where the highest captured value was 83 dBA, significantly exceeding the 45–52 dBA intervals recommended by WHO.

The RTE [12] magazine proposes the development of the noise monitoring system that uses a BeagleBone Black module as a controller of the noise sensors connected to it. It is configured in such a way that it can process and store data to later be presented through real-time graphics using the SIMORA software. Also, email and SMS notifications are sent to the attorneys in the areas for the recognition of offenders. This study focuses on capturing environmental decibels in areas of downtown Guayaquil, mainly bar areas with music. The system is located in the Las Peñas sector between the streets AV. October 9 and Esmeraldas. A 3 dBA increase was observed in peak hours. This study was able to establish a system in which users are notified of noise alerts caused in these areas and sanctions are applied to offenders according to the results of the system, thus work can be done to improve their quality of life.

In 2019, a design was carried out based on the implementation of Wireless Sensor Network (WSN) technologies with the use of Zigbee sensors [13]. The network design scenario includes the area of greatest socioeconomic activity within the city of Loja. Zoning of downtown areas was carried out to identify sources of CO_2 and noise emissions. In the project, an environment monitoring network is developed with wireless device technologies such as XBEE. The devices are configured as coordinating nodes and sensor nodes and data is sent to an end user interface in real time, for subsequent analysis. This study reveals the importance of the different wireless technologies, modules-controllers, and their configuration forms for optimization in a data network.

At the University of the Americas, a system was built with an XBee Pro 2B module that consists of a wireless sensor network which is made up of Nodes; a node is commanded by an ATmega328 microcontroller which works together with a GPS, as well as, a sound level meter that allows the noise level to be measured. The second stage consists of a BAN network which will allow knowing the status of people through non-invasive sensors. In the last stage, a graphical interface is created where the data obtained by the WSN network such as noise and its position can be viewed. In the data of the BAN network, the information of the people's status is tested and shown in another window of the interface [14].

A project developed by ESPOCH proposes a real-time system of wireless sensors based on development cards. The Faculty of Computer Science and Electronics was the area chosen to measure noise variations, locating three modules: supervision, storage, and warning. In addition, the use of Arduino Uno and Mega development boards were made, which are the processing elements of the modules. For the visualization of the data obtained in the supervision module, a virtual tool was developed through LabVIEW which allows it to observe the noise levels in graphical and numerical form. In tests carried out in the faculty, noise levels between 42 dB and 85 dB were detected, exceeding the permissible limits [15].

3 Location of the Study Area

The study was based on knowing the noise levels to which the Software Engineering and Information Technology students of the Faculty of Mathematical and Physical Sciences of the University of Guayaquil are exposed during the classes. The system was located in the commercial downtown of the city of Guayaquil on Baquerizo Moreno streets between Víctor Manuel Rendón and Francisco P. Icaza (see Fig. 1).

In the institution, more than 50% of the classrooms are in the north section of the establishment, so it is more exposed to the noise generated by vehicular traffic, informal vendors, labor strikes that usually occur near the campus, noise from college students who walk along the university sidewalk, people who work on the outskirts of the facilities daily as car attendants, among others. Guayaquil ranks 21st among the 25 most congested cities by traffic in the world, according to the INRIX 2018 report [16]. In addition, two conflicting schedules have been determined: 06H00 and 09H00 and from 17H00 to 20H00.

Considered as the first contribution to the ICF project "Noise pollution measurement systems in learning environments" approved by the university, the current state and the location of the building and above all due to COVID-19 pandemic restrictions the studies were just based on the faculty. The present investigation proposes two prototypes that allow determining the levels of environmental noise present during a working day inside the building. Currently the building has 30 classrooms distributed over the 3 floors. At least 60% of the total available classrooms do not have doors or windows suitable for isolating noise from internal or external sources.

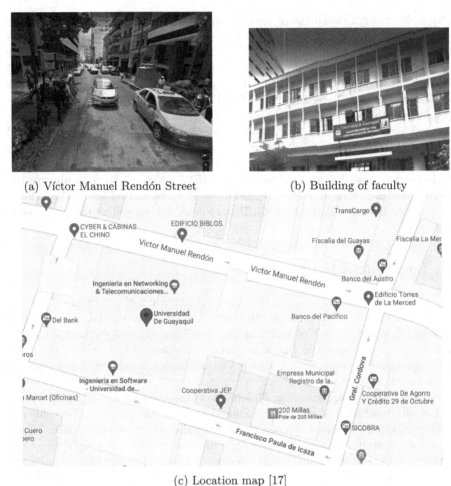

(a) Víctor Manuel Rendón Street   (b) Building of faculty

(c) Location map [17]

Fig. 1. Location of the faculty

4   Methodology

The study was carried out using the following methods and tools:

4.1   Methods

For the development of the proposal, two methodologies were implemented: descriptive and the PPDIOO methodology. In the first place, a survey was carried out on 98 students of the faculty to know the degree of impact of noise in the student community and to recognize the areas most exposed to environmental pollution during the academic day.

In the results of the poll, it turned out that 60.3% of students consider that there are interruptions due to high noise levels at the time of lessons. The building has different hours that go from 7H00 to 22H00, 90% indicate that in the hours of 12H00 to 14H00, 16H00 to 18H00 and 19H00 to 21H00, are the highest levels of environmental pollution due to external agents. In addition, the main sources of pollution include the following: 11.7% peddlers, 73.3% vehicles (public and private transport), 15% other sources. Finally, the building has 3 floors, 79% consider that the ground floor and first floor are the areas where the greatest number of interruptions from external sources are experienced from Víctor Manuel Rendon and Francisco P. Icaza streets. For the analysis of the noise levels present in the study area, the implementation of 2 prototypes based on hardware and free software based on IoT are proposed. The PPDIOO methodology guaranteed to meet the objectives of each stage [18].

4.2 Hardware and Software

Among the hardware and software elements implemented in the sensor network proposals are:

- Hardware
  - Sound sensors
    1. LM393 which has an adjustable acoustic detection level by means of a potentiometer integrated in it. This sensor has a gain adaptable to the reception of the microphone, additionally it has three external connection pins to a card or microcontroller.
    2. AA24 has the supply voltage is between (3.3–5) V, the measurement range of (30–130) dB, with a ± 1.5 dB variation in measurement.
  - Microcontrollers
    1. The Arduino UNO 5v/16 MHz board which is based on an ATMEGA328 microcontroller with 14 digital pins which are divided into: 6 PWM-type output pins and 6 analog input pins. This Arduino model was chosen because it has a number of libraries that will allow effective communication with the sensors and modules that are added to this microcontroller.
    2. The Esp32 board through the MQTT protocol header, the node connects to the configured Wifi network, which provides communication options such as: Wifi, Bluetooth and BLE. Allows connections to capacitive touch sensors, sound amplifiers, an SD card interface, Ethernet interface, and SPI interface.
    3. ESP8266 board containing a CPU-RISC with a 32-bit architecture, Tensilica Xtensa LX106 with a clock speed of 80 MHz. RAM memory is equivalent to a total of 64 KB of instruction type and 96 KB of data type. It works under the IEEE 802.11 b/g/n standard, which is WiFi technology uses SPI and I2C type protocols.

- Software
  1. ThingSpeak. This platform works under APIs, the most important is GitHub, which is a download server. It has unique channels, whether public or private, where the users store and publish their information. It handles a series of plugins where it facilitates the user to design applications in a native way, with HTML, CSS and JavaScript support. It is an IoT type platform which is compatible with several hardware and software platforms like Arduino, Raspberry Pi, Social Networks, MATLAB, among others. It also uses connections in mobile applications such as ThingTweet, ThingControl, React, among others.
  2. Ubidots. An easy-to-use, secure and widely used platform in IoT application ecosystems, it allows real-time monitoring of the noise levels obtained by the sensor network through the cloud with the configuration of a token assigned to the user. Ubidots offers a REST API compatible with HTTP and HTTPS that allows reading and writing data.

5   Prototypes

5.1   Prototype 1. Wireless Sensor Network

The first proposal consists of a wireless sensor network with the following elements: Sound Sensor AA204 in the data capture block, Esp8266 and Wifi Bluetooth in data transmission block and ThingSpeak platform and OLED display for the data visualization block.

The development of the sensor node is integrated by the microcontroller ESP8266 and a connection with the AA204 sound sensor. The analog data collected by the sensors will be processed by the microcontroller and the decibels corresponding to each range of sound captured will be obtained. The information captured in the environment (first floor of the building), for the microcontroller to process that information and through wireless communications (Wireless, Wifi), see Fig. 2.

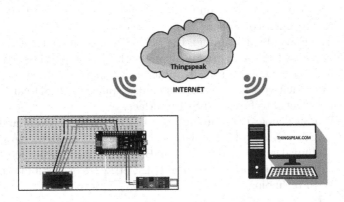

Fig. 2. Design of Prototype 1: Wireless Sensor Network

The node recollect the noise level data that is sent through the internet to the ThingSpeak platform which stores and displays the data in real time. The architecture of the first prototype with the creation of a database corresponding to the platform for IoT-type technologies called ThingSpeak, where the values from the sensor nodes are stored, files of type:.csv,. json, etc. Figure 3 is an example of the data measured in decibels by the sound sensor during half an hour at the faculty.

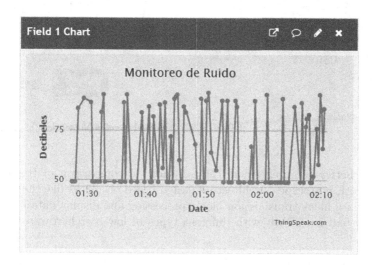

Fig. 3. Plot of noise levels data by ThingSpeak in real time

5.2   Prototype 2. Wired Sensor Network

The second proposal consists of a wired sensory network made up of 4 blocks for better understanding: Sound Sensor LM393 for data capture, Esp32 Wifi/Bluetooth for data transmission, Arduino UNO for data processing and Ubidots for data visualization.

The data processing block performs the reception, conversion and analysis of the data obtained by the sensor nodes, which are centralized by the Gateway to later be displayed in the software by means of a connection token, Fig. 4 shows the complete scheme of prototype 2. For the development of the code, it was necessary to import libraries corresponding to the module to be used with Esp32 (Espressif package), the Esp32 Dev Module was selected for Arduino. The next step was the declaration of variables of the values obtained by each sensor, declaration of the Esp32 communication module, pins used for each sensor, and MQTT client code to connect to the Wi-Fi network and send data to the sampling platform. The data is displayed by the Ubidots platform in real time, it could be customized and configured the graph and ranges, Fig. 5 shows an example of the noise level measured during one hour.

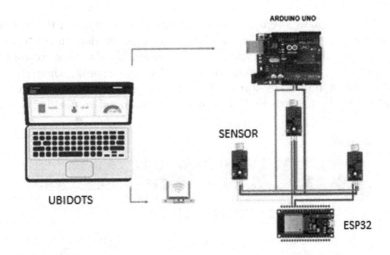

Fig. 4. Design of Prototype 2: Wired Sensor Network

For a better comprehension Table 1 shows a comparison of the architectures of both prototypes, architecture design based on blocks like the following: Capture data block transmission block, processing and display data block; each prototype had been built with different types of low cost hardware and open software.

Table 1. Prototype comparison: Block design architecture

Prototypes	Capture Data block	Transmission Block	Processing Block	Display data Block
Prototype 1	Sound sensor AA204	Wifi/ bluetooth	ESP8266	Thingspeak
Prototype 2	Sound sensorabreak LM393	ESP32 Wifi/ Bluetooth	Arduino UNO	Ubidots

6 Evaluation and Results

The methodology PPDIOO includes Operation phase where the exemplares were tested and calibrated with a professional sound level meter and a mobile sound level meter application, obtaining a minimum margin of error. After having verified the correct functioning of the prototypes, the noise levels were read for 5 days from 09H00 to 21H00 in a faculty classroom located on the ground floor in front of Víctor Manuel Rendón street. The data was stored by each open source application, which allows downloading in files with format .csv for graphic analysis as below.

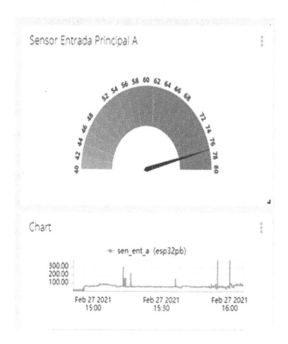

Fig. 5. Graphs of noise levels data in Ubidots in real time

Figures 6 and 7 show the noise levels captured in the tests, thus evidencing that the university community is exposed to a daily noise average of 67 dB during the work or academic day. Although these exposure levels are admissible and considered that 85 decibels (dB) for a maximum of 8 h is the maximum level of exposure without risks, we must reflect that the acoustic properties of the classrooms have a great impact on the noise level to which both students and teachers are subjected. According to one of the OMS recommendations for educational centers, the sound intensity should not exceed 35 dB (a) [19].

Indeed, after analyzing the results of the previous graphs, two peaks periods stand out, which are considered to be two important time bands, the first from 11H30 to 13H30 and the second from 18H00 to 20H0. Here the level of environmental pollution exceeds 70 dB. It is important to disclose these results to the university authorities so that they can consider whether it is feasible to suspend classes at these times or implement a plan to adapt the infrastructure of the classrooms in order to achieve improvements in soundproofing. This will raise awareness authorities and public organizations so that norms or laws are applied to control noise levels, in addition it is intended to encourage this type of studies in other educational institutions exposed to high levels of environmental noise.

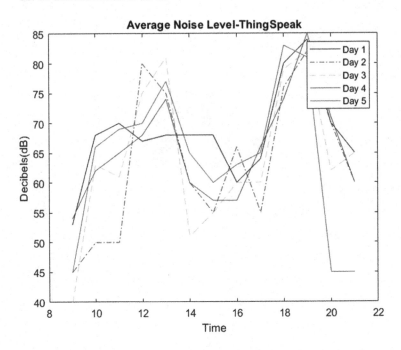

Fig. 6. Average noise levels measured for 5 days in location with Prototype 1

Based on the information, a sensor network design is proposed for monitoring environmental noise. The architecture consists in a star topology with 13 sensor nodes located on the different floors of the building, a base node, and a connection to the open source platform through internet; this proposal will allow monitoring the study area and collect more data that may be useful for future jobs. See Fig. 8.

This work is part of an ICF project - "Noise pollution measurement systems in learning environments" for the University of Guayaquil. Thanks to the authorities for the information-collecting despite being closed due to the pandemic caused by COVID- 19, the participation of the students is also appreciated: Erika Andaluz, Gladys Rigchag, Julio Sanchez and Roberto Ponce.

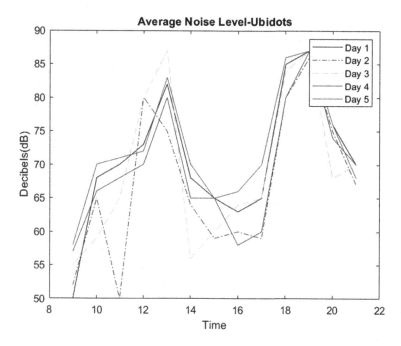

Fig. 7. Average noise levels measured for 5 days in location with Prototype 2

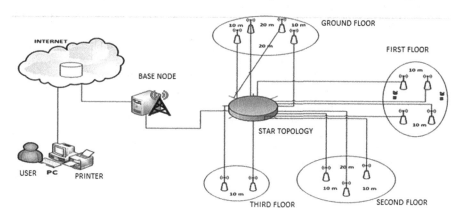

Fig. 8. Noise sensor network design

7   Conclusions and Future Work

The results obtained from the monitoring of environmental noise in the Faculty of Mathematical and Physical Sciences facilities prove the results of the poll and confirm the need to take measures and implement a system that is profitable, economical and for the benefit of the university community.

The sources of noise: the horns of cars and peddlers that remain in the surroundings of the building are the consequences that derive from a high exposure to noise. The current state of the classrooms would not be optimal for noise isolation, since most classrooms are without windows and doors causing external and internal noise to interfere with activities.

Two prototypes were proposed for a network of environmental noise sensors that will allow community to learn more about the noise pollution where the students are exposed.

This study was mainly focused on the faculty building but it will be addressed to other learning environments like schools and libraries. We are also proposing the development of noise maps on the campus of the university as another contribution for the community.

References

1. Ramos, D.R.: Evaluación del Nivel de Ruido Ambiental y Elaboración de Mapa de Ruidos del Distrito de Sachaca - Arequipa 2016 (2017)
2. OMS: Sordera y pérdida de la audición, March 2021
3. Rodríguez-Manzo, F.E., Juárez González, L.: A qualitative exploration of urban environmental noise in Mexico City. Estudios Demograficos y Urbanos **35**(3), 803–838(2020)
4. Rosa, R.M.L.: Evaluación del ruido ambiental por tránsito aéreo y lapercepción del impacto en la salud de los habitantesresidentes del asentamiento humano 200 millas -callao. resreport, UNIVERSIDAD NACIONAL MAYOR DE SAN MARCOS (2017)
5. Eulalia Peris (EEA): Environmental noise in Europe, 2020 - Publications Office of the EU. Technical report (2020)
6. Presidencia de la Republica. Codigo Organico del Ambiente, April 2017
7. UDLA: Mapa del ruido en la zona urbana de Quito (2018)
8. ElUniverso: Guayaquil tendrá mapa de ruido en diciembre; médico sugiere quitar pitos a buses urbanos y prohibir venta de altoparlantes (2020)
9. Ruiz, J.M.: Mobile system for monitorization of noise pollution. Techreport, Universidad de Malaga, June 2020
10. Marjanović, M., Grubeša, S., Podnar Žarko, I.: Air and noise pollution monitoring in the city of zagreb by using mobile crowdsensing. In: 2017 25th International Conference on Software, Telecommunications and Computer Networks (SoftCOM), pp. 1–5 (2017)
11. Vásconez, C.R.C.: Sistema de monitoreo de nivel de ruido ambiental para el Casco Central de la Ciudad de Ambato (2018)
12. Villacreses, J., Munizaga, L., Velasquez, W.: Sistema integral para el monitoreo y control de los sonidos en bares y zonas céntricas de la ciudad en tiempo real. Revista Tecnologica ESPOL **29**(Diciembre), 28–37 (2016)
13. Mendieta, A.O., Garrochamba. Á.: Diseño de una WSN para el monitoreo de CO2 en el aire y niveles de ruido en la ciudad de Loja. *MASKAY* **10**(1), 20 (2019)
14. Lescano, S.L.S.: Sistema de medición de contaminación auditiva, empleando una red de sensores inalámbricos y sensores Ban (2016)
15. Madelaine, A., Moreno, P.: DiseNo e implementaci On de una red inalAmbrica de sensores inteligentes para el registro de lacontaminaci On acUsticaen la espoch basado en tarjetas de desarrollo (2016)

16. Pesantes, K.: Guayaquil, una de las 25 ciudades con más tráfico en el mundo, opta por trabajo comunitario en lugar de multas. Primicias (2019)
17. Google Maps: Location of faculty of mathematical and physical sciences (2021)
18. Tayeb, S., Latifi, S., Kim, Y.: A survey on IoT communication and computation frameworks: an industrial perspective. In: 2017 IEEE 7th Annual Computing and Communication Workshop and Conference (9CCWC 2017). Institute of Electrical and Electronics Engineers Inc., March 2017
19. Cohen, M.A., Castillo, O.S.: Ruido en la ciudad. Contaminación auditiva y ciudad caminable/Noise in the city. Acustic pollution and the walkable city. Technical Report 1 (2016)

ICT for Agronomy and Environment

Agrotechnology: Analysis of the Services Offered by Mobile Applications for the Agronomic Control of Orchards

Katty Lagos-Ortiz$^{(\boxtimes)}$ ⓘ, Vanessa Vergara-Lozano ⓘ, Andrea Sinche-Guzmán ⓘ, and Tany Burgos-Herrería ⓘ

Faculty of Agrarian Sciences, Agrarian University of Ecuador, Av. 25 de Julio, Guayaquil, Ecuador
{klagos,vvergara,asinche,tburgos}@uagraria.edu.ec

Abstract. Home gardens or small orchards are an appropriate alternative for families to produce and consume fresh and healthy products at low cost for a balanced diet [1].

In these days, households in several sectors of the country have chosen to build their gardens in community, to cover the need for food, as well as to become a savings mechanism due to the benefits that its production generates. However, the lack of knowledge regarding the requirements and care involved in making a garden, make many families lose their plantations or prefer to avoid doing so [2].

Nowadays, computer applications are used in many areas, likewise mobile phones have become an essential device. Technology has also proven to be immersed in agriculture, playing an increasingly important role, helping us to automate and take care of it, also helping to mitigate the inconvenience in the care and control of community gardens.

The present work proposes to carry out an analysis of the services offered by mobile applications for the agronomic management of orchards and the impact that Agrotechnology generates in the control of community gardens.

Keywords: Orchards · Agronomic control · Crops · Mobile applications · Agromatics · Agrotechnology · Community gardens · Urban gardens · Home gardens

1 Introduction

The Food and Agriculture Organization of the United Nations in its book entitled E-Agriculture Strategy Guide [3] defines E-Agriculture as an emerging field that focuses on improving agriculture by enhancing information and communication processes. Specifically, E-Agriculture involves the conceptualization, design, development, evaluation and application of innovative ways of using technology in the field of information and communication. Even contributing to the development of support institutions or public policies that allow increasing quality standards, complying with all the rules of agricultural and food practices.

© Springer Nature Switzerland AG 2021
R. Valencia-García et al. (Eds.): CITI 2021, CCIS 1460, pp. 173–187, 2021.
https://doi.org/10.1007/978-3-030-88262-4_12

An urban or community garden offers a number of benefits at the family level, at home it will allow you to obtain totally fresh seasonal fruits and vegetables. In addition, natural options may be used instead of pesticides to protect plants, so their advantages are in accordance with the objectives of the National Plan for Good Living; developing productive capacities to achieve food sovereignty, and on the other hand, encourages family participation, among others. In addition, they can become transversal socio-educational spaces that infuse an educational and social value, incorporating themselves in various areas and serving to promote a social culture committed to sustainability [4].

The importance of creating urban or community gardens is clear, since it is possible to produce quality food with good taste, reduce food losses, save money on food purchases, it is grown with quality and safety and family integration is strengthened [5]. Creating orchards within a community or family contributes to improving their quality of life, interacting, socializing and creating a harmonious environment between neighbors and relatives, as proposed by Dahnil [6] in his project for the creation of community and educational gardens that tries to integrate wireless sensor networks and mobile applications to monitor the gardens. He considers that the proposed application is feasible to build using the infrastructure available in domestic and school buildings, considering its minimum cost of implementation, easy handling and operation.

Agrotechnology has taken a wide space in agriculture, nowadays there are already mechanisms for the supervision and control of agricultural fields either by technological applications, use of drones or irrigation systems [7]. However, it must be considered that community gardens are very common complements for homes in recent years, especially in times of confinement due to the pandemic, however one of the main difficulties of owning a home garden is getting food or sown plants grow quickly and adequately, since in many cases there is only empirical knowledge and there are no scientific bases, specialized techniques for the control of this type of orchards, making it difficult to hire an expert in agronomy who can help satisfy the needs of household agricultural users.

In this way, it is possible to control many factors of the orchard or field without being present, through applications that provide us with information in real time of decisive agronomic variables for an adequate production of crops, such variables as: irrigation, temperature, wind speed, vegetation index are measured by sensors that send the information to mobile devices [8].

Access to mobile technology makes it possible to take work to the geographic region where it is needed, having a significant amount of information available at all times, which is an advantage in an innovation model among agricultural producers and buyers [9]. Thus, it is also possible to use tools such as sensors, big data and management software that is based on the use of sensors to monitor variables that influence a crop cycle, processing large amounts of data that allow making timely decisions or supplying some need for crops. Some mobile applications are available to be used and facilitate management regarding decisions in the field [10].

This work is structured as follows: Sect. 2 describes the relevant literature about applications that allow the care and control of crops. Then, Sect. 3 describes a categorization of android and iOS mobile applications based on their functionalities. Section 4 presents the quantitative evaluation of the characteristics of the analyzed applications. Finally, Sect. 5 presents conclusions and future research directions.

2 Related Work

Nowadays, the migration of people to the urban area has increased, which has caused a high rate of crops in cities, with the aim of encouraging this agricultural production in urban sectors the author of the article "Internet of Things (IoT) Applied to an Urban Garden" [11] proposes the development of a system that allows measuring, monitoring and automatic irrigation for this type of orchards using IoT and CO_2 sensors, humidity, luminosity, temperature, plant detection and additionally remote monitoring through a local area network, with the purpose that the agronomic control of an orchard is possible.

Many efforts have been made to create systems and applications that allow the implementation of care and control processes for crops and orchards. As detailed below, Gomar [12] presents a design and implementation of an irrigation and fertilizer automation system for a hydroponic garden on the Campus of the UPV of Gandía, until now periodically managed manually. It seeks to automate said garden so that it can be controlled and managed automatically through microcontrollers, trying to make it as efficient as possible and have the capacity to manage all the electronic devices that make it up. On the other hand, the electronic design of all the devices and materials necessary to achieve this purpose is generated and the implementation of a system for sending control emails in order to see the status of all the sensors in the system.

Stickel and Ludwig [13] present an urban garden care option consisting of stationary ultra-low voltage (ULV) devices in the garden, which would be powered by solar energy, a mobile device with the "Garden App" and a web-based backend, with the which attempts to monitor the growth of cultivated vegetables.

Lafuente [14] also presents a design for an automatic irrigation system to achieve an adequate use of water in an orchard, both the needs of the crop itself, as well as certain meteorological and environmental conditions that can cause the loss of water due to excessive evaporation of the same, must be analyzed. These quantities can be measured by using specific sensors. Currently, there is little free time available, so it is important to be able to automate as many tasks as possible through intelligent systems. The author has made a system composed of: a series of sensors that record environmental magnitudes, a control system that analyzes the data acquired by the sensors and determines the automatic activation/deactivation of irrigation, a communications interface that allows wireless connection, a Web page for interaction with the user and integration into a general home automation system of the home and as a result a prototype has been obtained in which the user can either manage the irrigation manually, or specify the conditions of soil moisture that will automatically determine the activation/deactivation of irrigation, also taking into consideration the environmental parameters collected by the sensors. The tests and simulations carried out demonstrate the proper functioning of the prototype and the functionalities that had been proposed or specify the soil moisture conditions that will automatically determine the activation/deactivation of irrigation, also considering the environmental parameters collected by the sensors.

Each of the efforts made try to include new applications that include technological contributions, such as blockchain, Internet of things, (IoT), precision agriculture (PA), Artificial Intelligence (AI) and are giving rise to smart agriculture (SA), which is making a strong foray into the current market with future forecasts. In this context VegIoT Garden [15], proposes a low-cost, modular and energy efficient IoT platform for SA, using commercial devices, with short and long-range communication protocols (IEEE 802.11 and LoRa), to improve the agronomic management of orchards through the collection, monitoring and analysis of sensor data, related to air and soil humidity and temperature. The infrastructure is completed with an Internet-enabled Home Node (HN) and an iOS-based mobile application, developed to simplify data visualization and plant health monitoring.

It is important to define that to conserve and maintain orchards a strong social commitment and recognition of the multiple potentialities of urban agriculture is necessary [16].

Efficiency in crop production, that is, producing more with less, is a challenge that must be addressed. Therefore, it is necessary to develop computer applications that help farmers and/or agronomy students to carry out activities such as the treatment of pests and plant diseases, production quality, among others. Currently, mobile technologies offer optimal and comprehensive solutions for agriculture. Therefore, it is important to adopt these technologies to perform daily agricultural tasks [17].

3 Mobile Applications for Crops and Orchards

Urban, community gardens and/or crops in small plots or within a home in the city have been spreading over the years, both in developed and developing countries thanks to ecologists. Growing vegetables, greens or perhaps fruits inside the house today is very popular because it helps to provide more sustainable food and avoid wasting time and energy since there is no need to transport food and there is less dependence on fossil fuels.

Due to the facts that the development of these orchards or crops favour a better quality of the products, it also represents a less expensive alternative in comparison with the traditional option. Nowadays, people have free access to the Internet, therefore it has become possible for people to obtain the information they need for cultivation and equipment from their homes and thus carry out its control and management by themselves [19]. For this purpose, they make use of mobile applications that allow them to analyse certain characteristics of the soil, control parameters that they must consider with their crops, guides about the selection of plants to be sown according to what the user needs, among others.

Mobile applications play an important role, because they allow the use of new technologies to improve the care of gardens and get a better measurement of the variables that affect the growth and health of plants.

The development of apps, focused on agriculture, not only arises as a technological advance but as a solution and response to the current situation of population growth and the interest in creating orchards in urban areas, in addition to climate change. These apps generate solutions with greater affordability to achieve positive results.

For the app selection process that was carried out through a direct search in the of-ficial mobile app stores, for Android in Google Play and for iOS in the App Store, using keywords such as orchards, home gardens, orchard care, cultivation, crop care, crop control, plants, hostile, harvest, when performing this search, 43 apps for Android and 52 for iOS were found, to select the apps, they were analyzed using one of the ASO tools (App Store Optimization), platforms that are online for analysis and data, which help to track user ratings or reviews, the income stream, an also offer download analysis. The tool used was SENSOR TOWER, an ASO solution designed to provide companies with information on application usage, competitor metrics and ad performance. Designed for application developers and SEO professionals, it is an online solution that helps users track and manage keyword history, CSV exports, revenue streams, and reports. Each of the apps found for both Android and iOS, being a total of 95, which were analyzed with Sensor Tower, this tool provides a rating ranging from A + to F, establishes a score for the app analyzed in few seconds. Where it evaluates, App Icon, Name and subtitle, Visibility and internationalization index, Estimated number of downloads per month and income, keywords for the ranking and positive or negative user reviews.

The apps selected for Android were rated from A to D−. And from iOS, the apps selected were rated from A + to C−.

The score according to Sensor Tower takes into consideration factors such as search position, graphics positions, app name, icon, number of downloads, download speed, and user rating. One of the main factors for visibility is search queries is the name of the application. Opinions also influence search results. User feedback influences app installs as a decision factor. The more installs an application has, the more chance it has of achieving a better ranking position. The average rating or the number of stars of an application is a factor that influences the conversion. Considering these factors that influence the rating, an average of the apps was obtained, giving as a result a global score for each one, as shown in Table 1 and Table 2.

Table 1. User ratings for Android Apps

No.	Mobile applications	Operating system	Score	Total score
1	PlantNet	Android	A	77
2	PlantSnap	Android	A	76
3	Urban garden and planting	Android	D−	42
4	Plantnote: Plant Diary & Water	Android	D−	42
5	Plant Care Reminder	Android	D−	44
6	Veggie Garden	Android	D+	49
7	Planter - Garden Planner	Android	D	46
8	Gardenize, Garden Diary	Android	D−	42
9	Moon & Garden	Android	D−	41
10	Gardroid - Vegetable Garden	Android	D−	41
11	Garden Tags	Android	D-	39
12	Flowerpot Orchards	Android	D	44
13	Yara CheckIT	Android	D	44

(*continued*)

Table 1. (*continued*)

No.	Mobile applications	Operating system	Score	Total score
14	Gardenate	Android	D–	37
15	How to Plant Vegetables - Vegetables at Home	Android	D–	28
16	How to Grow Vegetables	Android	D–	34
17	Plantsss	Android	D–	32

Table 2. User ratings for iOS Apps

No.	Mobile applications	Operating system	Score sensor tower	Total score
1	PictureThis	iOS	A+	82
2	PlantIn: Plant Identifier	iOS	A–	71
3	NatureID: Plant Identification	iOS	A–	73
4	Blossom - Plant Identification	iOS	A–	73
5	PlantNet	iOS	B+	68
6	PlantSnap - identify plants	iOS	A–	72
7	Plantyx	iOS	B–	63
8	Plantie	iOS	B–	60
9	Incognita flora	iOS	C+	58
10	Plant & Tree Identifier	iOS	C+	59
11	Plan Scan	iOS	C–	53
12	iplant - Plant Identification	iOS	C–	53
13	Agrobase - weed	iOS	C	55
14	Veggie Garden Planner	iOS	C–	52
15	Planter: Garden Planner	iOS	C–	49

Within this study, various types of mobile applications for both Android and iOS systems were reviewed, 17 were selected for Android and 15 for iOS. Those apps allow mainly to control the crops, provide guides to carry out their management and also allow us to detect any disease or virus within the crop through the use of artificial intelligence. For this reason, we have categorized the different applications according to their characteristics and use as shown in Table 3 and Table 4.

Table 3. Android System Apps categorized and analyzed

Operating system	Categories:	Applications
Android	Informational tool	7
	Management tools	8
	AI tools	2
Total Android Apps		17

Table 4. iOS System Apps categorized and analyzed.

Operating system	Categories:	Applications
iOS	Informational tool	1
	Management tools	7
	AI tools	7
Total iOS Apps		15

3.1 Informational Tools

Within this category, the mobile applications that allow having a guide of different crops that are stored in their databases stand out, but they do not allow real-time control of the crops.

They contain specific information with images and control sheets with times allocated for each activity to be carried out in the crop, also some have information on possible pests or viruses that can make the plant sick and free tutorials. These types of tools are intended to expand the knowledge of users so that they can give them the best care at home [20].

It is important to mention that one of the characteristics of the analyzed apps is the availability of information related to orchards or crops, care and controls, which can be used as a reference or as a mean of learning about crop management. This characteristic allows the user to make inquiries, also allow quick and easy access to information with friendly and visually attractive interfaces.

Apps for both Android and iOS focused on information management for crops have evolved in parallel with advances in ICTs, the support of geographic information systems (GIS) and more recently mobile applications and services are providing innovative options for the problem of obtaining agricultural information.

3.2 Management Tools

These applications are one of the most found within the analysis since they automate and increase the productive performance of orchards or crops because these tools can be used for measurement, monitoring and advice in any urban garden [11].

Some of the newest functions or characteristics in this category is that types of plants can accompany those that are already planted and the functionality to upload photos of the crops to interact with other users who have similar crops.

In this category are the apps that allow users to monitor their activities, collect data and record them, manage the administration of data related to the crop. With these apps the user can optimize daily tasks, improve response times, facilitating data collection for decision-making in order to potentiate the sustainable usage of the different crops available.

Mobile applications focused on the management of orchards or crops allow you to monitor the orchards independently, consulting their status and acting on them from anywhere. These applications allow delegating the most iterative tasks such as irrigation control based on temperature and humidity, and focusing on other more manual, enriching and educational tasks such as pruning or harvesting.

3.3 AI Tools

In this category are the applications that use Artificial Intelligence to control certain processes in the crop, such as identification of pests or diseases of the plant, detection of levels of the most important variables of the crop such as temperature and humidity.

Many problems that today occur in crops can be remedied through the use of Artificial Intelligence, but for this, sensors that can be purchased in addition to the use of the mobile device must be used [21].

In this category are the apps that allow identification of pests or diseases through the use of image processing techniques, this process begins with the capture of the image and then through an analysis of the captured image the existence or not of any disease or plague is determined, with this type of apps it is possible to make timely diagnoses, and therefore reducing losses.

The use of artificial intelligence has achieved the protection of crops through various factors such as climate change information, plant growth, the proper use of water, pesticides and herbicides, and helps in the efficient use of labour, productivity, improve quality and maintain soil fertility, for which mobile applications provide their respective recommendations.

4 Analysis of the Characteristics

The analysis of the categories was carried out based on the 32 mobile applications that were reviewed through the web and the Android and iOS virtual stores. This process was carried out by reviewing the functionalities that the applications had, forms of access and appraisal of the applications. Within each characteristic, several edges that are important when controlling the orchards were analysed.

The objective of the analysis was to identify the services offered by mobile applications for the agronomic control of orchards, which is why three important aspects were analyzed when choosing an application, such as the form of access, cost free or if a license or payment is required for an additional service (freemium), the second edge analyzed was the appraisal of the app, this appraisal was given by 3 values, such as the score obtained in the tool used to search the apps, the score given by the user and the ability of the tool to share the processes with other users. Finally, the third aspect analyzed were the functionalities (processes) that they possess for the management of the crop.

4.1 Access Forms

Within the forms of access, most of the applications are free, but with certain limitations in the functionalities that they have, which must be acquired with the payment of the license. Almost 97% of the applications are initially freemium.

4.2 App Rating

To estimate the appraisal of the applications, three identified characteristics were analyzed, among them: User score, Sharing between users and application downloads during the months of April and May 2021, to carry out this analysis weights were given to each characteristic in such a way adding the weights to obtain a total of 10 points. The assigned weight was established as follows: 3 points for user scores, 2 points for sharing among users, and 5 points for application downloads, and it was performed separately with each operating system. The Android applications that obtained the highest scores according to Table 5 were PlanNet from the IA Tools Category, Plantnote: Plant Diary & Water from the Informational Tool Category and Plant Care Reminder from the Management Tool Category.

Table 5. Android apps with their App Rating score

No.	Mobile applications	User score 3 points	Share between users 2 points	Downloads 5 points	Total score
1	PlantNet	2.76	1.6	2.90	7.26
2	PlantSnap	2.16	1.6	1.45	5.21
3	Plantnote: Plant Diary & Water	2.7	1.6	0.04	4.34
4	Plant Care Reminder	2.64	1.6	0.07	4.31
5	Garden Tags	2.22	1.6	0.04	3.86
6	Gardenize, Garden Diary	1.92	1.6	0.04	3.56
7	How to Plant Vegetables - Vegetables at Home	2.76	0	0.04	2.80
8	Flowerpot Orchards	2.7	0	0.04	2.74
9	Planter - Garden Planner	2.58	0	0.07	2.65
10	Moon & Garden	2.52	0	0.05	2.57
11	Gardenate	2.52	0	0.04	2.56

(*continued*)

Table 5. (*continued*)

No.	Mobile applications	User score 3 points	Share between users 2 points	Downloads 5 points	Total score
12	Plantsss	2.52	0	0.04	2.56
13	How to Grow Vegetables	2.46	0	0.04	2.50
14	Gardroid - Vegetable Garden	2.34	0	0.04	2.38
15	Yara CheckIT	2.34	0	0.04	2.38
16	Urban Garden and Planting	2.22	0	0.04	2.26
17	Veggie Garden	2.16	0	0.05	2.21

As can be seen in Table 6 the highest-scoring iOS apps were PictureThis from the IA Planter Tools Category: Garden Planner from the Management Tool Category and Agrobase - weed from the Informative Tool Category.

Table 6. iOS apps with their App Rating score.

No.	Mobile applications	User score 3 points	Share between users 2 Points	Downloads 5 points	Total score
1	PictureThis	2.88	2	3.13	8.01
2	PlantIn: Plant Identifier	2.7	2	0.52	5.22
3	PlantNet	2.76	2	0.42	5.18
4	PlantSnap - Identify plants	2.76	2	0.31	5.07
5	iplant - Plant Identification	2.7	2	0.03	4.73
6	Planter: Garden Planner	2.7	2	0.01	4.71
7	NatureID: Plant Identification	2.76	1	0.42	4.18
8	Tomato & Basilic	1.8	2	0.01	3.81
9	Plantie	2.82	0.4	0.10	3.32
10	Gaia - Holistic Patch Planner	2.82	0.4	0.01	3.23
11	Garden Planner	2.52	0.4	0.01	2.93
12	Veggie Garden Planner	2.52	0.4	0.01	2.93
13	V for Green	1.8	0.8	0.01	2.61
14	Agrobase - weed	2.58	0	0.01	2.59
15	Plant & Tree Identifier	1.8	0.6	0.02	2.42

4.3   Apps Functionalities

To carry out the analysis of the functionalities of the applications, the expert in orchards, Eduardo Rochina Eng., was consulted, who provides his professional services in the Community Gardens developed by the Mayor's Office of the City of Guayaquil, and identifies 5 specific functionalities as the most important ones when managing orchards. One of the most important functionalities is the alarms for irrigation, fertilizer, harvest, etc. as well as a schedule or planner of the activities, the compatibility between plants at the time of sowing, the photo diary that is important to see the growth and/or plant development and finally advice on sowing or sown vegetables. Each functionality was reviewed by the expert, assigning it a score between 0 and 1 with the following scale: 0 there is no functionality, (0.1 to 0. 3) there are functionalities but at least 4 of them do not carry out their process correctly; (0.4 to 06) exists but 3 of them do not carry out their process correctly; (0.7–0.9) exists but but 2 of them do not carry out their process correctly and 1 all the functionalities exist and work correctly.

As can be seen in Table 7 the Android applications that obtained the highest score were: How to Plant Vegetables - Vegetables at Home from the Informational Tools Category, PlantNet from the IA Tool Category and Gardenate from the Management Tool Category.

Table 7. Android apps with their App Features score

No.	Mobile applications	Total score
1	How to Plant Vegetables - Vegetables at Home	3.6
2	Plantsss	3.6
3	PlantNet	3.5
4	Gardenate	3.5
5	Gardenize, Garden Diary	3.5
6	Planter - Garden Planner	3.4
7	Plant Care Reminder	3.3
8	Garden Tags	3.2
9	Moon & Garden	3.1
10	Urban garden and planting	3.1
11	How to Grow Vegetables	3.1
12	PlantSnap	3.0
13	Flowerpot Orchards	3.0
14	Yara CheckIT	2.9
15	Plantnote: Plant Diary & Water	2.9
16	Veggie Garden	2.8
17	Gardroid - Vegetable Garden	2.5

Table 8. iOS apps with their App Features score.

No.	Mobile applications	Total score
1	PictureThis	5.0
2	Plant & Tree Identifier	5.0
3	PlantSnap - identify plants	5.0
4	PlantIn: Plant Identifier	4.0
5	Garden Planner	3.3
6	NatureID: Plant Identification	3.1
7	Veggie Garden Planner	3.0
8	Planter: Garden Planner	3.0
9	Tomato & Basilic	3.0
10	Gaia - Holistic Patch Planner	2.4
11	Agrobase - weed	2.3
12	Plantie	2.0
13	PlantNet	2.0
14	iplant - Plant Identification	2.0
15	V for Green	1.4

The iOS applications that obtained the highest score according to Table 8 were PictureThis from the IA Tools Category, V for Green from the Management Tools Category and Agrobase - weed from the Informative Tool Category.

Finally, combining the Assessment and Functionality scores of the applications reviewed by each operating system, the Apps that meet the majority of the analyzed characteristics were identified. Table 9 shows the applications with the highest scores by category and operating system.

Table 9. Mobile applications by categories most scored in the analysis

SW	Mobile applications	Rating score	Score functionality	Total score	Category
Android	PlantNet	7.26	3.5	10.8	AI Tools
	Plant Care Reminder	4.31	3.3	7.6	Management Tools
	Plantnote: Plant Diary & Water	4.34	2.9	7.2	Informational Tools
iOS	PictureThis	8.01	5.0	13.0	AI Tools
	Planter: Garden Planner	4.71	3.0	7.7	Management Tools
	Agrobase - weed	2.59	2.3	4.9	Informational Tools

Carrying out a comparative analysis of the main features reviewed and the rating given by the SensorTower Tool about the internationalization and user visibility, we identify in Table 10 that 2 applications (PictureThis and PlantNet) scored the best. These are the A and A + rated apps within the SensorTower Tool, so we could conclude that these applications are the ones that meet most of the necessary characteristics in apps to manage home gardens.

Table 10. Results with the SensorTower tool

Mobile applications		Score sensor tower	Score fun-ctionality	Rating score	Total score
Android	PlantNet	A	2,0	7,3	9,3
	PlantSnap	A	3,0	5,2	8,2
iOS	PictureThis	A +	5,0	8,0	13,0
	PlantSnap - identify plants	A−	5,0	5,1	10,1
	PlantIn: Plant Identifier	A−	4,0	5,2	9,2

The use of mobile applications becomes essential to improve the state of crops, since they provide tools to obtain better production, help in the prevention of diseases and pests and reduce negative effects, such the ones that are presented when neglecting to maintain the appropriate temperature in crops.

5   Conclusions and Future Work

Through this study, it was possible to verify that 100% of the applications analyzed have a Freemiun payment method, meaning that not all their functionalities are free, additionally we see that the best rated (PictureThis and PlantNet) are those that use artificial intelligence to control crops.

The SensorTower Tool was very helpful since it allowed to segregate from the total of applications that were initially considered. We chose to work with the applications that had the highest scores according to different evaluated indicators. When comparing the evaluation results with the study carried out in this article, it was confirmed that the chosen applications were the best scored in the tool.

Currently, it is essential that in the creation of mobile applications they have marketing strategies and App Store Optimization ASO since it is a tool that helps applications to position themselves in the first places of search engines and gives visibility to the app in Marketplace, managing to increase the downloads of the app. The ASO consists of applying a series of techniques to improve positioning, such as doing key-word research or optimizing the app, it is a job that must be renewed over time and must conform to the algorithms of the search engines with which it works. Positioning is essential in a new market where everything related to mobile devices is so dynamic.

On the other hand, the interest in finding ways and methods to facilitate, improve and learn mechanisms of care and control of orchards has motivated the creation of applications that meet this purpose. The use of technological tools has been shown to be an effective way to automate processes and integrate people or farmers into a world that was not known before. The inclusion of current mechanisms such as artificial intelligence, Big Data and Machine Learning are technologies that sow profits. These technologies make it easier for farmers to be able to anticipate natural events, diseases or pests, yields, processes and make the best decisions. It is possible today to find a range of applications, from those that allow early identification of diseases and damage assessment.

For future considerations of work applied to the orchards, it is recommended to include new technologies that handle artificial intelligence, computer vision, which could effectively allow the recognition of the problems that are affecting the orchards. Create predictive models to improve agronomic decision making, detection of nutritional deficiencies in crops, among other relevant applications that continue to strengthen this current innovative paradigm.

References

1. FAO: Huerto Familiar Integrado (2009)
2. Vergara-Lozano, V., Medina-Moreira, J., Rochina, C., Garzón-Goya, M., Sinche-Guzmán, A., Bucaram-Leverone, M.: An ontology-based decision support system for the management of home gardens. Commun. Comput. Inf. Sci. **749**, 47–59 (2017)
3. FAO: E-Agriculture Strategy Guide. The Food and Agriculture Organization of the United Nations and International Telecommunication Union, Bangkok (2016)
4. Barrón Ruiz, Á., Muñoz Rodríguez, J.M.: Los huertos escolares comunitarios: fraguando espacios socioeducativos en y para la sostenibilidad. Foro Educ. **13**, 213–239 (2015)
5. Arce Valladares, P.: Importancia de los Huertos familiares en la Seguridad Alimentaria y Nutricional. https://www.zamorano.edu/2019/12/20/importancia-de-los-huertos-familiares-en-la-seguridad-alimentaria-y-nutricional/
6. Dahnil, D.P., Hassan, R.: Wireless sensor networks: a framework for community and educational gardens. Adv. Sci. Lett. **24**, 1153–1157 (2018)
7. Kumar, A., Nath, S., Balpande, R., Kumar, P., Mishra, A., Kumar, V.: Decision support system for agro technology (DSSAT) modeling for estimation of rice production and validation. J. Pharmacogn. Phytochem. **8** (2019)
8. Red de Especialistas en Agricultura: Agrotechnology, a safe bet for startups. https://agricultrers.com/la-agrotecnologia-una-apuesta-segura-las-startups/
9. Maldonado, I., Monsalve, E.: Training for teacher management in the promotion and development of an environmental culture. Mundo Fesc. **7**, 98–105 (2017)
10. Campoconectado: The optimization of resources in Agro through technology. http://www.camponectado.com/index.php/2019/05/17/la-optimizacion-de-recursos-en-el-agro-a-traves-de-la-tecnologia/
11. Carrión, G., Huerta, M., Barzallo, B.: Internet of Things (IoT) applied to an urban garden. In: Proceedings - 2018 IEEE 6th International Conference on Future Internet of Things and Cloud, FiCloud 2018, pp. 155–161. Institute of Electrical and Electronics Engineers Inc. (2018)
12. Gomar, P., Cabrera, M., Marín-Roig, J.: Desarrollo de un sistema electrónico para controlar el crecimiento de las plantas de un huerto vertical hidropónico. Univ. Politècnica València Esc. Politècnica Super. Gandia (2020)

13. Stickel, O., Ludwig, T.: Computer supported urban gardening. In: Proceedings of the Conference on Designing Interactive Systems: Processes, Practices, Methods, and Techniques, DIS, pp. 77–80. Association for Computing Machinery (2014)
14. Lafuente, A.B., Lopez, A., Carlos, A., Sánchez, M.: Diseño y control domótico de un sistema de riego automático para un huerto urbano en el hogar. Universitat Oberta de Catalunya (UOC) (2019)
15. Codeluppi, G., Cilfone, A., Davoli, L., Ferrari, G.: VegIoT garden: a modular IoT management platform for urban vegetable gardens. In: 2019 IEEE International Workshop on Metrology for Agriculture and Forestry, MetroAgriFor 2019 – Proceedings, pp. 121–126. Institute of Electrical and Electronics Engineers Inc. (2019)
16. Morán Alonso, N., Luis Fernández de Casadevante, J.: A desalambrar. Agricultura urbana, huertos comunitarios y regulación urbanística. Hábitat y Soc. (2014)
17. Lagos-Ortiz, K., Medina-Moreira, J., Sinche-Guzmán, A., Garzón-Goya, M., Vergara-Lozano, V., Valencia-García, R.: Mobile applications for crops management. In: Valencia-García, R., Alcaraz-Mármol, G., Del Cioppo-Morstadt, J., Vera-Lucio, N., Bucaram-Leverone, M. (eds.) CITI 2018. CCIS, vol. 883, pp. 57–69. Springer, Cham. https://doi.org/10.1007/978-3-030-00940-3_5
18. Khajouei, A., Zare, D., Haghighi, A.B.: The feasibility of utilizing a mobile app for expansion of urban agriculture. In: CIGR-AgEng Conference, Aarhus, Denmark, 26–29 June 2016, Abstracts and Full Papers, vol. 1, pp. 1–7 (2016)
19. Samonte, M.J.C., Signo, E.P.E., Gayomali, R.J.M., Rey, W.P., Serrano, E.A.: Phyto: an IoT urban gardening mobile app. In: ACM International Conference Proceeding Series, pp. 135–139. Association for Computing Machinery (2019)
20. Free Apps Native: How to grow vegetables (2019)
21. Ghosh, I., Banerjee, G., Sarkar, U., Bannerjee, G., Das, S.: Artificial intelligence in agriculture: a literature survey artificial intelligence in agriculture: a literature survey view project site specific crop recommendation view project artificial intelligence in agriculture: a literature survey (2018)

Automation of Poultry Production Monitoring Through Web Services

Maritza Aguirre-Munizaga[1(✉)] [ID], Jorge Romero-Sánchez[1] [ID],
Jefferson Quinde-Gonzabay[1] [ID], and Teresa Samaniego-Cobo[1,2] [ID]

[1] Ingeniería en Ciencias de la Computación, Facultad de Ciencias Agrarias, Universidad Agraria del Ecuador, Av. 25 de Julio y Pio Jaramillo, P.O. BOX 09-04-100, Guayaquil, Ecuador
{maguirre,tsamaniego}@uagraria.edu.ec
[2] Ingeniería Industrial, Universidad Politécnica Salesiana, Robles 107 y Chambers, Guayaquil, Ecuador

Abstract. To comply with the implementation of this research, all the logical architecture was developed in free hardware and software, open-source, with a very low cost in the market. By using the Arduino microcontroller board, the sensors of ambient temperature, ambient humidity, toxic gases, soil moisture, food level, and water level were implemented. The Raspberry Pi4 minicomputer was also used as hardware so that the poultry keeper could upload the daily records of the poultry house and thus visualize all the environmental information of the poultry house in the developed web system. The validation of the results was focused on the costs and automation of decision making by the poultry managers, taking as a comparison the commercial systems used by large national and international poultry farms.

Keywords: Raspberry Pi · Poultry farm · Monitoring system · RESTful Web service

1 Introduction

In Ecuador some large companies and micro enterprises are fully dedicated to poultry farming, they use rustic methods to carry out their poultry meat production processes, which require a large number of human resources. According to data from the Food and Agriculture Organization of the United Nations in developing countries, the type of housing and equipment used allows monitoring of the climatic conditions provided to the chickens, but these houses are expensive and require significant poultry rotation to be viable [1]. In addition, there are high costs for water, electricity, and feeding for broiler type chickens. Currently, broiler farming is on the rise, due to its meat and eggs fast production [2].

For this reason, it is necessary to control environmental factors according to the age of the chickens, thus achieving direct benefits to the poultry farmer by reducing diseases and mortality of the chickens.

R. Valencia-García et al. (Eds.): CITI 2021, CCIS 1460, pp. 188–200, 2021.
https://doi.org/10.1007/978-3-030-88262-4_13

This has pressured national poultry companies to automate and technical their different processes, such as production monitoring and control, marketing, and finally its distribution, to optimize the company's processes and resources. Poultry production in Ecuador is one of the most significant sources of employment for people either in the countryside or in the city, thanks to the different processes needed for the production of broiler chickens, from the germination of seed, breeding in poultry farms, and concluding with the slaughter of these. A study carried out by the National Poultry Farmers Corporation indicates that the poultry industry in Ecuador generates around 25,000 direct sources of employment and around 50,000 indirect sources of employment [3].

Automation refers to the intervention of machines in the daily tasks performed by humans, thus eliminating human intervention, which benefits the majority of people engaged in this economic activity by allowing teams to be more productive, reducing errors in processes, improving integrity, and optimizing the time that can be invested in other priority tasks.

In Ecuador, a large number of people have dedicated themselves to the raising of poultry in artisanal poultry plants, seeing in them a very sustainable capital, many times without taking into account the proper control of their installations and even generating losses for the poultry farmer [4].

Sometimes, quick actions are taken to avoid the negative effects on the poultry, proposing that this proposal will be of low economic investment and that it will facilitate control from almost everywhere in the world through a web page. According to the documentary research, some sensors and components are used to automate the monitoring of production in a poultry farm. Therefore, factors such as low cost, effectiveness, and positive use of the sensors included in the systems architecture are considered [5].

This research generated the design of a prototype that allows the owners of poultry farms to control and monitor important processes to improve the development and production of broiler type fattening poultry that are carried out traditionally, allowing innovation in line with technological evolution [6]. The implementation of the system at the "Avícola Romero y Hnos" farm is presented as a case study. Section two presents the related works, section three the methodology used for the development, section four an evaluation of comparative factors of cost and use of the system, as well as relevant data collected in the same.

2   Related Works

In this study, an embedded system for monitoring a poultry farm was developed. For validation, the "Romero y Hnos." poultry farm was used as a case study, where technology based on the use of sensors was implemented to collect data on temperature ammonia levels, soil and environmental humidity, and water levels. Several types of research generated worldwide on this topic have been used as references. In Indonesia, research result shows that a web-based system can be used to monitor ammonia levels, chicken food weight, and ambient temperature. According to the authors, the farmer can monitor chicken farms via the web and receive SMS notifications about situations that need to be addressed immediately [7].

In other research conducted at the Agricultural University in Peshawar, in the North West Frontier province of Pakistan, a one day experiment is presented, where the feasibility and reliability of a WSN based poultry farm monitoring system are evaluated[8]. At the same time, studies are presented where the tests are carried out according to the criteria of connectivity, functionality, and delay. According to [9], in tests with gas, temperature, and humidity sensors there is a delay of between 5 and 19 s in information sending. It was also identified in this case that, this time can change because there are aspects that can inhibit the internet connection, such as the number of devices connected to a network.

In the State of Brunei, a research project was conducted that helped reduce the mortality rate of chickens to improve the productivity of the farm by automating the monitoring process of temperature, humidity, air quality level, and food feeder, Internet of Things (IoT) and Wireless Sensor Networks (WSN) was used [10].

3 Design and Implementation

3.1 Architecture

Free open-source hardware and software, which is accessible and inexpensive in the market, were used for the development of the entire logic architecture. The Arduino microcontroller board allowed the interconnection with the sensors in the shed.

The sensors and actuators were placed in strategic locations in the shed, away from direct contact with temperature control devices such as fans and electric heaters that could interfere with their correct operation.

The sensors were connected to our Arduino microcontroller board with an Ethernet Shield board, which is responsible for exporting the environmental variables obtained in the poultry house to a database located in a hosting service, as well as the poultry keeper can enter the daily records from the interface created and enabled in the Raspberry Pi4.

The parameters monitored are as follows:

- Ambient temperature.
- Ambient humidity.
- Toxic gases.
- Soil moisture.
- Food level.
- Water level.

The Raspberry Pi4 minicomputer serves as a computer for the poultry housekeeper to upload the daily records of the poultry house and visualize all its environmental information in the developed system.

Figure 1 shows the type of architecture chosen, which is a three tiers client-server architecture.

Layer 1 shows the interface, which allows the user to interact directly with the system or vice versa, its function is to pass the actions performed by the client within the presentation layer to the business layer. In this case Raspberry Pi works as a computer and allows access to the system.

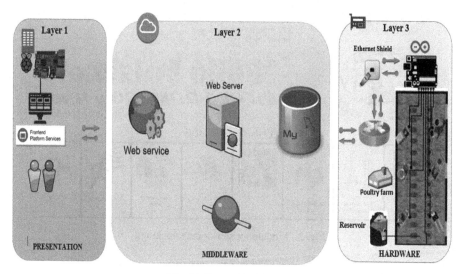

Fig. 1. System architecture

Layer 2 is the data access layer (Middleware), the same that allowed storing the values collected by the sensors used in the project, the basic function is to store and return data to the business layer. It should be noted that the platform uses web services, so it is characterized for being multiplatform and distributed. In this layer the RESTful Web services [11], are also used to allow the management of web services with defined methods, and handles the XML protocol, so that each service is identified only with a single URI.

Layer 3 is the business layer (Hardware), it processes the information and sends the answers after the process. This layer communicates with layer 1 to receive the request and present the results and with layer 2 to request the database manager to store or retrieve data from it.

3.2 Methodology

As part of the development of this project, the coding of the web system was carried out using the following tools:

- Bootstrap – Framework
- Php – Programming language
- Mysql – Database
- JavaScript – Descriptive graphics

C++ language was used for the programming of the different sensors and actuators, considering that several tests were needed with the end user since he uses the application.

Figure 2 shows a view of the interface that allows us to track the information from the sensors.

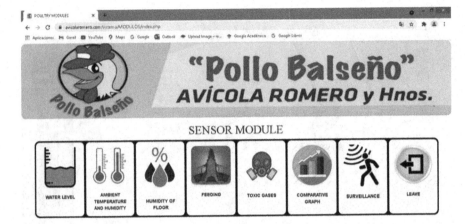

Fig. 2. Module for sensor data tracking.

At the Arduino microcontroller level, the connection of the sensors with their respective libraries was implemented. These components are based on parameters that help validate if threshold values are exceeded, if this occurs, corrective processes are automatically initiated to help reduce the mortality rate of chickens on the farm. The sensors used are detailed below:

Ultrasonic Sensor
This sensor was used to measure the level of chicken feed inside the poultry house. A range was established for issuing alerts according to the level of the chicken feeders, if the distance is greater than 50 cm "it is out of range", if the distance is less than 49 cm and greater than 30 cm "the feeder is full" if the distance is less than 29 cm and greater than 5 cm "the feeder is half full" and if the distance is less than 5 cm "the feeder is empty".

Dht11 Sensor
It measures the humidity and temperature of the environment, we use it because of its low cost and ease of use. Besides, it also works with libraries that facilitate the use of formulas.

Water Level Sensor
An ultrasonic sensor was used to measure the approach of water, due that this sensor has two cylinders, one of which emits an ultrasound that bounces off the objects and the other cylinder receives the captured signal.

The water reservoir has a size of 2 m high, where the following ranges have been established:

If the reservoir is greater than 1 cm and less than 40 cm "Reservoir_Low_River" if the reservoir is greater than 40 cm and less than 130 cm "Reservoir_Medium", and if the reservoir is greater than 130 cm and less than 201 "Reservoir_Full".

Carbon Dioxide Sensor

The gas sensor used to measure air quality [12], it is used for the detection of NH3 (ammonia), NOx, alcohol, benzene, smoke, CO2, etc.

It was used to detect carbon dioxide gas inside the poultry house since this type of gas is harmful to the health of the chickens. A range was established to measure air contamination with carbon monoxide. If the value of the sensor is less than or equal to 55 ppm "the air is normal" if the value is greater than or equal to 56 and less than or equal to 65 "the air contains some CO2" if the value is greater than or equal to 74 and less than or equal to 350 "carbon dioxide".

Ammonia Sensor

The sensor used to measure gas, specifically for ammonia. We have selected this sensor since the presence of ammonia in chickens is harmful to their health. The functionality of the sensors is as follows: it is initialized in the off state, once turned on it begins to collect data, if the sensor status is high "detect ammonia" and if it remains in the low state "No ammonia present".

Hygrometer Sensor

A sensor specifically used to read the amount of moisture in the surrounding soil is used to measure the humidity of the poultry litter inside the house. A range was established with respect to humidity, if the humidity value is greater than 70 "Wet litter" and if the humidity value is less than or equal to 68 "Dry litter".

The storage part of the database is done by sending information through the GET method.

To generate a web interface that allows monitoring and displaying the parameters and sensors mentioned above, the following modules were generated:

Production Control Module

The module allows keeping a record of the important data that the poultry farm produces daily, among them, we have the mortality record, which consists of keeping the number of chickens that die for a certain period belonging to a specific flock.

Food Registration

Stores the number of bags that are consumed by the chickens in a flock during the day. Food reception allows keeping track of the type of feed that is received and how many bags are purchased.

Average Weight

Stores the total weight of a selected sample of chickens to keep track of the weight of certain flocks, the result is obtained through the following formula:

$$\text{Average weight} = \text{Number of chickens/weight pounds} \qquad (1)$$

Closing Lot
It has three sub-modules, which are: closing average weight per flock, which is responsible for closing the flock, since it records the closing date or the day on which the chickens are sold, in addition, we must calculate the weight with which the closing has been generated with the following formula:

$$\text{Closing weight per lot} = \text{pound net/chickens sold} \tag{2}$$

Closing Weight Per Lot
It allows to record the percentage of death of a given flock, the number of chickens in the flock, and the number of chickens that have died at the flock closing date. The formula used is as follows:

$$\text{Mortality rate closure} = (\text{Total dead chickens} * 100)/\text{Number of incoming chickens} \tag{3}$$

Closing Food Consumed by Lot
It records with the closing date the quantity of bags of feed consumed by a given batch. The formula used is as follows:

$$\text{Closing food consumed per lot} = \text{Bag}_1 + \text{Bag}_2 + \text{Bag}_3 + \text{Bag}_n \tag{4}$$

Poultry Data Recording Module
In this module, the data of the poultry farm are registered in the database, such as new users (manager, administrator, poultry house manager, veterinarian), new flocks that enter the different poultry houses, entry of the poultry houses, the baby chickens suppliers, the entry of the diseases that will be associated with the daily deaths of the chickens, the registration of the types of balanced feed used by the poultry farm, as well as the registration of the breeds of broiler chicken with which the poultry farm woks [13].

4   Results

In the implementation of the Embedded System for the poultry farm [14]; first, the costs were evaluated and then the execution times of the sensors and system performance. The methodology used for this estimation is the cost benefit analysis, in an area of approximately 802 square meters, since in relation to the average price of the sensors, its benefit in time factor for the activities carried out in the poultry farm is evaluated. As part of the implementation, the sensors that automate the various activities detailed in Table 1 were acquired.

- Cost estimation: The cost comparison of commercial hardware and the hardware implemented in the poultry farm of the case study was performed.
- Time estimation: The utilization times in the different activities of the farm were evaluated manually and using the system developed.

4.1 Cost Estimation

Based on the first evaluation (costs), which is shown in Table 1, the cost of each of the functionalities implemented to carry out the different activities of the system was evaluated, identifying that the system has a cost decrease of 69.06% which is equivalent to $834.49 in system savings over systems currently on the market.

Table 1. Hardware cost comparison

Activities	Average in the market	System costs	Cost differencing (system-market)	%
Control of ambient temperature in the shed	$176,63	$34,50	$−142,13	−80,5%
Humidity control of the environment in the shed	$135,67	$23,96	$−111,71	−82,3%
Evaluation and monitoring of toxic gases	$141,90	$25,68	$−116,22	−81,9%
Soil moisture control	$381,96	$40,83	$−341,13	−89,3%
Food level tracking	$256,21	$153,91	$−102,30	−39,9%
Water level monitoring	$106	$85,00	$−21,00	−19,8%
Total	$1.198,37	$363,88	$−834,49	−69,6%

The table shows the reduced cost value and percentage.

4.2 Time Estimation

In the second evaluation, the human resources (10 people) of the farm "Avícola Romero y Hnos." were taken as a case study and were asked to perform the different activities that are generally used for the monitoring of poultry production. The analysis compares the time taken by the people performing each of the activities with and without the use of the web system, identifying that in total the implemented technology reduced the time by 85.38%.

In Table 2, we can see that the activities had a greater reduction in time with the use of the application than they normally perform take to perform the same activities without the system and with the help of their assistant. In addition to the fact that manual work is often inefficient, it is also cumbersome and error prone.

4.3 System Information

The implementation of the web system was carried out integrating both the hardware and software developed so that they work together and thus the users of the poultry farm could have a more adequate management of the control and monitoring in the poultry fattening cycle having all the values centralized in the system.

Table 2. Time comparison with the use of the system

Activities	Average time in manual activities (minutes)	Average time with use of the system (minutes)	Time difference with use of the system	%
Calculation of mortality rate	50	1,2	−48,8	−97,6%
Food level check	15	0,3	−14,7	−98,0%
Water level check	5	0,3	−4,7	−94,0%
Temperature and humidity control in the house environment	5	1,2	−3,8	−76,0%
Soil moisture control	15	1,2	−13,8	−92,0%
Air quality validation	20	1	−19	−95,0%
Overall Average	2,052	0,3	−1,752	−85,38%

The table shows the reduced time value and percentage.

Figure 3 shows the main menu options, highlighting the production control module and the sensor monitoring; additionally, reports can be used, as well as adding data from the sheds.

WELCOME: "Jefferson - Administrator"

CONTROL AND MONITORING AUTOMATION SYSTEM POULTRY FARM "ROMERO & HERMANOS"

MAIN MENU

| PRODUCTION CONTROL MODULE | SENSOR MODULE | POULTRY DATA RECORD MODULE | GENERAL REPORTING MODULE | POULTRY INFORMATION | GET OUT OF THE SYSTEM |

Fig. 3. Main system view

Figure 4 shows the descriptive statistics obtained by the ammonia and carbon monoxide sensors. This monitoring is applied in the implementation, given that if the temperature is not controlled, the chickens become ill with bronchitis, a viral disease that causes sneezing, coughing, and obstruction of the respiratory tract, and in the latter case death [15].

The level of ammonia and carbon monoxide in the environment depends on the humidity in the poultry litter since humidity should be between 20% and 35%.

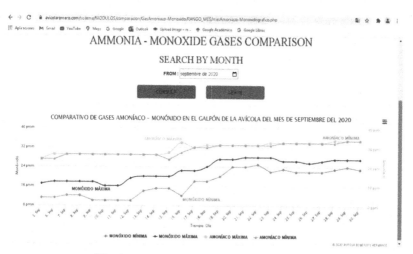

Fig. 4. Ammonium and carbon dioxide levels

Figure 5 shows the mortality results of a flock of chickens, the total number of chickens that entered and the total number of chickens that died in their developmental stage, a well as the percentage of mortality. Due to the use of the soil moisture and toxic gas sensor implemented, levels of gases detrimental to poultry health were controlled, significantly reducing the rate of disease.

Figure 6 shows the result of the flock named PAMPA001 (PAM001). The graph compares a previous flock and the flock that was automated, showing all the results so that the administrator can observe the percentage of mortality, total weight, total dead chickens, total food consumed, and total incoming chickens.

This study also allowed sending an automatic alert notification to the user via WhatsApp, SMS, and email. It is also emphasized that thermal comfort is a conclusive element in broiler production since it allows a relationship between chicken consumption and chicken meat production. Despite the automation technology available, poultry farming still depends on an expert to observe the process and set these control parameters. Hence, a framework created for monitoring and decision making in poultry farming is referred to [16]. In this research, the architecture of a plant that takes advantage of emerging modern technologies is generated, such as sensor networks, control theory, and remote monitoring, to manage temperature and humidity within a poultry house. The result provides a web-based monitoring system.

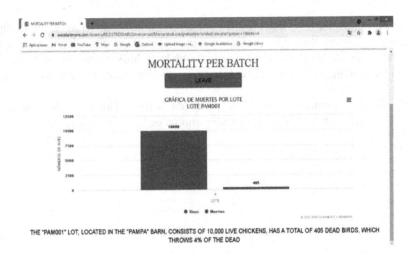

Fig. 5. Batch mortality PAM001

Fig. 6. Comparative production values

5   Conclusions and Future Work

With the implementation of this poultry system developed with the use of free software and hardware, low cost, and easy access, the goal proposed at the beginning of the project of making a system based on the control theory in the poultry farm "Romero & Hermanos" was achieved. At the same time, we were able to successfully meet the requirements that were determined during the information gathering process.

Nowadays the Romero & Hermanos poultry farm has a self-managed system that allows them to improve the control and monitoring of the most important critical processes for the development of broilers. It allows them to visualize directly on a web platform where all the data sent by the sensors are stored and at the same time to generate management reports that help make important decisions and corrections of the processes that are going out of the normal parameters or that in turn influence the development and production of broilers. In the future, we expect to implement a mobile application that will allow us to obtain important notifications directly through a smartphone and to add the systematization of the farm's accounting situation, including e-billing.

Thanks to the low cost of this poultry system, compared to other systems used by large national and international poultry companies that range in price from $60,000 to $150,000 US dollars, this research conducted at the Agrarian University of Ecuador has become a great help for small and medium poultry producers at the national level thanks to the scope and potential it offers them, thus having the necessary tools to maintain competitiveness in the market with their main rivals that threaten to wipe out these small poultry companies.

References

1. Food and Agriculture Organization of the United Nations: Poultry Development Review (2013)
2. Meluzzi, A., Sirri, F.: Welfare of broiler chickens (2009). https://doi.org/10.4081/ijas.2009. s1.161
3. Revista Lideres: More than 50 million birds are raised in the fields and sheds. https://www. revistalideres.ec/lideres/50-millones-aves-crian-campos.html. Accessed 17 June 2021
4. avicultura.info: The interview with Pablo Anhalzer, president of CONAVE in Ecuador. https:// avicultura.info/en/the-interview-with-pablo-anhalzer/. Accessed 20 June 2021
5. Bea, J.G., Cruz, J.S.D.: Chicken farm monitoring system using sensors and Arduino micro-controller. In: ACM International Conference Proceeding Series (2019). https://doi.org/10. 1145/3361570.3361607
6. Zheng, H., Zhang, T., Fang, C., Zeng, J., Yang, X.: Design and implementation of poultry farming information management system based on cloud database. Animals **11**, 1–15 (2021). https://doi.org/10.3390/ani11030900
7. Budiarto, R., Gunawan, N.K., Nugroho, B.A.: Smart chicken farming: monitoring system for temperature, ammonia levels, feed in chicken farms. In: IOP Conference Series: Materials Science and Engineering (2020). https://doi.org/10.1088/1757-899X/852/1/012175
8. Murad, M., Yahya, K.M., Hassan, G.M.: Web based poultry farm monitoring system using wireless sensor network. In: Proceedings of 6th International Conference on Frontiers of Information Technology, FIT 2009 (2009). https://doi.org/10.1145/1838002.1838010
9. Masriwilaga, A.A., Al-hadi, T.A.J.M., Subagja, A., Septiana, S.: Monitoring system for broiler chicken farms based on Internet of Things (IoT). Telekontran J. Ilm. Telekomun. Kendali dan Elektron. Terap. 7 (2019). https://doi.org/10.34010/telekontran.v7i1.1641
10. Hambali, M.F.H., Patchmuthu, R.K., Wan, A.T.: IoT Based Smart Poultry Farm in Brunei. In: 2020 8th International Conference on Information and Communication Technology, ICoICT 2020. Institute of Electrical and Electronics Engineers Inc. (2020). https://doi.org/10.1109/ ICoICT49345.2020.9166331
11. Paredes-Valverde, M.A., Alor-Hernández, G., Rodríguez-González, A., Valencia-García, R., Jiménez-Domingo, E.: A systematic review of tools, languages, and methodologies for mashup development. Softw. Pract. Exp. **45**, 365–397 (2015). https://doi.org/10.1002/SPE. 2233
12. Arduino: Gravity: Analog CO2 Gas Sensor I Arduino Official Store. https://store.arduino.cc/ usa/gravity-analog-co2-gas-sensor. Accessed 20 June 2021
13. Sassi, N.B., Averós, X., Estevez, I.: Technology and poultry welfare, /pmc/articles/PMC5082308/ (2016). https://doi.org/10.3390/ani6100062

14. Sinduja, K., Jenifer, S.S., Sri Abishek, M., Sivasankari, B.: Automated control system for poultry farm based on embedded system. Int. Res. J. Eng. Technol. **3**, 2395–2456 (2016)

15. Choukidar, G.A., Dawande, N.A.: Smart poultry farm automation and monitoring system. In: 2017 International Conference on Computing, Communication, Control and Automation, ICCUBEA 2017. Institute of Electrical and Electronics Engineers Inc. (2018). https://doi.org/10.1109/ICCUBEA.2017.8463953

16. Lorencena, M.C., Southier, L.F.P., Casanova, D., Ribeiro, R., Teixeira, M.: A framework for modelling, control and supervision of poultry farming. Int. J. Prod. Res. **58**, 3164–3179 (2020). https://doi.org/10.1080/00207543.2019.1630768

A Brief Systematic Review of the Latest Advances in IOT Platforms in Agriculture

Elke Yerovi$^{(\boxtimes)}$ (iD), Carlota Delgado-Vera (iD), Wilson Molina-Oleas (iD), and Laura Ortega-Ponce (iD)

School of Engineering in Computing and Informatics, Faculty of Agrarian Sciences, Agrarian University of Ecuador, Av. 25 de Julio y Pio Jaramillo, P.O. BOX 09-04-100, Guayaquil, Ecuador
{eyerovi,cdelgado,wmolina,lortega}@uagraria.edu.ec

Abstract. Iot or Internet of Things is an innovative advance in technology that helps interconnectivity between smart devices and machines helping to reduce human intervention. The use of IOT platforms, their architectures, network technologies and devices allow to improve the efficiency and productivity of any type of industry or mass production, this research is focused on one of the most important fields which is agriculture. The Internet of Things (IoT) is related to millions of applications and various devices throughout the world that communicate with each other and can exchange data and perform cooperative tasks without the intervention of human beings. Considering the aforementioned facts, relevant information is provided for farmers and researchers with a clear perspective of the technologies, devices, architecture, network and sensors used in IoT, in addition to the solutions that IoT provides in the agriculture field.

Keywords: Internet of Things (IoT) · Agriculture · Architecture · Technology · Platform

1 Introduction

The need for technology in the agricultural field according to the authors [1] comes from a greater motivation to feed an entire population around the world; through the years the agricultural area has evolved to facilitate all processes and satisfy the needs through applications developed for agriculture. The authors from India [2] indicates that the IoT called as the Internet of Things is used to interconnect objects, humans and devices. There are different Internet Protocols that the IoT uses to connect several equipment with sensors and the environment to each other. Subsequently, the use of the Internet of Things in agriculture solves most of the challenges nowadays, giving solutions such as: IoT provides the techniques to control farms remotely and control operations with robot and actuator devices; IoT used for pesticides and fertilizers; IoT improves food quality monitoring systems and remotely controls product shipping locations; and IoT also is able to provide wearable devices to analyze health and sustainability issues.

According to the authors [3] the IoT benefits from some computer systems, such as smart systems, sensors and devices to computers in the cloud. In general, the Internet

© Springer Nature Switzerland AG 2021
R. Valencia-García et al. (Eds.): CITI 2021, CCIS 1460, pp. 201–215, 2021.
https://doi.org/10.1007/978-3-030-88262-4_14

and mobile communications facilitate the spatio-temporal connection between separate people with common experiences. Currently, the technological evolution is monitored by the devices that are installed in the physical and virtual scope of IoT.

With the advancement of technology, smart agriculture uses (ICT) as a means to increase production and economic benefits with the aim of reducing the impact on the environment. The authors [4] mention that one of the key elements of smart agriculture is agricultural management through information systems based on IoT (SIAF) that can process, monitor, plan, make decisions that support the administration of the farm.

Panamanian authors [5] indicate that the use of Information and communications technology (ICT) and the Internet of Things (IoT) allow the analysis of large amounts of data related to crops, through monitoring, supervision, processing, soil conditions, microclimatic, irrigation, fertilization among others. They also indicate that the connection of processes and people allow the capture of events and data, from which it can be stated that:

a) People's behaviour can be learnt. Assets and processes.
b) It is possible to improve corrective or preventive actions to external or internal states.
c) It is possible to increase or modify business processes within the aspects in the agricultural field such as crop control, quality management, food preservation or products transport that can be improved taking into account the requirements that lead to ICT applications where an analysis must be developed, functional design, development and implementation.

Finally, with the help of the Internet of Things, everything is implemented in the everyday lives of customers and recognized organizations, equipped with sensors and associated with the web, the IoT provides the solutions to the existing agriculture challenges.

This research will focus on describing the IoT or Internet of Things system, for which its concepts, architectures and technologies used for its implementation in agriculture will be described. IoT allows connecting different devices which generate information, and it can be processed and presented in reports to make better decisions when sowing and harvesting [6].

The work starts from the identification of the meaning of IoT in the present and future, based on personal experiences in the basic use of IoT in agriculture, then it is intended to establish concepts and later a series of investigations focused on the architecture is identified. It is important to explain the technologies embedded in devices and the technology applied with them, all of these topics in the area of agriculture.

2 Planning and Analisis of the Review

Using the Kitchenham Methodology methodology, who proposes a method for conducting systematic reviews, in order to guide researchers to evaluate and interpret related research for a particular research question, the search strategy, the search chain, inclusion/exclusion criteria, quality assessment, data extraction and data synthesis; thus obtaining a better result of IoT's in agriculture.

In order to carry out this research, three guiding questions were asked, which prompted the systematic review methodology. The focus of the question is to identify trends in the use of IoT in agriculture, considering the architectures used for the development of the platform that allows efficient and quick management. The research questions are related to the following topics; technologies, tools used by the IOT in agriculture, both hardware and software, type of architecture, how is it formed and proposals that have been designed or proposed to provide a solution in agriculture through the application of the Internet of Things.

2.1 Source Selections

Table 1 shows the sources where the systematic literature review was carried out, including virtual libraries that are listed below. In addition, the type of bibliographic source and period of publication of the files is specified. It is necessary to mention that the review was carried out on articles that contain the keywords according to the search.

Table 1. Search and source chain

Virtual Libraries	Type of Bibliographical source	Search applied to	Language
Science Direct	Electronic books	Key words	English
IEEE Explorer	Scientific papers		
Elsevier	Conferences		
Springer			
ACM DL Digital Library			

These databases were last searched on June 20, 2021 and the search results are exported to BibTeX format which is then downloaded and stored in the Mendeley reference. For the ACM digital library, the export function only for the BibTeX format exporting the citation data of the literature, but not the abstracts. Therefore, Mendeley Web Importer uses the Chrome plug-in that allows the citation information, including the abstract, to be imported directly into Mendeley.

2.2 Search Strategies

Once the search sources have been defined, it is necessary to describe the processes and criteria for the selection and evaluation of studies. Search criteria were applied in order to reduce the probability of bias. It should be considered that the inclusion and exclusion criteria should be based on the research question. Therefore, we have established that the studies should present new initiatives (for a maximum of 5 years) that consider the trend in the use of IOTs in agriculture, the results that are presented in Table 2.

As strategies in the most relevant research papers between 2017 and 2021. Due to language limitations, only studies written in English were considered. The search strings used were:

– (IoT in agriculture) and (evolution of IoT)
– (IoT technology) or (devices used in IoT)
– (IoT Plataform) or (sensors used in IoT)
– (IoT Architecture) or (IoT Layers)

Table 2. Scientific database search criteria

Knowledge area combination	Rank	Knowledge area	Search result
(IoT in agriculture) and (evolution of IoT)	2016–2021	Engineering and computing	30
(IoT technology) or (devices used in IoT)	2017–2021	Engineering and computing	58
(IoT Platform) or (sensors used in IoT)	2017–2021	Engineering and computing	38
(IoT Architecture) or (IoT Layers)	2017–2021	Engineering and computing	26

2.3 Inclusion and Exclusion Criteria

We discarded those articles that were not directly related to the use of the Internet of Things in the domain of Agriculture. In addition, we use the following exclusion criteria:

• Research papers not written in English.
• Master and PhD thesis.
• Duplicate research papers obtained from Google Scholar and Web of Scence.

The inclusion criteria for the information from the primary studies consisted of articles about the different types of platforms, architectures, technologies and tools used by IOT's for the development of applications that help automate processes in agriculture. Therefore, we browsed Google Scholar and the SCOPUS database using the keywords "tools", "platforms", "systems", "IoT technologies", "architectures", among others.

3   Literature Development and Review

This section presents the execution of the systematic review that consisted of the search for research works related to trends in the use of IoT in agriculture in addition to its architecture, in selected digital libraries, considering the inclusion and exclusion of criteria. In addition, this review provided answers to the research questions presented in Sect. 2.1. These responses are discussed in the following sections.

3.1 Technology and Tools Used in Agriculture Both Hardware and Software

The Internet of Things (IOT) is defined as a network of physical objects, in which different devices of all types and sizes are connected, such as vehicles, smartphones, telephones, electrical appliances, toys, cameras, medical instruments and industrial systems, animals, people, buildings, all connected, all communication and information exchange based on stipulated protocols to achieve smarts environment, positioning, tracking, security and control and even real-time personnel online monitoring, online update, process control and administration [7,8].

In recent years, the use of technology in applications focused on human life has become widespread, which through the use of the IoT has spread to different areas such as; home, transportation, community, and nationwide in; remote monitoring, smart grids, infrastructure and defense [9]. IoT-based solutions are being developed to automatically maintain and monitor agricultural farms with minimal human involvement. Smart agriculture based on IoT consists of four main components [10] physical structure, data acquisition, data processing and data analysis.

According to the literature reviewed, the authors [11] mention that there are various criteria to apply IoT in agriculture, in this case it provides a classification of IoT applications for smart agriculture according to seven categories, such as: smart monitoring, smart water management, agrochemical applications, disease management, smart harvesting, supply chain management and smart farming practices. It must be considered that the Internet of Things is made up of devices connected to each other, whose purpose is to monitor, process and temporarily store blocks of data. The technology used is becoming more and more intelligent in the processing of this data, thus being the communication more real and effective in a direct or indirect way [12]. The article Internet of things (IoT) and agricultural unmanned aerial vehicles (UAV) in smart agriculture, mentions that IoT adopts various enabling techniques, such as wireless sensor networks, cloud computing, big data, embedded systems, protocols and security architectures, communication protocols and web services. On [13] the authors proposed an Internet of Things (IoT) sensing platform that provides information on the state of the soil and the surrounding environment in terms of pH, humidity, texture, color, air temperature and light; additionally, it combines computer vision to further analyze and understand the characteristics of the soil. The purpose of the System was to carry out adequate control of plant growth, obtaining better products and increased productivity. On [14] the researches presented a framework, which was called AgriTech, optimizing various agricultural resources (water, fertilizers, insecticides, and labor) in agriculture using IoT. Farmers could monitor crops and farmland remotely using a mobile terminal device. On [15] the authors proposed a decision support system (DSS) based on the integration of wireless sensors and actuation network technology (WSAN). Suggested actions were aimed at reducing water waste and improving crop yield according to climatic conditions. In "Precision Agriculture Design Method Using a Distributed Computing Architecture on Internet of Things ContextSe" [16] proposes a distributed communication architecture using technologies, the objective of which is to help farmers to develop intelligent systems in both current and new facilities. On [17] introduces the SWAMP architecture, platform, and system implementations highlighting platform replicability and, as scalability is a major concern for IoT applications, includes a performance analysis of FIWARE components used on the platform.

It can be indicated that the technologies [18] used for the implementation of the internet of things in agriculture would be classified according to the technology used such as the use of sensors, data transmission technology, sensor network technology and big data technology:

a. **Cloud Computing:** By using this technology, there is generalized access to shared resources through the network and thus operations can be carried out [19]; in the field of informatics it is considered as a solution to facilitate data processing through the use of sensors, actuators and many other integrated devices [20, 21]. The authors [22] implemented a private IoT Cloud platform for precision agriculture and ecological monitoring, precision agriculture is used focusing on remote monitoring and IoT technology. Cloud computing is a great ally in the application of IoT in agriculture, for data processing in the efficient use of inputs such as fertilizers and pesticides, livestock control, indoor agriculture, greenhouses, cost reduction and stables, fish farming, monitoring of storage in water tanks, fuel tanks and updates made in Back-end, easy and fast development including collaboration with other systems in the cloud. At a technological level, there are advantages of using IoT with WSN networks in agriculture such as: high scalability, fault tolerance, low cost, long life, reconfigurable systems, information security, farmland management, quality of service (QoS) and dynamic management.

b. **Big Data Analysis and Self-Learning:** Big data analysis provides methods for the control and monitoring of different crops and their different stages [23]. The analysis of this (big) data would allow farmers and companies to extract value from it, improving their productivity [24]. In unsupervised learning, one of the most used algorithms is neural networks, because they provide optimal solutions at a high level. Intrusion detection has been performed using neural network principles and technology; Another important feature of the neural networks is that they provide modules for detection and data training [25]. Through the use of deep neural networks, an IoT-based hydroponic system allows to control the growth of the crop [26]. A project [27] that uses sensors to acquire the data of the temperature and humidity variables, both in the air and in the soil, to apply an automatic control, keeping a breakeven for the development of tomato seeds on a platform that allows to simulate the ideal conditions of the crop, it is free hardware.

c. **Networks and Communication Protocols:** The agricultural IoT network consists of different types of reach networks for communications. Several network technologies help to design a crop by using communication between sensors that allows obtaining soil data through tests such as pH, humidity, nutrient content, humidity, temperature. It is important to obtain the results of soil tests to obtain a high yield and generate good quality [28]. Communication protocols are the backbone of an IoT-based agricultural network system to run the applications [29]. They are also used to exchange data or information about products through the network. Use of a sensor network based on an IoT framework for monitoring and control in the agriculture field, using Thinkspeak technologies (IoT platform to collect and store sensor data in the cloud), with use of the MQTT protocol [30].

d. **Robotics:** In smart agriculture, multiple Agribots have been developed with the purpose of minimizing the amount of work by farmers by increasing the speed of production through advanced techniques. Agribots perform elementary functions like weeding, spraying, sowing, etc. All these robots are controlled through the use of IoT to increase the productivity of crops and the efficiency of the resources used. A multisensor robotics approach has been proposed for land characterization and mapping [31].

3.2 Type of IoT Architecture Used for Agriculture

Several reference architectures have been provided for IoT [32, 33, 34, 35]. In general, IoT files are represented as a layered architecture. According to Fig. 1, the reference architecture includes the following layers: device, network, session, application, business, management and security. The device layer consists of physical devices and sensors, this layer identifies and collects data and specific information generated by sensors and physical devices. The collected data is passed to the network layer. In essence the device layer bridges the gap between the physical world and the digital world. The network layer provides functionality for network connectivity and transport capabilities, this layer is also called the transport layer. This layer securely transmits the data collected from sensors to the session layer. The transmission medium can be wired or wireless.

Finally, the session layer is responsible for service management and consists of functions to configure up and down the association between the IoT endpoints.

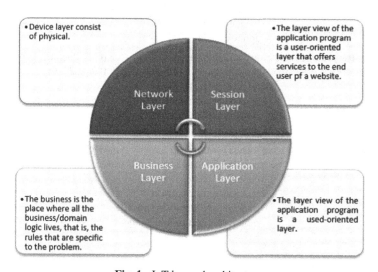

Fig. 1. IoT layered architecture

According to the review of articles from 2017 to the present time, it is summarized that the massification of IoT, it is important to consider some design aspects to establish standards of architectures for IoT, among them:

- Objective experimentation in order to break with the classic laboratory scheme.
- Scale to experiment with the real world.
- Heterogeneity, because the future of the IoT consists of a great diversity of devices integrated with other infrastructure and service delivery platforms. IoT devices are many, made up of heterogeneous nodes (sensors, actuators, QR and NFC tags, and mobile phones based on a sensing platform).
- Mobile, devices must interact with others in real-world scenes, and they must be transparent to users.
- User support and participation of the end user, which is the search for cost reduction to reach the end user and the segmentation of services and applications for smart cities.
- Reliability, to ensure smooth, uninterrupted operation.

Next, Table 3 presents a summary of the main architectures found in different works.

Table 3. P Main architecture in the IoT paradigm

Architecture	Description	Reference
Four layers	Sensor layer, hub and network layer, service management layer, and finally, application layer	(Hegde 2010) (Chen & Jin 2012)
Five layers ITU	The sensing layer, the access layer, the network layer, the mediation layer, and the application layers	(Chen & Jin 2012)
Alerts with Raspberry PI and Modem NBN	IoT solution based on projected light and sound alert by means of a Raspberry Pi card (Development Board), an NBN modem, a network power supply and a backup battery	(Gill, Phennel, Lane, & Phung 2016)
Three layers	Layers for devices, transmission and logic for control, such layers being: wireless sensor networks, transmission network, and data monitoring and central analysis	(Honghui et al. 2017)

(*continued*)

Table 3. (*continued*)

Architecture	Description	Reference
ICN (Information- Centric Networking)	Its key component is the hub, which acts as an intermediary communication element between clients and IoT devices. It promotes communication to an IoT device in two categories: 1) information that is dynamically generated by the reception of primitive controls; 2) information available on the device	(Suarez et al. 2016)
IoT – Bigdata – Data Mining	They apply two techniques called Canonical Polyadic Decomposition (CPD) and Tensor-Train Network (TT) to optimize the grouping of data in IoT systems, achieving a high compression rate for heterogeneous samples and thus significantly saving memory space, which makes Grouping of large volumes of data with low-end devices possible	(Zhang, Yang, Chen, & Li 2017)
Common three layers	An application layer (adding data, saving it, analyzing it and monitoring it), a network layer (network management and data processing) and the perception layer (sensor and actuator networks), this architecture is used to promote a data collection, analysis and transmission solution for the development of a security base and monitoring devices for agriculture	(Kodali, Soratkal, & Boppana 2017), (Lin & Yu 2013) y (Wu, Liu, Li, & Wang 2014)

(*continued*)

Table 3. (*continued*)

Architecture	Description	Reference
IoT Cloud	With data processing and mining techniques, cloud platforms such as; Software as a Service (SaaS), Platform as a Service (PaaS) and Infrastructure as a Service (IaaS) all with acronyms in English, which provide tools for different IoT applications	(Kataoka, Uchihira, & Ikawa 2016)
IoT, WSN y Machine Learning	It uses a WSN (Wireless Sensor Network) wireless network architecture using Xbee devices that according to (XBee.cl, 2018) "are integrated solutions that provide a wireless means for interconnection and communication between devices using the IEEE 802.15.4 and Zigbee protocol", meanwhile, data entries are analyzed on a server with pre-established rules to issue early alerts through messages	(Patil & Thorat 2016)
Sensor node	Types of nodes are grouped such as gas reading (air pollutants, CO_2, O_2 and NO_2) and environmental conditions (temperature, humidity and acceleration), the data of the nodes are transmitted through ZigBee to a base station to be processed and thus create a decision tree and classifications of the data as translations for the user, the product of this study is a fuzzy matrix to predict conditions based on the knowledge of the system	(Edwards- Murphy, Magno, Whelan, O'Halloran, & Popovici 2016)

(*continued*)

Table 3. (*continued*)

Architecture	Description	Reference
EPC (Electronic Product Code)	It supports radio frequency and is an initiative to innovate and develop industry-driven standards, some components developed in it include: extended support of static data, integration to dynamic data, compatibility with non-IP devices, integration of an actuator interface, integration optional federated and extended discovery services and software agents	(Uckelmann et al. 2011)

3.3   Trend of Use of IoT in Agriculture

New technologies, genetics, precision agriculture, the use of sensors and actuators, and big data suggest that agribusiness is becoming a technology industry. Labor productivity in the Agricultural sector is the highest compared to other sectors such as utilities and manufacturing [36].

Precision agriculture deals with the very precise monitoring and control of land crops in order to manage the spatial and temporal variability of the soil. Smart logistics in agriculture includes: traceability, safety and quality of food, in addition to the handling of food, it imposes the dimension of perishability [37].

Modern agriculture does not end on the farm, it requires several processes during production time. It consists of five main elements

- Agriculture production.
- Input from the value chain that links producers with agrochemical agricultural equipment, seeds and biotechnology companies.
- Production value chain (processors, exporters, supermarkets, etc.).
- Lateral services (financial, transport, logistics, IT, etc.).
- Public goods (research, sanitary and phytosanitary services, etc.)

According to [36] mentions that Latin America is improving its agricultural production and exports. For example, the share of imports in US fresh fruit sales increased from 23% in 1975 to 53% in 2016, with 90% of Latin American origin. The share of vegetable imports increased from 6% to 31% (USDA, 2018 and 2019). Latin America has a great opportunity in agribusiness, however, the implementation of modern technology still has a long way to go. Several factors are having an impact, the main one being that more than 50% of the farms are small farms (less than 2 hectares) and operated by a family; which have neither the knowledge nor the money to invest in technology and improve their production. According to the 2018 Statista report, Latin Americans use only two connected devices on average, in comparison with 11.5 devices for northamericans.

According to a study carried out by Logicalis in November 2018, almost 50% of the companies participating in the study declared that they are not planning to implement IoT in their companies. The most important barrier to adopting IoT is the financial aspect [38]. Current trends in the application of IoT in agriculture, according to the article "An Overview of Internet of Things (IoT) and Data Analytics in Agriculture: Benefits and Challenges", is based on the following areas: technological innovations, application scenarios; business and marketability [39].

4 Discussion

The bibliographic review allowed to investigate and establish the current state of the trend of technologies applied to agriculture in Latin America, in Table 4 the IoT solutions have been classified according to the areas of agriculture.

Table 4. Soluciones OIT en Agricultura

Soluciones IOT	Description
Climate variables	They create certain climatic environments to favor the development of certain foods and plantations
Smart inventors	Sensors capable of detecting climatic parameters and regulating them to maintain optimal conditions
Agricultural drones	Know from the cloud the most exhaustive details of the plantations and apply proper fertilizers and treatment
Monitoring and precision	Know from the cloud the most exhaustive details of the plantations and apply proper fertilizers and treatment
Smart pest control	Greater monitoring and control of the pest population
Efficient management of resources and profitability	Total knowledge about the conditions of the crop
Precision farming	Anything that makes agricultural practices more controlled and precise

Agriculture is a field of application extremely susceptible to the application of systems based on the IoT paradigm, its diversity and complexity lie in the number of incident variables, the granularity of the range of technological application for each crop, the particular characteristics of each plant, the techniques of the planting, cultivation and harvesting process, the support for packaging and transport processes, and of course, the disposal of the food to the end user.

5 Conclusions

The deployment of an architecture supported in IoT for smart agriculture has been achieve by taking advantage of the great flexibility and functionality offered by the combination of low-cost hardware tools and free software. It is important to recognize that the possible applications of IoTs are numerous and diverse, being used in different scenarios such as health, homes, environment, water, industrial control, agriculture, among others.

Some of the most prominent technologies that are combined with IoT to develop agricultural solutions are wireless sensor networks, cloud computing, middleware systems and mobile applications [39].

To be successful in modern agriculture, companies must innovate and customize products and value chains to adapt to changing market requirements. It is also important that regional governments invest in technology and empower the ecosystem.

References

1. Spanaki, K., Sivarajah, U., Fakhimi, M., Despoudi, S., Irani, Z.: Disruptive technologies in agricultural operations: a systematic review of AI-driven AgriTech research. Ann. Oper. Res. (2021). https://doi.org/10.1007/s10479-020-03922-z
2. Kaur, H., Singh, A., Kaur, M.: Agriculture and IoT: the literature review. Int. J. Adv. Sci. Technol. 29, 2475–2490 (2020)
3. Mohammadi, V., Rahmani, A.M., Darwesh, A.M., Sahafi, A.: Trust-based recommendation systems in Internet of Things: a systematic literature review. Hum.-Centric Comput. Inf. Sci. 9, 21 (2019). https://doi.org/10.1186/s13673-019-0183-8
4. Fischer, J.E., Crabtree, A., Colley, J.A., Rodden, T., Costanza, E.: Data work: how energy advisors and clients make IoT data accountable. Comput. Support. Coop. Work (CSCW) 26(4–6), 597–626 (2017). https://doi.org/10.1007/s10606-017-9293-x
5. Roca Marí, D.: Analysis and Simulation of Emergent Architectures for Internet of Things. TDX (Tesis Dr. en Xarxa) (2017)
6. Parvez, B., Haidri, R.A., Kumar Verma, J.: IoT in agriculture. In: 2020 International Conference on Computational Performance Evaluation (ComPE), pp. 844–847 (2020). https://doi.org/10.1109/ComPE49325.2020.9200035
7. Vermesan, O., Friess, P.: Internet of Things: converging technologies for smart environments and integrated ecosystems. Presented at the (2013)
8. Dorsemaine, B., Gaulier, J.-P., Wary, J.-P., Kheir, N., Urien, P.: Internet of Things: a definition & taxonomy. In: 2015 9th International Conference on Next Generation Mobile Applications, Services and Technologies, pp. 72–77 (2015). https://doi.org/10.1109/NGMAST.2015.71
9. Vashi, S., Ram, J., Modi, J., Verma, S., Prakash, C.: Internet of Things (IoT): a vision, architectural elements, and security issues. In: 2017 International Conference on I-SMAC (IoT in Social, Mobile, Analytics and Cloud) (I-SMAC), pp. 492–496 (2017). https://doi.org/10.1109/I-SMAC.2017.8058399
10. Farooq, M.S., Riaz, S., Abid, A., Abid, K., Naeem, M.A.: A survey on the role of IoT in agriculture for the implementation of smart farming. IEEE Access. 7, 156237–156271 (2019). https://doi.org/10.1109/ACCESS.2019.2949703
11. Friha, O., Ferrag, M.A., Shu, L., Maglaras, L., Wang, X.: Internet of Things for the future of smart agriculture: a comprehensive survey of emerging technologies. IEEE/CAA J. Autom. Sin. 8, 718–752 (2021). https://doi.org/10.1109/JAS.2021.1003925

12. Boursianis, A.D., et al.: Internet of Things (IoT) and agricultural unmanned aerial vehicles (UAVs) in smart farming: a comprehensive review. Internet of Things, 100187 (2020). https://doi.org/10.1016/j.iot.2020.100187

13. Oliveira-Jr, A., et al.: IoT sensing platform as a driver for digital farming in rural. Africa (2020). https://doi.org/10.3390/s20123511

14. Giri, A., Dutta, S., Neogy, S.: Enabling agricultural automation to optimize utilization of water, fertilizer and insecticides by implementing Internet of Things (IoT). In: 2016 International Conference on Information Technology (InCITe) - The Next Generation IT Summit on the Theme - Internet of Things: Connect your Worlds, pp. 125–131 (2016). https://doi.org/10.1109/INCITE.2016.7857603

15. Viani, F., Bertolli, M., Salucci, M., Polo, A.: Low-cost wireless monitoring and decision support for water saving in agriculture. IEEE Sens. J. **17**, 4299–4309 (2017). https://doi.org/10.1109/JSEN.2017.2705043

16. Ferrández-Pastor, F.J., García-Chamizo, J.M., Nieto-Hidalgo, M., Mora-Martínez, J.: Precision agriculture design method using a distributed computing architecture on Internet of Things context. Sensors **18** (2018). https://doi.org/10.3390/s18061731

17. Kamienski, C., et al.: Smart water management platform: IoT-based precision irrigation for. Agriculture (2019). https://doi.org/10.3390/s19020276

18. Naveen, S.: Study of IoT: understanding IoT architecture, applications, issues and challenges (2016)

19. Kumar, J.S., Patel, D.R.: A survey on internet of things: security and privacy issues. Int. J. Comput. Appl. **90** (2014)

20. Botta, A., de Donato, W., Persico, V., Pescapé, A.: Integration of cloud computing and Internet of Things: a survey. Future. Gener. Comput. Syst. **56**, 684–700 (2016). https://doi.org/10.1016/j.future.2015.09.021

21. Pavón-Pulido, N., López-Riquelme, J.A., Torres, R., Morais, R., Pastor, J.A.: New trends in precision agriculture: a novel cloud-based system for enabling data storage and agricultural task planning and automation. Precision Agric. **18**(6), 1038–1068 (2017). https://doi.org/10.1007/s11119-017-9532-7

22. Bajceta, M., Sekulić, P., Krstajic, B., Đukanović, S., Popovic, T.: A private IoT cloud platform for precision agriculture and ecological monitoring. Presented at the (2016)

23. Gill, S.S., Chana, I., Buyya, R.: IoT based agriculture as a cloud and big data service: the beginning of digital India. J. Organ. End User Comput. **29**, 1–23 (2017). https://doi.org/10.4018/JOEUC.2017100101

24. Kamilaris, A., Kartakoullis, A., Prenafeta-Boldú, F.X.: A review on the practice of big data analysis in agriculture. Comput. Electron. Agric. **143**, 23–37 (2017). https://doi.org/10.1016/j.compag.2017.09.037

25. Liu, X., et al.: Application of temperature prediction based on neural network in intrusion detection of IoT. Secur. Commun. Netw. **2018**, 1 (2018). https://doi.org/10.1155/2018/1635081

26. Mehra, M., Saxena, S., Sankaranarayanan, S., Tom, R.J., Veeramanikandan, M.: IoT based hydroponics system using deep neural networks. Comput. Electron. Agric. **155**, 473–486 (2018). https://doi.org/10.1016/j.compag.2018.10.015

27. Kalathas, J., Bandekas, D.V., Kosmidis, A., Kanakaris, V.: Seedbed based on IoT: a case study. J. Eng. Sci. Technol. Rev. **9** (2016)

28. Navulur, S., Sastry, A.S.C.S., Prasad, M.N.: Agricultural management through wireless sensors and Internet of Things. Int. J. Electr. Comput. Eng. **7**, 3492–3499 (2017). https://doi.org/10.11591/ijece.v7i6.pp3492-3499

29. Al-Sarawi, S., Anbar, M., Alieyan, K., Alzubaidi, M.: Internet of Things (IoT) communication protocols: review. In: 2017 8th International Conference on Information Technology (ICIT), pp. 685–690 (2017). https://doi.org/10.1109/ICITECH.2017.8079928

30. Jaishetty, S.A., Patil, R.: IoT sensor network based approach for agricultural field monitoring and control. IJRET Int. J. Res. Eng. Technol. **5** (2016)

31. Milella, A., Reina, G., Nielsen, M.: A multi-sensor robotic platform for ground mapping and estimation beyond the visible spectrum. Precision Agric. **20**(2), 423–444 (2018). https://doi.org/10.1007/s11119-018-9605-2

32. Köksal, Ö., Tekinerdogan, B.: Architecture design approach for IoT-based farm management information systems. Precision Agric. **20**(5), 926–958 (2018). https://doi.org/10.1007/s11119-018-09624-8

33. Khattab, A., Abdelgawad, A., Yelmarthi, K.: Design and implementation of a cloud-based IoT scheme for precision agriculture. In: 2016 28th International Conference on Microelectronics (ICM), pp. 201–204 (2016). https://doi.org/10.1109/ICM.2016.7847850

34. Vuran, M.C., Salam, A., Wong, R., Irmak, S.: Internet of underground things in precision agriculture: architecture and technology aspects. Ad Hoc Netw. **81**, 160–173 (2018). https://doi.org/10.1016/j.adhoc.2018.07.017

35. Triantafyllou, A., Sarigiannidis, P., Bibi, S.: Precision agriculture: a remote sensing monitoring system. Architecture (2019). https://doi.org/10.3390/info10110348

36. Moreira, M.M., Stein, E.: Trading Promises for Results: What Global Integration Can Do for Latin America and the Caribbean. Inter-American Development Bank (2019). https://doi.org/10.18235/0001886

37. Sundmaeker, H., Verdouw, C., Wolfert, S., Freire, L.P.: Internet of food and farm 2020. In: Digitising the Industry - Internet of Things Connecting the Physical, Digital and Virtual Worlds, pp. 129–151 (2016)

38. Cerioni, T., Malandrin, L.: IoT Snapshot Latam 2018, 24 (2018)

39. Elijah, O., Rahman, T.A., Orikumhi, I., Leow, C.Y., Hindia, M.H.D.N.: An overview of Internet of Things (IoT) and data analytics in agriculture: benefits and challenges. IEEE Internet Things J. **5**, 3758–3773 (2018). https://doi.org/10.1109/JIOT.2018.2844296

Author Index

Printed in the United States
by Baker & Taylor Publisher Services